EDITOR
PATRICIA J. BAUER
Emory University

MANAGING EDITOR
ADAM MARTIN
Society for Research in Child Development

EDITORIAL ASSISTANT
STEPHANIE CUSTER
Society for Research in Child Development

THE CHANGING NATURE OF EXECUTIVE CONTROL IN PRESCHOOL

EDITED BY

*Kimberly Andrews Espy, University of Arizona and
University of Nebraska-Lincoln*

WITH COMMENTARY BY

Michael T. Willoughby

Patricia J. Bauer
Series Editor

MONOGRAPHS OF THE SOCIETY FOR RESEARCH IN CHILD DEVELOPMENT

Serial No. 323, Vol. 81, No. 4, 2016

WILEY

Boston, Massachusetts   *Oxford, United Kingdom*

THE CHANGING NATURE OF EXECUTIVE CONTROL IN PRESCHOOL

CONTENTS

COMMENTARY

I. EXECUTIVE CONTROL IN EARLY CHILDHOOD

C. A. C. Clark, N. Chevalier, J. M. Nelson, T. D. James, J. P. Garza, H.-J. Choi, and K. A. Espy

This article is part of the issue "The Changing Nature of Executive Control in Preschool" Espy (Issue Editor). For a full listing of articles in this issue, see: http://onlinelibrary.wiley.com/doi/10.1111/mono. v81.4/issuetoc.

Executive control (EC) is a central construct in developmental science, although measurement limitations have hindered understanding of its nature and development in young children, relation to social risk, and prediction of important outcomes. Disentangling EC from the foundational cognitive abilities it regulates and that are inherently required for successful executive task completion (e.g., language, visual/spatial perception, and motor abilities) is particularly challenging at preschool age, when these foundational abilities are still developing and consequently differ substantially among children. A novel latent bifactor modeling approach delineated respective EC and foundational cognitive abilities components that undergird executive task performance in a socio demographically stratified sample of 388 preschoolers in a longitudinal, cohort-sequential study. The bifactor model revealed a developmental shift, where both EC and foundational cognitive abilities contributed uniquely to executive task performance at ages 4.5 and 5.25 years, but were not separable at ages 3 and 3.75. Contrary to the view that EC is vulnerable to socio-familial risk, the contributions of household financial and learning resources to executive task performance were not specific to EC but were via their relation to foundational cognitive abilities. EC, though, showed a unique, discriminant relation with hyperactive symptoms late in the preschool period, whereas foundational cognitive abilities did not predict specific dimensions of dysregulated behavior. These findings form the basis for a new, integrated approach to the measurement and conceptualization of EC, which includes dual consideration of the contributions of EC and foundational cognitive abilities to executive task performance, particularly in the developmental context of preschool.

Corresponding author: Caron Clark, email: caron.clark@unl.edu
DOI: 10.1111/mono.12268

Young children often appear to live in the moment. They lack the foresight to recognize that grabbing a toy from another child's hand may result in swift retaliation. Preschoolers point out the same color over and over, even when their daycare teacher has moved on to another task. They can move almost instantaneously from a state of happy laughter to an outright tantrum. They run and scream when you wish them to sit still and quiet, and they unabashedly make loud, negative appraisals of the appearances of passers-by. These behaviors generally are overlooked by adults, as it is understood that young children lack the abilities necessary to independently modulate their thoughts, feelings, and behavior. In psychological terms, they lack executive control (EC), the set of tertiary mental processes that coordinate and manage sensory-perceptual inputs, motor outputs, and other lower-level processes to regulate and support intentional, goal-directed thoughts and actions. We prefer the term "executive control" over the historic and more commonly used "executive function" to emphasize (i) the coordinating aspect endemic to direction toward a goal reflected in "executive" and (ii) the element of selective choice among alternatives that is elemental to "control." Additionally, the term executive control intentionally bridges the adult cognitive neuroscience and clinical/developmental literatures, which typically use the terms cognitive control and executive function, respectively. Finally, for ease of presentation, we will hereafter refer to the theoretical psychological construct as EC, and will employ the term executive to refer to the various tasks that are used to assess EC.

Historically, in adults, EC has been portrayed in a metaphoric way as the conductor of cognition and is considered essential for guiding adaptive behavior in situations where well-learned, automatic, or habitual responses are inappropriate or where goal-relevant behaviors compete with conflicting alternatives. In adults, this metaphor is particularly useful, as all "members of the orchestra," the fundamental sensory, perceptual, language, motor, and other subordinate mental processes, are considered mature, stable, and competent. The conductor's role in the orchestra is to direct, via emphasis, restraint and pacing, each professional musician to play in a manner toward a goal—an elegant, coordinated production—and not a cacophony of sounds that results from individuals playing in a disharmonious, uncontrolled manner. Conversely, the musicians provide the conductor with the actual sounds and music to be directed and coordinated, through interpretation of the changing musical notation.

As children age, developmental gains in EC support their successful coordination of mental processes in increasingly complex academic and social contexts. For instance, EC is involved in solving a simple subtraction problem, enabling the child to implement the correct arithmetic operation and ignore previous and now incorrect, competing representations. EC is involved in learning new motor skills such as skiing or skateboarding, coordinating and suppressing dominant motor responses so that the child is able to move forward and maintain balance. As children gain greater experience and practice, these abilities generally become more fluent and automatic and require less EC for successful execution. The role of EC in supporting children's self-regulation is perhaps even more conspicuous when it fails, for instance when a child calls his teacher by his mother's name or, more alarmingly, when she runs heedlessly into oncoming traffic despite repeated reprimands. As illustrated by these examples, EC is integral to flexible human behavior, allowing for adaptive responses in an ever-changing environment.

HISTORICAL ROOTS OF EXECUTIVE CONTROL

The original concept of EC in adults emanates from neurological case studies (e.g., Milner, 1963), from lesion studies with primates (e.g., Jacobsen, 1935), and from cognitive theories that distinguish between controlled and automatic, reactive cognitive processes (e.g., Shallice, 1988). Inherent to all of these literatures and to current definitions of EC is a focus on the distinction between complex, tertiary, goal-directed control capacities and subordinate, foundational cognitive abilities. These latter subordinate processes serve as a platform for EC, providing the content on which it can act, and broadly include, but are not limited to, vocabulary and other language abilities, visual/spatial perception, and motor processing. In adults, these processes are organized relatively discretely in circumscribed cortical areas and can be measured summarily with various tests of defined abilities (e.g., receptive or expressive vocabulary). Perhaps the most famous example of the neuropsychological distinction between voluntary control processes and more foundational cognitive abilities is the case of Phineas Gage (Harlow, 1848, 1993). After sustaining massive damage to the left orbitofrontal cortex, Gage showed marked changes in personality and behavior despite apparently intact verbal, sensory, visual/spatial perception, recall, and motor abilities. Similar discrepancies are highlighted in the writings of Luria (1973) and Damasio (1979) with respect to cases of injury to the prefrontal cortex. These individuals generally showed a preserved ability to remember and enact well-learned, habitual responses to stimuli in the environment and relatively spared sensorimotor perception and language. Nonetheless, closer observations revealed that these patients often were unable to cope with the demands of everyday life, lacking an ability to plan for the future or maintain steady jobs, focus attention, react with appropriate emotional intensity, grasp abstract ideas, or show expected behavioral restraint. Broadly, these case studies set up a distinction between well-learned, foundational cognitive abilities and complex, higher-order control processes that allow for goal-directed, flexible responses to immediate contextual demands.

On the basis of this neuropsychological literature, EC became inexorably linked to the prefrontal cortex. Indeed, many adult measures of EC are denoted as such based on their sensitivity to frontal lobe pathology. For instance, the Wisconsin Card Sorting Test, in some venues referred to as the gold standard measure of EC in adults, initially was validated by showing that performance on the task discriminated adults with injury to the frontal cortex from those with lesions in other brain regions (Milner, 1963; Robinson, Heaton, Lehman, & Stilson, 1980). Advancements in neurobehavioral imaging and assessment admittedly have facilitated a more sophisticated and nuanced understanding of the relation of EC to neural structure and function, and have underscored the importance of broader prefrontal systems, incorporating subcortical and parietal neural regions, for executive task performance (Carpenter, Just, & Reichle, 2000). However, mechanistic theories of EC derived from computational modeling continue to underscore the central role of prefrontal cortical regions in updating, maintaining, and inhibiting lower level perceptual representations without the need to concede to an imaginary homunculus (Hazy, Frank, Michael, & O'Reilly, 2007). Situating EC in its roots in the neurological case study literature, which traditionally has centered on isolating and attributing cognitive functions to discrete neural regions, lends an important premise of modularity and specialization to the concept of EC. In essence, it is the hierarchical distinction of EC from the set of more general, automatic, foundational cognitive abilities it coordinates that defines it as an independent psychological construct.

The characteristic profile of executive deficits coupled with relatively intact subordinate cognitive abilities, however, was observed in patients with frontal lesions (e.g., stroke, head injury) acquired in adulthood or late childhood. In the mature adult nervous system, the development of these various neural systems for processing linguistic, visual, and semantic information, as well as for programming motor outputs, is complete, and the relations among brain areas and systems are well-formed, discrete, and relatively stable. This high degree of modularity and automaticity in adults increases the salience of dissociations between impaired EC and these intact foundational cognitive processes. Yet, as pointed out by D'Souza and Karmiloff-Smith (2011), this dissociation represents the "end state" for development, and may not adequately reflect the start state or the dynamic developmental process of EC acquisition with age. In fact, evidence shows that infant and child brains are less modular than the adult brain; that is, cognitive processes are not as discretely mapped to specific neural regions in young children relative to adults (Ansari, 2010; Jacobs, 2011). If EC is to be meaningfully applied and its ontogeny properly elucidated, its measurement and conceptualization needs to be approached with recognition of these changes across development. In terms of the initial symphony analogy of the conductor and musicians who together deliver organized, enchanting music, in children, both the "conductor" and the "members of the orchestra" are undergoing fundamental changes as a consequence of development. That is, neither the conductor nor the musicians are accomplished professionals in childhood. Rather, the conductor has little experience in music interpretation, in what to amplify or dampen, or in how to pace the baton to guide the performers. The musicians also are still developing their respective musical talents. The present volume examines these issues through a longitudinal study focused on a particularly critical age range, the preschool period. Below, we contextualize the study of EC in early childhood, identify important issues with respect to its fundamental and potentially changing structure through childhood, and discuss the difficulties in distilling EC from more foundational cognitive processes over which it is conceptualized to exercise control.

EXECUTIVE CONTROL IN CHILDREN

During the late 20th century, the concept of EC emanating from adult case studies was extended gradually to younger ages. New measures suitable for children were created by simplifying adult neuropsychological paradigms; by using tasks that had long been used to study children's cognitive development but that seemed to encapsulate the planning or mental representation skills that commonly were ascribed to EC in adults; or by adopting paradigms used successfully in primate studies (e.g., Diamond & Goldman-Rakic, 1986; Espy, Kaufmann, McDiarmid, & Glisky, 1999; Frye, Zelazo, & Palfai, 1995; Welsh, 1991). The concept of EC offered a new, neuropsychological bent to concepts such as effortful control and self-regulation, terms similar to, and often used synonymously with, EC in the developmental field, but with different historical roots in the educational and temperament literatures that do not focus as directly on modular cognitive processes (McClelland & Cameron, 2012). Perhaps related to the origination and prominence of EC in the clinical neuropsychology literature, much of the initial developmental research on EC was conducted in clinical populations, including children with autism, phenylketonuria, and particularly children with attention deficit hyperactivity disorder (ADHD; Diamond, Prevor, Callender, & Druin, 1997; Ozonoff & Jensen, 1999). Deficits associated with "minimal brain dysfunction," the dated term for ADHD, bore marked similarities to the under controlled, impulsive or unmotivated behaviors associated with frontal lobe damage in adults (Wender, 1975). The concept of EC offered an important new lens for understanding the specific deficits in attention, inhibitory control, and emotion regulation often manifested by children with ADHD in the context of broadly intact foundational cognitive abilities (Pennington & Ozonoff, 1996; Schuck & Crinella, 2005).

11

The use of EC measures in the study of both typical and atypical development has proven productive. Young children's performance on executive measures predicts competence across multiple developmental domains, including theory of mind (Carlson & Moses, 2001), emotion regulation (Carlson & Wang, 2007), and behavior (Espy, Sheffield, Wiebe, Clark, & Moehr, 2011; Hughes, White, Sharpen, & Dunn, 2000). Perhaps the predictive value of EC is most impressive in the educational arena, where performance on executive measures is associated with attention and self-regulation in the classroom environment (Friedman et al., 2007; Schmitt, Pratt, & McClelland, 2014) and with academic achievement in literacy, vocabulary, and mathematics in preschoolers (Bull, Espy, & Wiebe, 2008; Bull, Espy, Wiebe, Sheffield, & Nelson, 2011; Clark, Pritchard, & Woodward, 2010; Clark et al., 2013; Espy et al., 2004; Welsh, Nix, Blair, Bierman, & Nelson, 2010) as well as in school-aged children and adolescents (Bull & Scerif, 2001; St Clair-Thompson & Gathercole, 2006; van der Sluis, de Jong, & van der Leij, 2007) even after controlling for the influence of general intelligence (Blair & Razza, 2007; Bull et al., 2011; although see Willoughby, Kupersmidt, & Voegler-Lee, 2012, as an exception). Individual differences in EC at preschool age not only are associated with concurrent academic achievement, but also predict academic performance at age 7 (Bull et al., 2008). Moreover, growth in EC skills over the kindergarten year predicts growth in academic skills over that same year (McClelland et al., 2007).

The strong predictive relation of early EC to a broad range of developmental outcomes motivates the study of its development in early childhood. With an increasing array of measures that are suitable for young children, studies have described manifestations of EC as early as the first year of life. The precursors for endogenous cognitive control are evident at 4 and 6 months of age, when infants show an increasing ability to orient or inhibit visual saccades to a target location based on a preliminary cue or repeated sequence (Johnson, Posner, & Rothbart, 1991; Sheese, Rothbart, Posner, White, & Fraundorf, 2008). Even more rudimentary measures, such as the length of time that children look at a stimulus, have been related to executive task performance at older ages, suggesting that there is a degree of heterotypic continuity in endogenous attention regulation that has implications for later EC (Cuevas & Bell, 2014). By 9 months of age, infants succeed at inhibiting their tendency to search for an object in a previously accurate "A" location and will reach instead to the new location where they most recently saw the object being hidden (Diamond, 1985). However, 10-month-old infants still show more perseverative looking at the "A" location than their 12-month counterparts, and substantial perseveration is evident even in 2-year-olds when there are more locations and more obstacles to retrieval (Watanabe, Forssman, Green, Bohlin, & von Hofsten, 2012; Zelazo, Reznick, & Spinazzola, 1998). By 11 months, infants also are able to suppress their impulsive tendency to reach directly for a toy that is obstructed by a transparent barrier (Diamond, 1990). Unlike children of younger ages, who try, sometimes repeatedly, to reach through the barrier, older infants will reach indirectly through a window to the side of the barrier. Taken together, it seems that infants possess a rudimentary ability to direct and control their visual attention or motor behavior according to the demands of the environment and that these early abilities may presage later individual differences in performance on EC measures.

Co-occurring with the rapid development of symbolic thought, self-representation, language and motor abilities that children exhibit over the toddler and preschool years, there is marked age-related improvement in performance on executive tasks. Between age 3 and 6 years, children become increasingly proficient at suppressing inappropriate prepotent responses (Carlson & Moses, 2001; Diamond, Kirkman, & Amso, 2002; Kochanska, Murray, & Harlan, 2000; Wiebe, Sheffield, & Espy, 2012). For instance, at age 3 years, children generally are unable to perform an action that conflicts with the action they are observing (e.g., tap a dowel once when the examiner taps twice), whereas children can easily execute such tasks by age 5.5 years (Diamond & Taylor, 1996). On a button-press response inhibition task, children's accuracy increased by 30% between age 3 and 5 years (Wiebe et al., 2012). Similarly, children show an increasing ability to delay gratification for rewards over the preschool years (Carlson, Mandell, & Williams, 2004; Kochanska et al., 2000). These simultaneous improvements on tasks that assess inhibition, but that vary significantly in their response requirements, language demands, and motivational features, suggest changes in core control processes across the early childhood period.

Together with these advances in inhibitory task performance, pre-schoolers also show marked improvements in their ability to apply rules flexibly according to changing task demands. The classic paradigm used to examine these changes is the standard dimensional change card sort (DCCS; Frye et al., 1995), a task in the same vein as the Wisconsin Card Sorting Test with explicit instructions for children to sort cards first by color and then by shape or vice versa. At age 2 years, children are unable to sort cards systematically, soon failing to sort by the rules and making arbitrary responses. Three-year-olds are able to sort cards using different rules that apply the same sorting dimension (e.g., sort shapes such that circles are binned with circles and then sort circles with squares), whereas by 5 years of age, children are able to apply rules flexibly across dimensions, that is, sort by color, then by shape (Zelazo, Frye, & Rapus, 1996). Complementing these findings, children's accuracy on the Shape School measure of cognitive flexibility increases from 30% to 95% from ages 3 through 5 years (Clark et al., 2013). Thus, by the time they enter elementary school, children generally show high levels of ̃ on basic executive measures, although smaller gains, primarily speed, are observed even in late adolescence and early adulthood (Best, Miller, & Jones, 2009; Cepeda, Kramer, & Gonzalez de Sather, 2001; Reimers & Maylor, 2005).

The above studies indicate quantitative gains in EC through the preschool years. Many theories of EC development imply that these changes are underscored by increasing representational processing or inhibitory control modulated by the prefrontal cortex (e.g., Diamond, 2001; Morton & Munakata, 2002). However, research and theory also suggests that children may undergo qualitative gains and transitions in EC, particularly during early childhood (Chevalier, Huber, Wiebe, & Espy, 2013; Munakata, Snyder, & Chatham, 2012). With age, preschool children become better able to process environmental cues to determine which relevant task goals they need to attain, and ultimately how to behave adaptively as circumstances change (Chevalier & Blaye, 2009). For instance, whereas the errors of younger preschool children on the Shape School are related predominantly to distracting or irrelevant stimulus features, this pattern changes so that children's errors gradually become more related to the appropriate task cues or features with advancing development (Clark et al., 2013). In other words, children become increasingly adept at attending to environmental cues that signal appropriate or inappropriate behaviors. A glare is now sufficient to curb a child's inappropriate behavior where an explicit reprimand was necessary at younger ages. Further, as children age, there appears to be a shift from a reactive mode of control, characterized by the recruitment of executive processes in the face of immediately unfolding events, to a proactive mode of control, where children anticipate and actively prepare for probable upcoming events (Chatham, Frank, & Munakata, 2009; Waxer & Morton, 2011). For example, children slowed their response times to achieve greater accuracy on a response inhibition task toward the end of their third year (Wiebe et al., 2012). Finally, with age, children may exert EC in an increasingly self-directed manner, endogenously determining what they need to do to achieve a goal instead of relying on external agents. For example, homework is done without any prompt from parents (Snyder & Munakata, 2010). Overall, these studies suggest that abrupt increases in the accuracy of children's executive task performance between 3 and 5 years may reflect underlying qualitative changes in the way that children are processing and responding to task demands.

NEURAL BASES OF EXECUTIVE CONTROL

The improvements in children's executive task performance discussed above correspond with patterns of neural maturation observed in structural and functional imaging studies. In functional magnetic resonance imaging

4

(fMRI) studies with adults, EC tasks elicit signal changes in a broad neural network encompassing prefrontal, anterior cingulate, basal ganglia, and parietal regions (Aron & Poldrack, 2006; Carter & Van Veen, 2007; Chambers, Garavan, & Bellgrove, 2009; Hwang, Velanova, & Luna, 2010). Activity in the prefrontal regions presumably allows individuals to maintain goal-relevant information in an active state, thereby biasing activity in the posterior regions that modulate subordinate cognitive processes through synaptic projections to those brain regions (e.g., Miller & Cohen, 2001). Notably, the prefrontal and inferior parietal cortical regions are the latest to mature during ontogeny, as evidenced by a longer peak in synaptic density (Huttenlocher, 1990) and a later peak in cortical gray matter density relative to sensorimotor regions (Giedd & Rapoport, 2010).

Neural growth is particularly rapid during early childhood, with the brain reaching 95% of its adult volume by age 6 years (Giedd & Rapoport, 2010). Nonetheless, it is important to note that neural development is not simply a case of quantitative, linear growth, but rather reflects qualitative reorganization of neural circuits and systems throughout the course of childhood and adolescence. For instance, results from electroencephalography (EEG) studies indicate that regional electrical activity in the brain becomes increasingly coherent with age (Boersma et al., 2011; Thatcher, 1992). Although few investigations have been conducted during the preschool period, graph theory analysis methods for fMRI data indicate that there is a movement from local functional connectivity to longer-range connectivity over childhood that correlates with the structural myelination of long-tract fibers, as well as with changes in axonal density and myelin thickness (Fair et al., 2007; Hagmann et al., 2010; Sherman et al., 2014; Wang, Zuo, & He, 2010; Yap et al., 2011). In essence, the architecture supporting neural transmission between regions is increasingly elaborated with age. The likely impact of this progressive change in connectivity is that the prefrontal cortex, via these long-distance fibers, is connected more effectively to subcortical and posterior regions that process sensory input, which then enables self-directed control of more subordinate, domain-specific cognitive processes.

Functional MRI studies also indicate changes in neural activation in response to executive tasks with age (e.g., Bunge, Dudukovic, Thomason, Vaidya, & Gabrieli, 2002; Hwang et al., 2010), with activation of prefrontal areas that correlate with higher executive task performance increasing progressively through childhood (Casey et al., 1997; Durston et al., 2006). Likewise, EEG studies indicate that, whereas most of the cortex is activated when infants perform working memory tasks, EEG power and coherence during working memory task performance is centralized at the frontal cortex by 4 years of age (Bell & Wolfe, 2007; Bell, Wolfe, & Adkins, 2007; Wolfe & Bell, 2004). Notably, higher 6–9 Hz power at frontal EEG electrode sites at 10 months of age also predicted higher executive task performance at age

4 years (Kraybill & Bell, 2013). In a study using near infrared spectroscopy, adults and preschoolers who passed a flexible sorting task showed a greater hemodynamic response in the inferior prefrontal cortex relative to children who perseverated during the switch phase (Moriguchi & Hiraki, 2009). This prefrontal activation pattern was present for all 5-year-old participants, whereas it was observed only in those 3-year-olds who were able to switch flexibly to a new sorting rule when required. Although more speculative, the neural network supporting EC has been hypothesized to change with age, with progressive specialization of inferior prefrontal cortex and increasing recruitment of dorsolateral cortex (Crone & Ridderinkhof, 2011). One study indicated that adults showed two distinct functional networks supporting EC, whereas these networks were largely integrated and indistinguishable in school-aged children (Fair et al., 2007). This increased specialization in adults likely reflects stronger connectivity between prefrontal and posterior regions (see Edin, Macoveanu, Olesen, Tegnér, & Klingberg, 2007, for evidence that increasing brain connectivity enhances working memory capacity with age). Collectively, then, neuroimaging studies indicate that neural activation becomes more focal and localized to prefrontal regions but also more interconnected across larger specialized networks with increasing age and efficiency of executive task performance. This progressive reorganization and specialization of neural systems with age underscores the need for measures and theories that recognize the developmentally dynamic nature of the relation between EC and other cognitive processes.

FRAMING EXECUTIVE CONTROL IN THE DYNAMIC DEVELOPMENTAL CONTEXT OF EARLY CHILDHOOD

Clearly, group and individual differences in performance on executive tasks are informative and there have been major advances in charting the developmental course and neural bases of EC. However, theoretical and measurement issues over the lifespan have hindered a coherent understanding of the true nature of EC, its course of development and its relations to important outcomes. One major issue is task "impurity" (Hughes & Graham, 2002; Miyake, Friedman, Emerson, Witzki, & Howerter, 2000; Rabitt, 1997). Given that EC typically is viewed to act on other subordinate processes, it is impossible for any executive task, even the best designed, to capture a pure representation of the EC construct alone. In practical terms, every task designed to assess EC uses words or pictures that must be processed or motor responses that must be selected and implemented to varying degrees. Therefore, every executive task necessarily requires the engagement of subordinate cognitive abilities to process the specific stimuli or response requirements. The ability to inhibit, maintain, or flexibly shift between these stimulus or response representations in the face of either irrelevant, previously correct, or competing representations is what defines EC—the key cognitive apparatus necessary to flexibly act or respond as determined by the particular cue or contingency. The EC process and the stimulus or response representations likely are mutually dependent and together enable the child's observed performance on the executive task.

The impact of task impurity may be especially dramatic in early childhood, when neural systems are undergoing massive reorganization and the mastery of basic semantic concepts varies dramatically among individual children. As an example, suppose children are asked to complete a traditional card sorting task with color and shape stimuli. Imagine preschool Child A has well-educated parents who have time in the evening to read to this child. The child's family is fortunate to have sufficient resources to send the child to a high-quality preschool. The child routinely hears adults highlight colors and shapes the child encounters in the everyday environment. The father, when he takes this child to the store, asks what color the red pepper is, and routinely points out the neighbor's red car in the adjacent driveway. In contrast, preschool Child B is living temporarily with her grandfather because her single mother lost custody. The grandfather works hard at the local warehouse and has little energy at the end of the day to do more than get dinner made, bathe the child, and get her off to bed. Child B attends a local daycare where the ratio of teachers to children is at the state maximum. The impact of such differences in the richness of the language environment related to these socioeconomic circumstances has been empirically quantified and well documented: children from families receiving public assistance are estimated to hear 30 million fewer words on average by age 3 years than are children from professional families (Hart & Risley, 1995). As a result of this richer language environment, Child A in our example likely will have a deeper, more coherent semantic representation of the color "red" than Child B.

In turn, these different experiences and resultant representations of color words and symbols may have an impact on executive task performance because executive tasks by definition require both (i) basic cognitive processing of the simple stimuli, in this case the color and (ii) engagement of the EC process to inhibit the distractor stimulus (the shape), maintain the relevant stimulus (the target color) or flexibly shift among stimuli as warranted by the condition at hand. On the one hand, variation in the representation of these stimulus properties and dimensions, color in our example, may enhance executive task performance, as Child A has more available cognitive resources to devote to maintaining the representation of "red" in working memory, in contrast to Child B who may have to devote more cognitive resources to recognizing and identifying the color before assigning it the verbal label, "red." Alternatively, a deeper, more coherent representation of "red" potentially may enhance the conflict demands of the stimulus for Child A because the representation of "red" is stronger as a result of experience and thus invokes greater demand for EC to manage irrelevant, previously seen, or competing representations (e.g., blue). With either alternative, individual differences in processing the visual, semantic, linguistic, and motor demands that fundamentally contribute to executive task performance are likely to be more pronounced during the rapid acquisition of these foundational cognitive abilities in early childhood. Individual variability in these foundational abilities may therefore cloud the accurate measurement of EC and scientific efforts to properly characterize it as a distinct construct.

Two basic methods commonly have been used by researchers in an attempt to address the task impurity problem fundamental to the measurement of EC: experimental manipulation via repeated conditions and latent variable modeling (discussed below). To parse EC itself from task-specific foundational cognitive demands, experimental studies with adult participants often employ stimulus materials that are similar in their perceptual stimulus and response demands, but have varying degrees of conflict or interference. The amount of interference in a given task condition is assumed to be proportional to the amount of EC required to complete the task and the difference in performance between the conditions with and without conflict should uniquely reflect the individual's EC proficiency. Although this discrepancy method intuitively addresses the task impurity problem and certainly has been applied successfully with children, and even preschoolers (e.g., Chevalier et al., 2012; Davidson, Amso, Anderson, & Diamond, 2006; Zelazo, Müller, Frye, & Marcovitch, 2003), its application in developmental studies carries unique challenges. Practically, tasks that rely on the repetition of stimuli that vary only in nuanced cues are not feasible for use with young children, who quickly lose interest and motivation to do the task at all. Researchers often need to administer shorter tasks that vary considerably in their stimulus properties or response demands in order to maintain child interest and motivation. More fundamental to EC measurement though, stimulus features may interfere to greater or lesser degrees depending on the age and proficiency of the child (Ellis & Oakes, 2006). The Stroop task, where participants name the ink color of color words (e.g., "red" for the word "green" written in red), is a classic example in this respect, as the interference created by semantic information of the word varies as a function of the automaticity of children's reading skills (i.e., the red of the ink color only interferes with the green of the written word if the child can read fluently). To overcome this difficulty, nonexecutive task demands are reduced as much as possible in measures for young children by using perceptual stimuli, such as color and shape matching, which are presumed to be well learned even in children, and thus more automatic. This assumption of automaticity may be reasonable in an 8-year-old child, but is more tenuous in a 4-year-old. As noted in our example above, the strength and integration of perceptual and symbolic representations for these types of stimuli vary tremendously among individual children. Differences in experience and familiarity with stimuli or responses may alter the nature of the executive task for different children, essentially requiring EC to different degrees depending on the individual child's proficiency in the relevant foundational cognitive abilities.

The other common approach to the task impurity problem is to try to parse EC through the application of latent modeling approaches, specifically confirmatory factor analysis (CFA). In psychometric theory, an individual's level of skill or ability on the unobserved construct (e.g., EC) is inferred on the basis of task performance. Classical test theory has been the foundation for describing the relation between unobserved constructs and individual performance on a specific task. One of the main assumptions of classical test theory is that the observed score (X) consists of an individual's true score (T) and a random error (E) as written

$$X = T + E.$$

In classical test theory, the true score cannot be directly observed. Thus, in studies that use the observed score obtained directly from a single executive task administered to the child, such as the total number correct on a go/no-go task, the dependent variable does not directly reflect the latent construct of interest, in this case, EC. Rather, the obtained score includes both the individual's true ability, as well as error variance.

Latent modeling methods (i.e., CFA) explicitly parse the true score from task-specific error variance by modeling the shared variance across a battery of tasks, which are theorized to measure a common, underlying construct. The variance that overlaps across these multiple tasks is extracted as the primary factor(s) of interest and theoretically reflects the reliable, true score, while the nonoverlapping variance specific to each task is parsed into separate error terms. Furthermore, the error (E) can be either random (i.e., related to idiosyncrasies of the particular day, test session, or child—the child did not eat breakfast that day and the child's hunger had an impact on performance on that particular day) or systematic (i.e., related to some unmeasured issue that, if measured, would account for some meaningful variation in performance across subjects). Distinguishing systematic error from random error can be important because systematic error may be meaningfully related to performance. For instance, systematic error may relate to a method effect (e.g., all tasks require a manual response, and thus variations in manual proficiency may systematically predict the observed variable to some degree) or a nuisance construct that is not of interest. Latent variable modeling allows us to explicitly model random and systematic error as well as the substantive constructs of interest in the same model.

In latent variable modeling, the individual tasks or measures, typically referred to as "indicators" of the latent variable of interest—here EC—are administered to a comparatively large number of subjects to sufficiently model individual variability. The investigator first derives a series of a priori models to represent the theoretical structure of the latent variable and evaluates the mathematical fit of each theoretical model against the obtained data. In general, the relation between each indicator or task and the construct

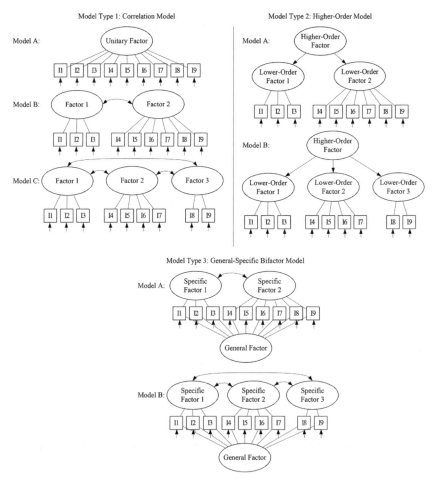

FIGURE 1.—Schematic representation of the various EC latent factor model types.

of interest is quantified by a loading and the resulting unexplained error term also is estimated for each indicator.

Suppose there are nine indicators derived from the nine executive tasks that have been administered to a given sample. Figure 1 graphically represents several generic models that might best represent the hypothesized structure of EC. Each model is derived from theory and the overall purpose is to empirically test the fit of each hypothesized model and/or compare the fit of competing models to determine which is best supported by the observed data. Model Type 1 shows correlation models, the most common type of latent variable model, used to examine and represent latent EC structure. In Model Type 1: Model A, the covariance among the observed indicators is hypothesized to best be accounted for by a single, unitary factor. Note that the factor captures only the variance that is shared among the nine administered executive tasks whereas the variance that is not shared is captured in error terms for each indicator. Models B and C are alternative correlation models that indicate that more than one factor, possibly two to three factors, underlie the covariance among the observed indicators; the factors can be hypothesized to be correlated as shown, although this assumption is not a necessity of latent variable modeling. If Model A provides a better or more parsimonious fit to the data relative to the other models, then findings provide empirical support for a unitary structure: one factor can be used to describe the true score performance across the nine dependent variables that were measured directly from the subject. Correspondingly, significant improvement of model fit for Model B or Model C would provide support for a fractionated EC structure, where there is more than one latent construct that describes performance on these nine tasks.

THE APPLICATION OF LATENT VARIABLE MODELING TO INVESTIGATE EXECUTIVE CONTROL

The task impurity problem and measurement challenges surrounding EC are central to debates regarding its fundamental organization, which, according to test theory, can be conceptualized as the latent structure. Although early theoretical models viewed EC as unitary (Baddeley & Hitch, 1974; Norman & Shallice, 1986), the term has come to include an extensive list of processes, such as working memory, flexibility, inhibitory control, goal abstraction, planning, self-monitoring, initiative, judgment, and fluency (Anderson, 2008; Tranel, Anderson, & Benton, 1994). There is ongoing debate as to whether and how these specific executive subcomponents can be distinguished from the broader EC rubric. In their seminal study, Miyake, Friedman, Emerson, Witzki, and Howerter (2000) used latent variable modeling to test competing theoretical structures for EC in a sample of young adults. They examined the pattern of loadings for a wide variety of executive measures selected a priori to assess: (i) inhibition of spontaneous and/or irrelevant responses; (ii) information updating in working memory; and (iii) set-shifting, that is, the ability to switch between multiple tasks. The findings provided support for three separate, but moderately correlated, factors, suggesting a fractionated EC structure composed of these three somewhat differentiated subcomponents. Applying the same statistical method to two other independent samples led these authors to revise their model and propose that EC can be best represented as a single, common process, hypothesized to reflect goal maintenance in prefrontal regions, along with related, yet separable set-shifting-specific and updating-specific components (Friedman, Miyake, Robinson, & Hewitt, 2011; Friedman et al., 2008). Of particular note is that this modified model does not include an inhibition-specific component over and above the common EC process. This view that EC encompasses two to three partially separate components now dominates adult models of EC (although see McCabe, Roediger, McDaniel, Balota, & Hambrick, 2010, for an alternative view).

In children, latent variable modeling also has been applied to identify the organization of EC at different developmental periods, although results are less consistent than in adults. Partially separable components have indeed been found from middle childhood through adolescence using these latent methods (Brydges, Fox, Reid, & Anderson, 2014; Huizinga, Dolan, & van der Molen, 2006; Lee, Bull, & Ho, 2013; Lehto, Juujärvi, Kooistra, & Pulkkinen, 2003), although models in middle childhood sometimes have failed to differentiate inhibition from set-shifting components (St Clair-Thompson & Gathercole, 2006; van der Sluis et al., 2007). Studies from different laboratories administering different executive task batteries to preschoolers, though, have yielded a very different pattern of results. During the preschool period, several studies incorporating different tasks have found that a unitary EC factor is preferred (Fuhs & Day, 2011; Hughes, Ensor, Wilson, & Graham, 2010; Wiebe, Espy, & Charak, 2008; Wiebe et al., 2011; Willoughby, Blair, Wirth, & Greenberg, 2010, 2012), where the inclusion of more than one latent variable does not significantly improve model fit. As an exception, Miller, Giesbrecht, Müller, McInerney, and Kerns (2012) found that a two-factor solution incorporating an inhibitory control and a working memory factor was preferred in a preschool sample, depending on the types of indicators used to represent EC, and argued on this basis that the structure of EC identified through latent modeling was dependent on the nature of the indicators chosen to represent it. Notably, the sample size in their study was small. Lerner and Lonigan (2014) also found that a two-factor model, incorporating independent working memory and an inhibitory control components, was preferred over a one-factor model as early as age 4 years, although the correlation between the factors was .95 and significantly higher than for 5-year-old children (.65).

22

Similarly, using very simple response inhibition and interference suppression tasks, Gandolfi, Viterbori, Traversi, and Usai (2014) found that a unitary model was preferred in a sample of toddlers, while a two-factor model was preferred in 3- to 4-year-old children. With some exceptions, then, even factor analytic studies that have made use of the same EC tasks at different age points suggest that EC may be less differentiated in younger than in older children.

Although it is unclear when, or in what manner, the structure of EC changes with development, there are many reasons why EC may be organized somewhat differently in young children relative to adults. The most tempting explanation, of course, is that EC abilities differentiate and become more specialized or fractionated with advancing development (Shing, Linden-berger, Diamond, Li, & Davidson, 2010). However, other alternatives are plausible. The nature of EC itself may be fundamentally unique in younger children, as preschool children may employ a developmentally distinct approach to executive tasks, bounded by the immaturity of their nervous system and prefrontal systems in particular (Chevalier et al., 2013). Regardless of the explanation, we have thus far been unable to demonstrate measurement invariance in our studies that use latent variable modeling of EC in preschoolers, despite our use of identical tasks across this age period (Nelson, James, Chevalier, Clark, & Espy, 2016; Wiebe et al., 2008, 2011). Instead, the relations between the EC construct and the manifest executive tasks used to characterize it appear to differ at different ages. This pattern suggests a change in the way that EC relates to children's performance on executive tasks across the preschool period. Collectively, then, studies employing latent variable modeling have contributed important insights into the nature and importance of EC across the lifespan. However, they also raise the important question of whether and how the nature of EC and its relation to manifest executive task performance changes with ontogeny, particularly in the critical early childhood period.

ALTERNATIVE LATENT VARIABLE MODELING APPROACHES TO EXECUTIVE CONTROL

What other approaches might be used to tackle the issue of task impurity and better elucidate the organization of EC and its relation to outcomes in this preschool period where multiple cognitive systems are undergoing rapid development? Delineating latent variable modeling in more detail, including some of the assumptions and limitations of this statistical method, may reveal a productive new strategy. Studies that have employed latent variable methods to date have capitalized on the administration of multiple tasks, ideally differing in their nonexecutive demands. These investigations have not explicitly examined the role of foundational cognitive abilities that are

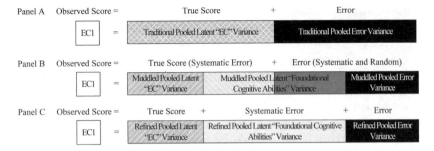

FIGURE 2.—Schematic representation of sources of variance contributing to executive task performance. The first formula, in line with classical test theory and the correlation model, assumes that all shared variance among the executive tasks is accounted for by latent EC. All other variance is classified as error, whether unaccounted for systematic variance or random variance. What we propose in the second formula is that the executive tasks also contain a portion of systematic shared variance attributable to foundational cognitive abilities, resulting in a muddled latent EC true score, where the shared, systematic foundational cognitive abilities variance across all executive tasks is included with the latent EC variance. Systematic foundational cognitive abilities variance not shared across all executive tasks is contained within the error variance. Without accounting for a separate foundational cognitive abilities latent variable, the model latent EC variance will resemble the first two segments of the second formula. When the model, however, does account for the systematic foundational cognitive abilities variance shared across the executive tasks, a refined latent EC true score, a refined latent foundational cognitive abilities true score and a refined error term co exist, as displayed in the third formula. We acknowledge that the refined pooled error variance in Panel C may include other sources of systematic variance not accounted for in our model.

invoked by the stimulus- or response-processing demands of the executive tasks. Generally, studies have rested on the assumption that the shared variance reflected in the latent executive construct/s is entirely specific, and that variance pertaining to task-dependent foundational cognitive abilities is embedded entirely in the error term (e.g., Lee et al., 2013; van der Sluis, de Jong, & Van der Leij, 2004). In Figure 2, Panel A, which describes the assumptions of classical test theory, note that there are two contributors to performance—the true score, in this case EC, and the remainder—error. That error term, in theory, includes everything that is not EC, namely, random error pertaining to the day, context, or child, as well as systematic differences associated with variation in foundational cognitive abilities, which, together with EC, drive observed performance. In fact, it is not fully clear from these models whether the shared variance captured by the latent variables entirely reflects EC per se, or whether this latent also captures foundational cognitive abilities. The tradition has been to assume that all of the overlapping variance across tasks can be ascribed specifically to EC, perhaps a reasonable assumption in an adult with relatively modularized neural systems and stable, mature cognitive abilities. However, there may also be systematic variance that is common to all measures but is not reflective of the specific executive demands of the task, including, for example, the language abilities needed to

24

process task instructions, the visual and spatial processing to recognize and identify the picture stimulus and its features, or the motor skills needed to select and produce a response. Thus, even with the latent variable modeling strategy, some subordinate foundational cognitive processes that are coordinated by EC and yet also drive task performance may remain embedded within the EC factor score, despite our best intentions to segregate these influences into the error term. Without additional parameters to capture systematic, shared variance related to foundational cognitive abilities, some of this variance likely will be contained in the EC factor, which in turn will not solely reflect EC as intended.

Preferably, then, the statistical model used to characterize the nature of EC would include at least two components: a specific executive process reflected by EC, as well as a stimulus-/response-driven subordinate factor reflective of the processing contribution of various foundational cognitive abilities. This idea is depicted visually in Figure 2, Panel C where task performance on all measures now is broken into three parts—the specific EC true score (in darker gray), general foundational cognitive abilities (in light gray), and the remaining error (in black). With this conceptualization, task performance is represented and modeled as a dualistic relation between EC and the general foundational cognitive abilities it coordinates. The metaphorical conductor and the musicians work together in an interdependent manner to produce smooth, beautiful music. Note that the variance pertaining to general foundational cognitive abilities is systematic and, as shown in Figure 2, Panel B, is composed of both task demand-related error variance previously ascribed to the error term, as well as true score variance previously ascribed to EC that in fact represents the foundational cognitive component processes that are controlled by EC. If these respective, systematic contributions to observed executive task performance can be modeled explicitly, perhaps EC in the preschool period can be better defined and our understanding of its role in shaping developmental outcomes enhanced.

In this volume, we argue that an alternative type of confirmatory factor analysis, the bifactor approach, may have utility for further examining the task impurity problem, particularly the unique challenges posed for EC measurement in the preschool period. Although integrated into this research area only recently (Friedman et al., 2008), the bifactor model often is used in circumstances where a general and a domain-specific factor(s) may be contributing together to performance on a task, and the inter related contribution of each of these factors is of interest. As shown in Figure 1: Model Type 3, in a bifactor model, each indicator is specified to load simultaneously onto a general factor and onto a specific factor. These double loadings indicate the potential for both a general and a specific factor to influence a child's performance on a task. In other words, an observed task score can be assumed to be influenced by multiple abilities that all affect performance.

Historically, bifactor models were developed in the context of research on intelligence (Holzinger & Swineford, 1937). In these models, task performance was believed to reflect both a general factor, "g," and more specific abilities of particular interest. Recently, the application of bifactor models has been extended to various research questions, including psychopathy (Patrick, Hicks, Nichol, & Krueger, 2007), health outcomes (Reise, Morizot, & Hays, 2007), achievement tests (DeMars, 2006), psychiatric diagnostic screening (Gibbons, Rush, & Immekus, 2009), and ADHD (Toplak et al., 2009).

In previous applications of the general-specific bifactor approach to characterize EC organization in adults, a general EC factor was modeled along with specific working memory and shifting factors, without consideration of the influences of foundational cognitive abilities because in most studies with adults, these abilities are presumed stable, well-learned, and fairly automatic. Here, we propose that using a bifactor model approach to simultaneously model the foundational cognitive abilities invoked by the processing demands of executive tasks in addition to EC may have utility for elucidating the dualistic contributions of these processes to well-controlled, smoothly executed task performance. Children need to complete both an executive task battery and some separate measure(s) of foundational cognitive abilities

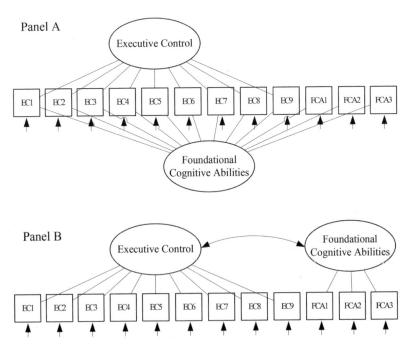

FIGURE 3.—Proposed bifactor model of EC and foundational cognitive abilities.

designed not to include strong executive demands (e.g., discrete tests of vocabulary, visual/spatial perception, or motor speed) in order to segregate these respective systematic influences on observed test performance. Because all executive measures are hypothesized to require foundational cognitive abilities in at least some degree, all measures would load onto the foundational cognitive ability factor, but only measures hypothesized to require EC would load onto an EC factor.

Restated in latent modeling terms, the contribution of each latent construct to each observed task is estimated in the measurement model. This measurement model consists of one general factor, hypothesized to reflect the amalgam of foundational cognitive abilities that are necessary for stimulus or response processing across all 12 measures in this case, and another factor(s), hypothesized to be EC, which captures the covariance only among the nine executive measures (see Figure 3, Panel A). Of note, the residual error for each indicator also is estimated in the bifactor approach and captures random error that affects children's performance on a task on a given day or in a particular moment. If the bifactor approach has explanatory power, the residual variance is hypothesized to be smaller than in traditional latent variable models that do not consider the influence of foundational cognitive abilities (compare the size of the error term between Panels A and C in Figure 2).

Of final note, the bifactor approach differs from our attempts in previous studies to consider alternative influences of shared task demands (Wiebe et al., 2008). In these models, alternative influences were modeled in an all or none fashion using a model similar to Figure 1, Model Type 1:B. Computerized tasks were modeled as a separate latent from noncomputerized tasks, for example. Unlike the bifactor approach, these past models did not consider simultaneously the relations of task stimulus- or response-characteristics to the common EC latent. Furthermore, the bifactor approach is not the same as a covariate model (see Figure 3, Panel B). In covariate models, the correlation between the covariate and the construct of interest is used to adjust for the relation of the covariate to an outcome so that two, independently defined constructs essentially compete with each other to explain variance in the dependent measure. Covariate models therefore do not allow one to evaluate whether, and to what degree, task performance itself is dependent on different constructs. As illustrated in Figure 3: Panel B, the assumption in covariate models is that the executive tasks are unidimensional EC indicators. EC correlates with foundational cognitive abilities at the construct level, but the executive tasks themselves are not assumed to assess these foundational abilities. In this parameterization, there is no way to determine how much of the executive task performance may actually be attributed to the influence of foundational cognitive abilities. In contrast, the bifactor model represents the executive tasks themselves as multidimensional and reliant on both EC and foundational cognitive abilities. The interest is in determining whether the control process that has two respective contributions, the specific EC and subordinate foundational cognitive abilities, both of which are developing in the preschool period, may contribute differentially to task performance. It should now be clear that the bifactor model is a particularly promising means to investigate the structure and development of EC in the pivotal preschool age period where different brain regions are at different stages of maturation. By modeling foundational cognitive abilities and EC simultaneously, we also may be able to better elucidate how each construct relates to variations in children's experiences and to important developmental outcomes.

USING THE BIFACTOR APPROACH TO BETTER UNDERSTAND EXECUTIVE CONTROL IN EARLY CHILDHOOD

As highlighted above, the measurement and conceptual issues surrounding EC in early childhood have hindered understanding of its true nature, its developmental course, and its relations to other constructs and outcomes. Disentangling EC from the foundational cognitive abilities that it regulates may enhance the specificity of its measurement and provide advantages in characterizing the true nature of EC and its links to predictors and outcomes of interest.

The studies in this volume make use of the bifactor approach to (i) evaluate the validity of a segregated EC construct with a view to shedding additional light on the potentially dynamic latent structure of EC across the preschool age range; (ii) identify how sociodemographic risk may relate to EC and foundational cognitive abilities to improve our understanding of possible mechanisms of individual differences; and (iii) examine the relation of early EC and foundational cognitive abilities to core dimensions of developmental psychopathology. We used the bifactor model to consider the respective influences of EC and subordinate foundational cognitive abilities that also are rapidly developing and differ among preschoolers in this dynamic developmental period. To assess these foundational abilities, we drew upon discrete standardized tests that demonstrate high content and test-retest reliability, have been subject to rigorous validation procedures, and are designed to capture cardinal cognitive abilities that relate to the stimulus and response processing demands. Our goal was to take a translational approach and use a psychometrically sound characterization of the key foundational cognitive abilities that may be involved in executive task performance, in a manner that is feasible in assessment of young children who have a very limited time window of systematic effort, attention, and endurance.

Chapter II describes our approach to sampling, assessment, and latent variable modeling. In line with our global aims, Chapter III focuses primarily on the application of this bifactor method at different points spanning the preschool period to evaluate the respective influences of EC and foundational cognitive abilities on executive task performance. Specifically, we simultaneously allowed executive tasks administered at each of the longitudinal follow-up points to load on an EC factor and onto a foundational cognitive ability factor. Chapters IV and V are focused on the application of this bifactor model to individual differences in development. We examined the relation of different dimensions of children's early socio-familial settings to their executive task proficiency in Chapter IV, with the goal of better characterizing potential mechanisms of effect. Chapter V probes the predictive relation of EC identified with the bifactor approach to empirically determined dimensions of dysregulated, hyperactive, inattentive, impulsive behaviors, which in the clinical/developmental psychopathology literature would be referred to as ADHD symptoms. Here we use the developmental terminology given the monograph audience, but in keeping with a translational approach, utilize measurement tools that span both approaches. Chapter VI provides cross-cutting conclusions, with an eye toward broader implications for developmental science.

II. THE PRESCHOOL PROBLEM SOLVING STUDY: SAMPLE, DATA, AND STATISTICAL METHODS

T. D. James, H.-J. Choi, S. A. Wiebe, and K. A. Espy

This article is part of the issue "The Changing Nature of Executive Control in Preschool" Espy (Issue Editor). For a full listing of articles in this issue, see: http://onlinelibrary.wiley.com/doi/10.1111/mono. v81.4/issuetoc.

The goals set forth in Chapter I to study executive control (EC) in early childhood were examined using data from the Preschool Problem Solving Study. Here, we describe the study participants, data collection procedures, and measures used across the subsequent three chapters. In addition, the current chapter presents and elaborates on the manifest behavioral data collected for each executive and foundational cognitive ability measure central to models of latent EC tested in Chapter III. Finally, the chapter details and provides rationale for the chosen estimation and evaluation methods used for the latent modeling in Chapters III, IV, and V.

PARTICIPANTS

The sample consisted of 388 typically developing preschool children. Study participants were recruited from two Midwestern study sites, a small city and a rural tri-county area. Techniques used to recruit the sample included birth announcements, local preschools, the local health department, doctor's offices, and word of mouth. Prior to enrollment in the study, parents

Corresponding author: Tiffany James, email: tjames6@unl.edu
DOI: 10.1111/mono.12269
© 2016 The Society for Research in Child Development, Inc.

completed a telephone screening. Children were excluded from study participation if they had known delays in development or language or a diagnosed learning or behavioral disorder, if the primary language spoken in the home was not English, or if the family planned to move out of the area during the study timeline. Children with parent-reported diagnosed developmental or language delays that were reported to emerge after enrollment also were excluded subsequently from the analyses.

The cross-sectional forms of data analysis conducted in this monograph use data from a longitudinal study that utilized a lagged sequential design (Schaie, 1965) to evaluate practice effects that are confounded with developmental change in a single cohort longitudinal design. Figure 4 summarizes the study design and cohort retention at different age points. The majority of the children were enrolled at age 3 years (3;0 cohort; $n = 228$), with smaller groups of children enrolled at 3 years 9 months (3;9 cohort; $n = 57$), 4 years 6 months (4;6 cohort; $n = 55$), and 5 years 3 months (5;3 cohort; $n = 48$). Due to the nature of this design, children recruited at later ages had missing data (i.e., planned missing observations) at ages prior to their enrollment. Of the 228 eligible children enrolled at 3 years, 96% were seen at the 3 years 9 months assessment, 93% were seen at the 4 years 6 months assessment, and 92% were seen at the 5 years 3 months assessment. Of the 57 eligible children enrolled at 3 years 9 months, 91% were seen at the 4 years 6

	3 years, 0 months	3 years, 9 months	4 years, 6 months	5 years, 3 months
3;0 cohort (n=228)	Measures administered: EC Task Battery CAARS-S, EC-HOME, LISRES-A, SWP	Measures administered: EC Task Battery	Measures administered: EC Task Battery	Measures administered: EC Task Battery CBCL, SNAP-IV, WJ-III BIA
	100% Completed	96% Completed	93% Completed	92% Completed
3;9 cohort (n=57)		Measures administered: EC Task Battery CAARS-S, EC-HOME, LISRES-A, SWP	Measures administered: EC Task Battery	Measures administered: EC Task Battery CBCL, SNAP-IV, WJ-III BIA
		100% Completed	91% Completed	89% Completed
4;6 cohort (n=55)			Measures administered: EC Task Battery CAARS-S, EC-HOME, LISRES-A, SWP	Measures administered: EC Task Battery CBCL, SNAP-IV, WJ-III BIA
			100% Completed	100% Completed
5;3 cohort (n=48)				Measures administered: EC Task Battery CAARS-S, CBCL, EC-HOME, LISRES-A, SNAP-IV, SWP,WJ-III BIA
				100% Completed

FIGURE 4.—Summary of sampling methods and data collected at different age points in the Preschool Problem Solving Study.

31

months assessment, and 89% were seen at the 5 years 3 months assessment. All of the 55 eligible children enrolled at 4 years 6 months were seen at the 5 years 3 months assessment.

Sampling was stratified based on sex and sociodemographic risk, defined by enrollment in public medical assistance or enrollment in free school lunch, or based on Health and Human Services poverty guidelines, as programs in these two regions use the same poverty guideline for enrollment qualification. Children considered at sociodemographic risk comprised 44.1% of the sample. The sample consisted of 195 girls and 193 boys. The racial/ethnic breakdown was 286 non-Hispanic Whites/Caucasians, 20 African Americans, 1 Asian American, 31 Hispanics, and 50 multiracial children. At the 3-year assessment, children's mean age was 3 years 5 days ($SD = 14$ days; Range $= 2.92$–3.08 years); at the 3 years 9 months assessment children's mean age was 3 years 8 months 30 days ($SD = 16$ days; Range $= 3.67$–3.83 years); at the 4 years 6 months assessment children's mean age was 4 years 5 months 29 days ($SD = 15$ days; Range $= 4.42$–4.58 years); and at the 5 years 3 months assessment children's mean age was 5 years 2 months 26 days ($SD = 15$ days; Range $= 5.17$ to 5.33 years). The distribution of maternal education was 19% high school graduate or less; 37% some college, and 44% college graduate or greater ($M = 14.97$ years, $SD = 2.37$ years).

PROCEDURES

Trained research technicians conducted a home visit within a 4-week window of the target enrollment age. At the home visit, the mother completed questionnaires, including the Life Stressors and Social Resources Inventory-Adult Form (LISRES-A; Moos & Moos, 1994), and a research technician completed the Early Childhood Home Observation for Measurement of the Environment (EC-HOME; Caldwell & Bradley, 1984) with the mother. The first lab session was completed within approximately one week of the home visit. At this lab visit, the mother completed a background interview and the Satisfaction with Parenting Scale from the Inventory of Parent Experiences (SWPS; Crnic, Greenberg, Ragozin, Robinson, & Basham, 1983), and the child completed a battery of child-friendly executive tasks. Subsequent lab sessions were completed every 9 months within 2 weeks before or after the target age until completion of the study. Each lab session was video recorded and lasted approximately 2 hr with a scheduled break. At the final lab session, a trained research technician administered the WJ-III Brief Intellectual Assessment (Woodcock, McGrew, & Mather, 2001) to the child. For all tasks except modified Snack Delay, the mother remained in the room with the child during the lab sessions, completing a background interview and forms rating the child's behavior and home environment. At the final lab session, the mother completed the Child Behavior Checklist for Ages 1½–5 (CBCL/ 1½–5; Achenbach & Rescorla, 2000) and the SNAP-IV Rating Scale (SNAP-IV; Swanson, Sandman, Deutsch, & Baren, 1983). After each lab session, the child received a small toy for their participation and the mother received a gift card as compensation. Participants who completed the entire longitudinal study received an additional gift card bonus.

MEASURES

The executive tasks administered to preschoolers varied in stimulus type, presentation format, and response requirements with the goal of sufficiently holding the preschool child's interest within and across tasks to maximize the amount of data that could be collected. Tasks were designed with varying a priori demands on working memory, inhibition, and flexible shifting. Because the end-goal was to model individual variation across the preschool period, the same measures were administered at each time point. The downside of this measurement approach is that performance, even in preschoolers, may be subject to practice effects. Specific efforts, such as changing the colors and shapes of containers used in delay tasks, were implemented to try to minimize carryover across sessions. Tasks also were administered in a fixed order to hold possible carryover effects constant across participants, see Table 1 for the order of administration.

A brief description of each executive task is in Table 1. Measures of working memory included the Nine Boxes task (adapted from Diamond et al., 1997), the Delayed Alternation task (Espy et al., 1999; Goldman, Rosvold, Vest, & Galkin, 1971), and the Nebraska Barnyard task (adapted from the Noisy Book task; Hughes, Dunn, & White, 1998). Measures of inhibition included the Big-Little Stroop task (adapted from Kochanska et al., 2000), the Go/No-Go task (adapted from Simpson & Riggs, 2006), the Shape School task–Inhibit condition (Espy, 1997; Espy, Bull, Martin, & Stroup, 2006), and the modified Snack Delay task (adapted from Kochanska, Murray, Jacques, & Koenig, 1996; Korkman, Kirk, & Kemp, 1998). Measures of flexible shifting included the Shape School task–Switching condition (Espy, 1997; Espy et al., 2006) and the Trails task–Switching condition (modified from Espy & Cwik, 2004).

Nebraska Barnyard was administered on the computer using Perl v5.8.8 (Active-State Software, Vancouver, BC, Canada). Big-Little Stroop, Go/No-Go, and Shape School were administered on the computer using E-Prime 1.1 (Psychology Software Tools, Pittsburgh, PA, USA) or SuperLab (Cedrus, San Jose, CA, USA). Trained undergraduate students and researchers coded the child's behaviors offline for Nine Boxes, Nebraska Barnyard, Big-Little

TABLE 1

Description	Order of Administration	Examples
Working Memory		
Nine Boxes: Task requires children to keep the previously searched boxes of varying color in mind to find the reward in the unsearched location	1	
Delayed Alternation: Task requires children to keep the last reward location in mind over a delay to retrieve the reward in the alternate location	5	
Nebraska Barnyard: Task requires children to recall progressively increasing sequences of animals and correctly reproduce the sequence on the touch screen	9	
Inhibition		
Big–Little: Task requires children to name the smaller picture embedded in the larger picture while suppressing naming the larger picture shape	2	
Go/No-Go: Task requires children to press the button for fish stimuli and suppress pressing the button for shark stimuli	4	
Shape School–Inhibit: Task requires children to name the color of the stimuli with happy faces and suppress naming the stimuli with sad faces	6	
modified Snack Delay: Task requires children to maintain a snowman-like posture despite accessibility to a snack and the researcher's verbal and visual distractions.	8	
Flexible Shifting		
Shape School-Switching: Task requires children to name the color of the stimuli without hats and name the shape of the stimuli with hats	7	
Trails–Switching: Task requires children to alternate stamping paired dog and bone stimuli of progressively increasing size	3	

Stroop, Shape School, modified Snack Delay, and Trails using Noldus Observer Video-Pro 5.0.31 (Noldus Information Technology, Wageningen, the Netherlands). Delayed Alternation was scored by the researcher during the session. For these scored or coded tasks, interrater reliability was calculated from redundant offline coding or scoring from the videos filmed during the assessment on a random sampling of 20% of files, which is reported below with the description of each task. Children responded via button press and the button box recorded the response accuracy information for Go/No-Go.

For Nine Boxes (9B), the researcher placed nine small figurines in nine boxes, which differed in color and shape on the lid, as the child watched. The child was asked to find all of the figurines by selecting one box for each trial. Between trials during a 15-second delay, the box locations were rearranged out of the child's sight. The task was discontinued when the child found all nine figurines, when the child made five consecutive errors, or after 20 administered trials. The dependent measure selected was the longest run of consecutive correct responses. All four ages had complete data. Interrater reliability for the coding of this task was 96%.

During Delayed Alternation (DA), a treat was hidden, out of the child's sight, beneath one of two identical cups on a testing board. Whenever the child correctly retrieved the reward, the treat location alternated to the other location. Between trials, the child needed to remember the previous reward location across a 10-second time delay, including researcher verbal distractions. Up to 16 trials were administered, although the task was discontinued if the child made nine consecutive correct responses. Children who reached nine consecutive correct responses prior to the end of 16 trials were given credit for the remaining responses. The selected dependent variable was the maximum number of consecutive correct responses minus the maximum number of consecutive incorrect responses. There was one missing data point at 3 years and 3 years 9 months, respectively, both due to task noncompletion. There were no missing data at the latter two ages. Interrater reliability for the scoring of this task was 100%.

Nebraska Barnyard (NB) is a complex span task administered with nine colored buttons, initially with pictures of animals, arranged in a 3×3 grid on a computer touch screen. The button colors corresponded to the animal (e.g., a brown button for the cow, a white button for the sheep) and the computer produced the corresponding animal sound when the child pressed the button. During the training trials, children were introduced to the game with the animal pictures on the buttons to learn which buttons represented which animals. Children received a score of 0 if they could not name the majority of the animals to continue to the test trials ($n = 8$). For the test trials, the animal pictures were removed. The test trials began with nine trials with a sequence length of only one. After these trials and starting with sequences of two animals, up to three trials were administered at each span length. The researcher read the sequence and the child attempted to reproduce the sequence in the correct order on the touch screen. If a child correctly reproduced the first two trials, the third trial was skipped and the child was given credit for it. The sequence length continued to increase until the child was unable to correctly reproduce any of the three trials. The selected dependent measure was a correct trial total (One sequence length trials = .33 per trial, All other trials = 1 per trial). At 3 years, six children did not have data for this task due to task noncompletion. All other ages had complete data. Interrater reliability for the coding of this task was 96%.

For Big–Little Stroop (BL), line drawings of everyday objects embedded with smaller pictures were presented on the computer screen. The smaller embedded pictures either matched the larger object or were different than the larger object. A brief presentation (730 ms) of just the larger object preceded the presentation of the full trial that included the embedded smaller pictures. The child attempted to name the smaller embedded picture while suppressing a verbal response to the larger picture when it conflicted with the smaller picture. During the training phase, children unable to correctly name the majority of the objects to continue to the test trials were assigned a score of 0 ($n = 3$). The selected dependent measure was the proportion of correct responses on the conflict trials; half of the 24 test trials were conflict trials. At 3 years, five children were missing data; at 3 years 9 months, two children were missing data; at 4 years 6 months, one child was missing data; no children were missing data for this task at 5 years 3 months. Missing data was due to audiovisual malfunction or task noncompletion. Interrater reliability for the coding of this task was 99%.

Go/No-Go (GNG) is a computer game where pictures of colored fish and sharks were presented on the computer screen. Children were instructed to press the button to "catch" the fish stimuli and not press the button for shark stimuli to "let it go." When the child pressed the button, feedback was given as a fish in a net for fish trials and as a broken net for shark trials. No feedback was given if the child did not press the button. After an interval of 1,000 ms between trials, the stimulus appeared on the screen until the child pressed the button or for 1,500 ms. Each block of eight trials included six fish and two shark trials presented as one shark trial following two fish trials and the other shark trial following four fish trials. Forty test trials were administered, of which 25% were shark trials. The selected dependent measure was d prime (d') which is the standardized difference between the hit rate and the false alarm rate (calculated by subtracting the z-score value of the hit rate right-tail p-value from the z-score value of the false alarm rate right-tail p-value; Macmillan & Creelman, 2005). Trials with response times faster than 200 ms were excluded as they are assumed to be responses to the previous trial. Six children were missing data at 3 years, three children were missing data at 3 years 9 months, and one child was missing data at 5 years 3 months. Missing data was due to audiovisual malfunction or task noncompletion.

For Shape School–Inhibit condition (SSI), cartoon stimuli, introduced through a story of school children, were presented on the computer screen. To prime the prepotent color-naming response, 12 trials were administered during a control condition where children named the colors of the neutral faced stimuli. Children who could not accurately name the colors of the stimuli and move onto the inhibit condition received a score of 0 for the inhibit condition ($n = 38$). During the inhibit condition, children named the color of the stimuli with a happy face and suppressed naming the stimuli with a sad face. Eighteen trials were administered, of which six were inhibit trials. The selected dependent measure was the proportion of correct responses on inhibit trials. At 3 years, 37 children were missing data; at 3 years 9 months, 12 children were missing data; at 4 years 6 months, 2 children were missing data; no children were missing data at 5 years 3 months. Missing data was due to audiovisual malfunction, examiner error, or task non-completion. Interrater reliability for the coding of this task was 99%.

During modified Snack Delay (mSD), the researcher instructed the child to remain frozen like a snowman, without moving or talking, with his/her hands on a placemat and feet planted on the floor. This task lasted for 240 seconds during which the snack was left in sight of the child and the examiner provided scripted distractions (e.g., coughing, dropping pencil) and left the room for a fixed time period. The selected dependent measure was a summary score of hand movement. Children were given 1 point for each 5-second epoch with no hand movement, .5 point for each 5-second epoch with some hand movement, and 0 points for each 5-second epoch with lots of hand movement. This was summed across all epochs prior to the child eating the snack or the end of the task at 240 seconds. Fourteen children were missing data for this task at 3 years, 8 children were missing data at 3 years 9 months, one child was missing data at 4 years 6 months, and one child was missing data at 5 years 3 months. Missing data was due to audiovisual malfunction, examiner error, or task noncompletion. Interrater reliability for the coding of this task was 91%.

For Shape School–Switching condition (SSS), cartoon stimuli, intro-duced through a story of school children, were presented on the computer screen. During a control condition, 12 trials were administered to prime the shape-naming response, where the child named the shapes of the stimuli wearing hats. Children who could not accurately name the colors or shapes of the stimuli received a score of 0 for the switching condition ($n = 75$). During the test trials, children named the color of the stimuli without hats and named the shape of the stimuli with hats. Fifteen trials were administered, of which 10 were switching trials. The selected dependent measure was the proportion of correct responses on switching trials. At 3 years, 76 children were missing data for this task. At 3 years 9 months, 34 children were missing data and at 4 years 6 months, 5 children were missing data. There were no missing data at 5 years 3 months. Missing data was due to audiovisual malfunction, examiner error, or task noncompletion. Interrater reliability for the coding of this task was 99%.

During Trails–Switching condition (TRB), children were presented a storybook of a family of dogs. Two control conditions were administered to train the child in identifying size sequencing prior to the switching condition. In the switching condition, children were asked to stamp the dogs then their matching bones beginning with the smallest dog and bone pair moving up to the largest dog and bone pair. The selected dependent measure was an efficiency score computed by dividing the total number of correct stamps by the total number of stamps. Forty-nine children were missing data at 3 years, 14 were missing at 3 years 9 months, three were missing at 4 years 6 months, and nine were missing at 5 years 3 months. Missing data was due to audiovisual malfunction, examiner error, or task noncompletion. Interrater reliability for the coding of this task was 95%.

The Verbal Comprehension, Concept Formation, and Visual Matching measures are standardized tests from the WJ-III Brief Intellectual Assessment. For all of these standardized tests, item difficulty increased across trials and the researcher discontinued the test if the child met the termination criteria. Given the cross-sectional nature of the analyses, the raw score of each test was used.

The Verbal Comprehension test measures four different aspects of language development, including picture vocabulary, synonyms, antonyms, and verbal analogies. To test picture vocabulary, children identified pictures of a variety of objects by pointing in the first two trials and responding verbally in subsequent trials. For synonyms and antonyms, the researcher read a word and the child provided the synonym or antonym. To test verbal comprehension, the researcher read three words of an analogy and the child completed the analogy with the correct fourth word. Reliability for these subtests in 3–6 year olds ranges between .88 and .90 (Woodcock et al., 2001).

Concept Formation measured visual/spatial perception by requiring children to use categorical identification and reasoning. The first part of the test required children to identify the different object among a set of similar objects, and the second part of the test required children to identify the reason why a particular object was different from the set of presented objects. Reliability for this test in 3–6 year olds ranges between .86 and .94 (Woodcock et al., 2001).

Visual Matching tested processing speed with two versions. In the first version, children pointed to the two matching shapes in a row of 4–5 shapes. In the second version, children circled two matching numbers in a row of six numbers. Per standardized procedures, the researcher first administered version 1 and then administered version 2 only if the child demonstrated acceptable performance on version 1 and understanding for the rules of version 2 during a practice test. The researcher discontinued the test if the child had not finished in the given time limit (2 minutes for version 1 and 3 minutes for version 2). Reliability for this test in 3–6 year olds ranged between .93 and .95 (Woodcock et al., 2001). Forty-one children were missing data on these tasks as they were not available for their anticipated final session for reasons such as living out of the area or inability to schedule the appointment.

BEHAVIORAL DATA

Descriptive statistics and Pearson correlations for all measures are presented in Tables 2 and 3, respectively. As expected, the mean accuracy performance for each task in the executive battery increased across the four ages, as seen in Figure 5. For some of these tasks, floor effects were seen at the youngest age. Not surprisingly, due to the rapid cognitive development over the preschool period, ceiling effects began to appear at the latter two ages for some of the tasks, particularly for Big-Little Stroop and Shape School–Inhibit condition. The distribution of some of the tasks at certain ages was less than desirable with skewness and/or kurtosis greater than 3 or less than -3. For these cases, outliers were trimmed to three standard deviations above and below the mean. The trimmed measures are Delayed Alternation at 3 years, Big-Little Stroop at 4 years 6 months and 5 years 3 months, Go/No-Go at 5 years 3 months, Shape School–Inhibit condition at 4 years 6 months and 5 years 3 months, Shape School–Switching condition at 5 years 3 months, and Trails–Switching condition at 4 years 6 months. Trimming resulted in an improvement for all of the measures, however, less than ideal distributional properties remained for Big-Little Stroop at age 4 years 6 months (skewness $= -2.14$; kurtosis $= 4.07$) and 5 years 3 months (skewness $= -1.96$; kurtosis $= 3.89$) and Shape School–Inhibit condition at 4 years 6 months (skewness $= -2.65$; kurtosis $= 6.33$) and at 5 years 3 months (skewness $= -3.01$; kurtosis $= 9.35$), which was not surprising given the ceiling effects that appeared at these ages for these tasks. Correlations between the executive tasks were low to moderate, as in other studies in which a large task battery was administered to a preschool sample (e.g., Hughes et al., 2010). The modest correlations suggest a need for a latent EC construct and the consideration of modeling additional sources of shared variance among the executive tasks.

Practice effects were minimal and only seen with two executive tasks. Practice effects were significant for Nine Boxes at ages 4 years 6 months $F(2, 316) = 3.09$, $p(.047)$ and 5 years 3 months $F(3, 360) = 3.92$, $p(.009)$. Post hoc analyses revealed that at 4 years 6 months, the 3;0 cohort had a significantly

39

TABLE 2

Descriptive Statistics for Preschoolers' Cognitive Task Performance at Different Assessment Points

Task (Outcome Measure)	Age	N	M	SD	Observed Range	Skewness	Kurtosis
Nine Boxes (9B) (Longest consecutive correct run)	3;0	228	4.32	1.60	2–9	0.85	0.42
	3;9	276	4.92	1.71	2–9	0.32	−0.57
	4;6	319	5.23	1.79	2–9	0.47	−0.60
	5;3	364	5.73	1.87	2–9	0.12	−0.85
Delayed Alternation (DA) (Longest correct run–longest incorrect run)	3;0	227	−0.37	3.96	−16 to 16	−0.10	4.83
	3;9	275	2.61	4.85	−10 to 16	1.33	2.00
	4;6	319	5.99	5.51	−5 to 16	0.65	−0.63
	5;3	364	7.52	5.80	−6 to 16	0.35	−1.23
Nebraska Barnyard (NB) (Correct trial total)	3;0	222	2.88	1.57	0–9	0.68	0.85
	3;9	276	4.90	2.07	.33–10	0.43	−0.33
	4;6	319	6.98	2.60	0–13	0.21	−0.77
	5;3	364	8.91	2.41	2.33–15.67	−0.48	−0.13
Big–Little (BL) (Proportion correct [conflict trials])	3;0	223	.29	.29	0–1	0.98	−0.18
	3;9	274	.64	.34	0–1	−0.73	−0.98
	4;6	318	.85	.23	0–1	−2.37	5.32
	5;3	364	.94	.11	.08–1	−3.97	22.58
Go/No-Go (GNG) (d prime)	3;0	222	0.25	0.74	−1.37–2.39	0.65	0.06
	3;9	273	1.38	1.01	−1.26 to 3.11	−0.33	−0.69
	4;6	319	2.30	0.82	−.57 to 3.11	−1.31	1.50
	5;3	363	2.74	0.53	−.16 to 3.11	−1.96	5.15
Shape School–Inhibit (SSI) (Proportion correct [inhibit trials])	3;0	191	.38	.42	0–1	0.55	−1.43
	3;9	264	.75	.37	0–1	−1.16	−0.27
	4;6	317	.92	.21	0–1	−3.16	9.92
	5;3	364	.95	.15	0–1	−4.61	23.91
Modified Snack Delay (mSD) (Hand movement score)	3;0	214	12.21	11.42	0–48	0.79	−0.23

(Continued)

TABLE 2. (Continued)

Task (Outcome Measure)	Age	N	M	SD	Observed Range	Skewness	Kurtosis
	3;9	268	17.96	10.93	0–44.5	0.00	−0.59
	4;6	318	21.85	9.40	0–44	−0.36	0.15
	5;3	363	25.54	9.84	0–48	−0.35	0.17
Shape School–Switching (SSS) (Proportion correct [switching trials])	3;0	152	.26	.26	0–1	0.56	−0.65
	3;9	242	.57	.29	0–1	−0.38	−0.71
	4;6	314	.73	.24	0–1	−0.79	−0.01
	5;3	364	.84	.19	0–1	−1.77	3.84
Trails–Switching (TRB) (Efficiency score)	3;0	179	.70	.19	.07–1	−0.44	−0.10
	3;9	262	.82	.13	.38–1	−0.71	0.25
	4;6	316	.86	.12	.18–1	−1.23	3.10
	5;3	355	.90	.11	.52–1	−0.92	0.10
Verbal Comprehension (VC)	Exit	347	464.29	13.10	434–502	0.01	−0.52
Concept Formation (CF)	Exit	347	460.58	16.99	418–508	0.24	−0.24
Visual Matching (VM)	Exit	347	456.18	11.97	411–486	−0.43	0.50

TABLE 3

Pearson Correlations Between Measures of Executive Control and Foundational Cognitive Abilities at Each Age

Age 3;0

Measure	9B	DA	NB	BL	GNG	SSI	mSD	SSS	TRB	VC	CF
DA	.07										
NB	.13*	.20*									
BL	.07	.23*	.30*								
GNG	.02	.09	.15*	.19*							
SSI	−.02	.18*	.27*	.36*	.27*						
mSD	.07	.02	.26*	.24*	.23*	.26*					
SSS	.03	.16*	.58*	.25*	.15	.50*	.17*				
TRB	.02	.06	.33*	.20*	.14	.27*	.31*	.27*			
VC	.05	.17*	.50*	.24*	.27*	.35*	.25*	.37*	.28*		
CF	.09	.15*	.34*	.28*	.13	.30*	.25*	.30*	.18*	.57*	
VM	.19*	.16*	.32*	.20*	.16*	.15*	.19*	.19*	.17*	.45*	.40*

Age 3;9

	9B	DA	NB	BL	GNG	SSI	mSD	SSS	TRB	VC	CF
DA	.09										
NB	.14*	.19*									
BL	.08	.22*	.43*								
GNG	.11	.11	.25*	.27*							
SSI	.05	.12*	.33*	.36*	.42*						
mSD	.08	.09	.20*	.23*	.30*	.25*					
SSS	.14*	.17*	.35*	.51*	.33*	.48*	.22*				
TRB	.04	.07	.18*	.13*	.09	.28*	.10	.20*			
VC	.07	.19*	.42*	.39*	.26*	.33*	.24*	.39*	.20*		
CF	.05	.17*	.33*	.36*	.30*	.27*	.16*	.42*	.19*	.57*	
VM	.12	.21*	.32*	.31*	.27*	.26*	.15*	.27*	.05	.45*	.40*

Age 4;6

	9B	DA	NB	BL	GNG	SSI	mSD	SSS	TRB	VC	CF
DA	.09										
NB	.17*	.23*									
BL	.07	.13*	.34*								
GNG	.02	.18*	.25*	.19							
SSI	.00	.10	.20*	.10	.31*						
mSD	.16*	.23*	.29*	.16*	.31*	.22*					
SSS	.07	.18*	.37*	.40*	.33*	.29*	.30*				
TRB	.10	.15*	.21*	.15*	.14*	.17*	.17*	.25*			
VC	.10	.12*	.45*	.29*	.27*	.18*	.20*	.34*	.02		
CF	-.04	.14*	.35*	.25*	.27*	.15*	.28*	.27*	.05	.57*	
VM	.07	.17*	.34*	.30*	.25*	.18*	.22*	.24*	.08	.45*	.40*

Age 5;3

	9B	DA	NB	BL	GNG	SSI	mSD	SSS	TRB	VC	CF
DA	.11*										
NB	.17*	.14*									
BL	.14*	.11*	.38*								
GNG	.16*	.23*	.30*	.25*							
SSI	.03	.05	.13*	.17*	.10						
mSD	.23*	.03	.24*	.21*	.21*	.15*					
SSS	.12*	.07	.28*	.28*	.23*	.23*	.19*				
TRB	.09	.13*	.17*	.18*	.12*	.12*	.12*	.22*			
VC	.03	-.02	.53*	.34*	.31*	.15*	.14*	.27*	.13*		
CF	.02	.02	.39*	.25*	.30*	.11*	.18*	.26*	.12*	.57*	
VM	.06	.05	.34*	.26*	.30*	.05	.13*	.30*	.05	.45*	.40*

Note. 9B = Nine Boxes, DA = Delayed Alternation, NB = Nebraska Barnyard, BL = Big-Little, GNG = Go/No-Go, SSI = Shape School–Inhibit, mSD = modified Snack Delay, SSS = Shape School–Switching, TRB = Trails–Switching, VC = Verbal Comprehension, CF = Concept Formation, VM = Visual Matching.
*$p < .05$.

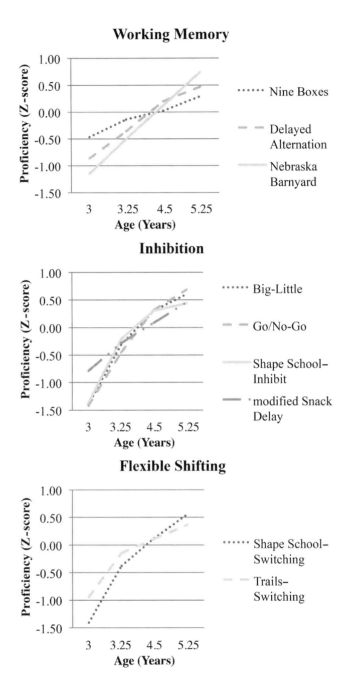

FIGURE 5.—Mean age-related gains in performance for executive measures of working memory, inhibition, and flexible shifting across the preschool period.

higher maximum consecutive correct run than the 4;6 cohort. At 5 years 3 months, the post-hoc analyses revealed that the 3;0, 3;9, and 4;6 cohorts had a significantly higher maximum consecutive correct run than the 5;3 cohort. Trails at age 3 years 9 months also had a significant practice effect with the 3;0 cohort having a significantly higher efficiency score than the 3;9 cohort.

MODEL ESTIMATION

The following three chapters all employ latent modeling to address the proposed questions. For a latent modeling approach, maximum likelihood estimation (MLE) has well-known optimal properties such as efficiency, consistency, and lack of bias, that is, the variance of MLE is at a minimum (efficiency), MLE converges to the true parameter values as sample size increases (consistency) and MLE neither over- nor underestimates the parameter (unbiased). The underlying principle of MLE is to determine parameter estimates that maximize the probability of the observed data (Fisher, 1922). However, these properties hold only if the model is true and the data meet a set of assumptions, including independent observations, multivariate normality, continuity, and large sample size (Bollen, 1989; Kline, 2010). In practice these assumptions are often violated and the observed data are nonnormal or categorical. In such cases, MLE yields biased standard errors that can have a significant impact on hypothesis tests of parameter estimates and threaten the validity of the study findings. To accommodate such violations and obtain robust estimates with more accurate standard errors, alternative estimators have been proposed, including robust MLE (e.g., MLR in Mplus). MLR has several advantages. It is recommended for small- or medium-sized samples (Yuan & Bentler, 2000) and using MLR, one can handle missing data through full information maximum likelihood estimation under either the missing at completely random (MCAR) or missing at random (MAR) assumptions for incomplete data. MLR is less sensitive to model misspecification. That is, it may yield smaller standard errors and outperform other estimators (e.g., WLSMV) even when a model is slightly misspecified because MLR uses a full information matrix as opposed to using a limited information matrix from the data. Given that some variables in the current study showed nonnormality or were ordinal, we utilized MLR to estimate model parameters throughout the monograph.

MODEL EVALUATION

Once a model is specified and parameters are estimated, how well the model fits the observed data should be assessed before interpreting results.

Various fit indices have been developed and can be classified into three bins: absolute fit indices, incremental fit indices, and information-based fit statistics (Bollen, 1989; Hu & Bentler, 1999). Absolute fit indices assess how well the imposed model reproduces the sample data and includes the root mean squared error of approximation (RMSEA). Second, incremental fit indices, also known as comparative fit indices, including Bentler's Comparative Fit Index (CFI; Bentler, 1990), assess the improvement in fit by comparing a target model with a more restricted, nested model. Finally, fit statistics based on information criteria attempt to balance goodness of fit with parsimony and include the Akaike information criterion (AIC; Akaike, 1987) and Bayesian information criterion (Schwarz, 1978). For AIC and BIC, the degrees of freedom of a model or sample size is included to penalize model complexity. These indexes are particularly useful for comparing models that are not nested.

The choice of how to use incremental and information-based fit statistics depends on whether the competing models are nested within one another. Generally speaking, Model A is nested within Model B if Model A is a special case of Model B; that is, Model A can be specified by constraining some of the parameters in Model B. For comparing the relative fit of the nested models, the difference between the χ^2 values for two nested models can be used as the χ^2 difference that follows the χ^2 distribution with degrees of freedom equal to the difference in degrees of freedom for the two models. When several competing models or theories exist, model fit indices can be used to determine which model best represents the data. It is worth noting that a good fit is a necessary, but not sufficient, condition to decide which model is the most apt or preferred one. Theoretical justification and the overarching tenet of parsimony are important in combination with statistical evidence in selecting a final model. It is recommended to use multiple fit indices, as well as theory, to determine the best fit model (Jaccard & Wan, 1996; Marsh, Wen, & Hau, 2004). It is common to use the χ^2 difference test, CFI, RMSEA, AIC, and BIC together for model comparison. For the χ^2 difference test, the significance of the change in value given the change in degrees of freedom provides model fit information. For other indices, the following have been recommended as criteria for a good fit: $CFI \geq .95$, $RMSEA \leq .06$ (Hu & Bentler, 1999). For AIC and BIC, smaller values indicate better fit. More detailed criteria for evaluation of model fit can be found in Byrne (1998), and Hu and Bentler (1999).

As discussed in the previous section, we applied a latent modeling framework via MLR estimation for the forthcoming chapters. More specifically, in Chapter III, latent variable modeling was used to explore the structure of EC and the influence of foundational cognitive abilities in executive task performance using the bifactor approach. In Chapter IV, exploratory factor analysis (EFA) was used to establish the factor structure underlying variables used to describe children's socio-familial risk and then integrated with structural equation modeling (SEM) to investigate the relation of these social background characteristics to children's EC and foundational cognitive abilities. MLR with numerical integration was used in Chapter V employing SEM to investigate the relation of EC and foundational cognitive abilities to dimensions of dysregulated child behavior. The estimation method specific to each study will be described in more detail in each chapter.

This study used these data and methods to better understand the nature of EC and its relation to predictors and outcomes, as we investigated the dualistic contribution of EC and foundational cognitive abilities to executive task performance through explicit modeling via the bifactor approach. A critical α of .05 was used for all significance tests. All descriptive and correlation analyses were conducted using SAS software 9.3. All latent models were estimated using Mplus version 7 (Muthén & Muthén, 1998–2010), with the exception of the EFA that was estimated using SAS 9.3. All latent models included the estimation of indicator error coefficients, although these coefficients are not graphed or reported in the figures for visual ease of presentation.

III. DISTINGUISHING EXECUTIVE CONTROL FROM OVERLAPPING FOUNDATIONAL COGNITIVE ABILITIES DURING THE PRESCHOOL PERIOD

J. M. Nelson, T. D. James, H.-J. Choi, C. A. C. Clark, S. A. Wiebe, and K. A. Espy

---

This article is part of the issue "The Changing Nature of Executive Control in Preschool" Espy (Issue Editor). For a full listing of articles in this issue, see: http://onlinelibrary.wiley.com/doi/10.1111/mono. v81.4/issuetoc.

Executive control (EC) is central for supporting the child to transition from a "wiggly, in the moment" preschooler to a self-regulated youngster who can navigate the increased expectations and demands of formal schooling. Therefore, determining when and how EC develops during the preschool period, how its development may be affected by malleable aspects of the child's socio-familial environment, and its implications for important outcomes, such as psychopathology, are central issues in developmental science with substantive implications for policy and practice. These important developmental questions cannot be effectively addressed in the absence of a comprehensive, developmentally informed measurement approach that represents EC in a manner truest to its neural basis and resultant cognitive structure.

Scientific understanding of the development of any psychological construct traditionally involves careful longitudinal measurement at meaningful intervals using tools that are sensitive to quantitative change. Research on the early development of EC is no exception—recent longitudinal studies have used this approach to delineate age-related, quantitative changes in children's performance on individual executive tasks administered

---

Corresponding author: Jennifer Nelson, email: jnelson18@unl.edu
DOI: 10.1111/mono.12270

repeatedly across the preschool period (e.g., Clark et al., 2013; Hughes & Ensor, 2007; Wiebe et al., 2012). From these studies, we have begun to deduce a typical early developmental trajectory of executive abilities, where on average, children show dramatic improvements in accuracy on executive tasks from age 3 to 6 years, with some indication of accelerated, perhaps qualitative, change in children's strategic approaches to executive tasks around age 4 years. Critically, however, evaluation of the rate and trajectory of individual growth in any latent construct, including EC, rests on an assumption of measurement invariance. That is, estimating the magnitude of quantitative change requires that exactly the same underlying construct is measured in an identical way at each assessment point. Unfortunately, there has been little empirical research evaluating the measurement invariance of executive tasks. Thus, studies that describe quantitative developmental changes on single executive tasks may not adequately describe growth at the level of the EC construct.

The overarching aims of the longitudinal preschool project described in this volume were to determine the latent structure and longitudinal growth of the EC construct across the preschool years utilizing CFA and longitudinal latent growth modeling methods. Earlier reports of these data supported a unitary EC structure at each of the four age points in preschool (Nelson, James, Chevalier et al., 2016; Wiebe et al., 2011), consistent with recent findings in many other research groups (Fuhs & Day, 2011; Hughes et al., 2010; Willoughby et al., 2010; Willoughby, Blair, et al., 2012). However, we have learned that the executive tasks in our data are not longitudinally invariant (Nelson, James, Chevalier et al., 2016). Specifically, based on earlier analysis of these data, the factor loadings for four of the seven executive tasks varied across the preschool age range, meaning that the degree to which latent EC drove manifest individual task performance varied significantly from one age point to the next for these tasks. Further, holding latent EC constant across age points resulted in instability in the executive task intercepts for the three tasks that demonstrated loading invariance, which suggests that other, unconsidered factors may be impacting on age-varying task performance. This inability to establish even partial measurement invariance across the four longitudinal time points in the study made it impossible for us to model latent growth in the EC construct. This lack of measurement invariance is not unique to our data: using item response theory models, Willoughby, Wirth, and Blair (2012) recently examined longitudinal measurement invariance of EC and found strict invariance for only two of their five tasks. In contrast, Hughes and colleagues (2010) had some success obtaining measurement invariance for their tasks, although they assessed EC at relatively later ages (age 4 and age 6) and only three tasks were administered at each time point.

In light of discovering that the EC construct does not appear measurement invariant across the preschool years, we sought to consider what these findings may mean, arriving at important questions about *what* latent models of EC are capturing and *how* to better capture the development of EC. These questions were the impetus for this monograph. Given what is known about the rapid and dynamic development of the brain in this age range (Huttenlocher, 1990; Thatcher, 1992), the change in EC may be better illustrated and modeled when allowing for qualitative, in addition to quantitative, change. After all, development is not simply improvement in a child's individual ability, as reflected by improved scores on a single task or measurement battery. It also entails qualitative change predicated on the dynamic interactions among the set of abilities a child draws upon to complete a particular task.

As described in more detail in Chapter I of this volume, the degree to which executive task performance also inherently requires young children to draw upon foundational cognitive abilities (e.g., the set of mental abilities that includes processing of sensory inputs, motor outputs, language, visual/spatial perception, and simple recall), as the targets of EC, points to the importance of explicating the dual, intertwined influences of EC and these other abilities when modeling the contributions to executive task performance. Indeed, our earlier results point to qualitative change in executive task performance across the preschool period, which may likely represent different degrees to which EC and other abilities bear on performance at different age points. Given that both sets of abilities are developing rapidly over the preschool years, and thus differ individually and systematically at any time point, the bifactor model seems a particularly useful methodological approach for providing a more accurate and precise understanding of the potentially changing nature of EC. Accordingly, the primary aim of the analyses presented in this chapter was to advance the field's methodological representation of executive task performance using the bifactor model, and thus evaluate the specification of the influences of EC and foundational cognitive abilities.

The process of determining the utility of the bifactor approach for modeling EC at each age also gave rise to an opportunity to more effectively revisit the question of which EC structure, in the context of the bifactor model, best captures observed executive task performance at different age points across preschool. Characterization of the structure of EC is important, as it represents a critical first step in explicating how individual differences in biology and experience impact on EC acquisition and how potentially fractionated components of EC may presage important outcomes of interest. Despite support for more fractionated views of EC as early as middle childhood (Huizinga et al., 2006; Lee et al., 2013; Lehto et al., 2003) and certainly into adulthood (Friedman et al., 2008; Miyake et al., 2000), available evidence to date across laboratories using different executive measures, samples and ages, indicates that a more parsimonious model fits data obtained across the preschool period (Fuhs & Day, 2011; Hughes et al., 2010; Nelson, James, Chevalier et al., 2016;

Wiebe et al., 2008, 2011; Willoughby et al., 2010; Willoughby, Blair, et al., 2012). Given this new application of the bifactor approach that considers the influences of EC and foundational cognitive abilities in an integrated manner, it is an open question whether a unitary structure of EC will best describe the executive task data obtained at different time points through preschool, or whether a fractionated structure may be plausible.

Against this background, a bifactor model capturing the respective EC and foundational cognitive abilities drivers of observed executive task performance was specified and fit separately at each of four age points spanning the preschool period: 3 years (3;0); 3 years 9 months (3;9); 4 years 6 months (4;6); and 5 years 3 months (5;3). We tested this model at each age point separately as the initial step in determining whether this newly proposed structure fit well to the data at each age. In order to determine how best to represent EC in these bifactor models, three series of models were employed. Although we have considered fractionated (2-factor) versus unitary models of EC structure previously (Nelson, James, Chevalier et al., 2016), in that study, two measures designed to assess flexible shifting were not yet fully coded and thus were not available for inclusion in the analyses. Therefore, for the purposes of this monograph, theoretically informed fractionated (2- and 3-factor) and unitary latent models of the executive task battery were reevaluated at each of the four age points in the study using traditional, unidimensional latent modeling to identify the preferred model of EC structure. Then, the bifactor model that incorporated both the EC and the foundational cognitive abilities factors was specified and fit at each age. The pattern of factor loadings at each age was examined to elucidate the relative contributions of EC and foundational cognitive abilities. Finally, alternative models were explored to ensure the selection of the preferred model that best fits or most parsimoniously describes these data. Delineating the precise structure of executive performance at each age point was crucial, as this represents the initial step toward testing measurement invariance of this new structure and subsequent longitudinal growth modeling, as well as forming the basis for analyses conducted in subsequent studies in this volume linking EC to predictors and outcomes.

METHOD

Detailed information concerning study participants, procedures, and measures is provided in Chapter II. Foundational cognitive abilities were indexed by the Verbal Comprehension, Concept Formation, and Visual Matching subtests (Woodcock et al., 2001), as cardinally reflecting the major abilities of language, visual/spatial perception, and motor speed expected to map onto the portion of executive task performance attributable to foundational cognitive abilities. A small number of children who participated in the study exit session did not complete the executive task battery at one or more earlier age points. Estimation methods in Mplus allowed for the retention of all children who completed the language, visual/spatial, and motor speed assessments in all models even if they were missing data from the executive tasks at a given age. Therefore, the final sample sizes included in analyses estimating the EC bifactor model were identical to the models that incorporated only executive task data for ages 3;0 and 5;3 and slightly larger for ages 3;9 ($N = 279$) and 4;6 ($N = 323$).

Data Analysis

Analyses were conducted in three steps. First, as a basis for determining how the bifactor approach might yield different findings from more commonly employed, unidimensional latent modeling methods, we examined the structure of EC using only executive tasks. In order to determine a model most representative of the observed executive task data, at each age, 1-, 2-, and 3-factor latent variable models were fit to the data. Figure 6 depicts

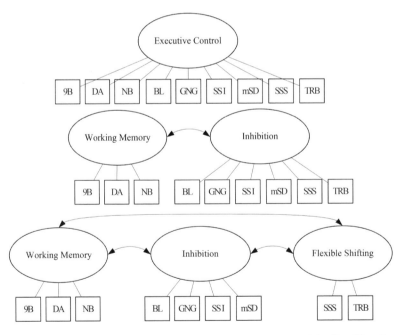

FIGURE 6.—Schematic representation of three EC structure models. 9B = Nine Boxes; DA = Delayed Alternation; NB = Nebraska Barnyard; BL = Big-Little; GNG = Go/No-Go; SSI = Shape School–Inhibit; mSD = modified Snack Delay; SSS = Shape School–Switching; TRB = Trails–Switching.

these 1-, 2-, and 3-factor models. Conceptually, the 1-factor model suggests that EC is best represented as a unitary construct, as suggested by early theoretical accounts of EC (Baddeley, 1986; Norman & Shallice, 1986), whereas the 2- and 3-factor models reflect fractionated theoretical models, where EC is best described as one or two distinct, yet correlated skills (as in Miyake et al., 2000). For the 2-factor model, observed executive task performance was hypothesized to be driven by independent Working Memory and Inhibition constructs. This 2-factor model is supported by theoretical ideas stressing working memory and inhibition as the basis for secondary EC skills, including flexible shifting (Diamond, 2013). In contrast, the 3-factor model included an additional, separate Flexible Shifting factor. Note that executive tasks that subsequently were constrained to load on the Flexible Shifting factor (Shape School–Switching, Trails) were loaded on the Inhibition factor in the 2-factor models given findings suggesting difficulty separating inhibition and flexible shifting demands in models of EC well into childhood (St Clair-Thompson & Gathercole, 2006; van der Sluis et al., 2007). Additionally, inhibition tasks and flexible shifting tasks are sometimes used interchangeably in the preschool age range (e.g., Garon, Bryson, & Smith [2008] list Reverse Categorization tasks as measures of complex inhibition, whereas such tasks have also been used to measure flexible shifting [Kloo, Perner, Kerschhuber, Dabernig, & Aichhorn, 2008]).

In all models, the residual error terms for the two Shape School indicators (i.e., from the Inhibit and Switching conditions) were allowed to correlate given that using two indicators from different conditions of the same task inevitably will result in some correlated error related at least in part to similarity in the stimuli and response format. Likelihood difference tests, the Bayesian information criterion (BIC), the root mean square error of approximation (RMSEA), and the comparative fit index (CFI) were used for model comparison. For likelihood difference tests, corrected for MLR estimation, if the χ^2 difference between nested models is statistically significant at the $p < .05$ level, the result indicates that the more complex model is better-fitting. Otherwise, the less complex model is preferred on the basis of parsimony (Bollen, 1989).

In stage 2 of the analyses, the model of EC structure identified in stage 1 of the analyses was extended to the bifactor model, where the standardized language, visual/spatial perception, and motor speed subtests were included to anchor the variance associated with foundational cognitive abilities across all tasks so that EC could be specified in the context of foundational abilities. In the bifactor models, all nine executive tasks were constrained to load on both the predetermined preferred latent EC structure and on the foundational cognitive abilities latent variable, whereas the language, visual/spatial, and motor speed subtests were allowed to load exclusively on the foundational cognitive abilities latent (hereafter abbreviated as FCA when referring to the latent variable, for brevity, in the Method and Results of this chapter). In line with the bifactor modeling approach, the EC and FCA latent variables were not allowed to correlate, making them orthogonal. The resulting factor loading pattern then was evaluated at each age. In particular, the pattern of differences in the strength of EC-related loadings at each age was noted to draw conclusions about changes in how each task was related to EC, after accounting for the relation of observed executive task performance to the FCA latent variable. RMSEA and CFI were used to determine the quality of fit of each EC bifactor model. The third and final phase of analyses involved follow-up model comparisons to determine the relative fit of these bifactor models compared to alternative models.

RESULTS

EC Structure

Table 4 includes the likelihood difference tests and fit statistics comparing the 1-, 2-, and 3-factor models of the executive task battery at each of the four age points. The task loadings on the latent factors for the three models at each age are displayed in Table 5. At age 3;0, the RMSEA and CFI indicated that both the 1- and 2-factor models provided reasonable fit to the data, and all tasks loaded significantly on the a priori specified EC demand. Notably, however, the correlation between the Working Memory and Inhibition factors in the 2-factor model was very high ($r = .90$, $p < .001$). Similarly, at ages 3;9 and 4;6, both the 1-factor and 2-factor models fit the data well, with all EC tasks loading significantly in both models at both ages, although the Working Memory and Inhibition factors were highly correlated ($r = .83$, $p < .001$, and $r = .83$, $p < .001$, at ages 3;9 and 4;6, respectively). At age 5;3, the RMSEA and CFI indicated that the 1-factor model also fit well and all executive tasks again had significant loadings. However, at this age, the 2-factor model resulted in a nonpositive definite latent variable covariance matrix, and the associated parameter estimates are considered unreliable. The same problem occurred at all four ages when attempting to estimate the 3-factor models. Although the matrices were nonpositive definite, the results from these 3-factor models estimated correlations above 1 for some of the latent factors, which may indicate a high degree of overlapping variance. Because of the estimation problems, the planned model comparisons involving the 3-factor EC models were not possible, so we focus on model comparison results for the 1- and 2-factor models.

The 1-factor model was retained as the preferred representation of EC at ages 3;0, 3;9, and 4;6 based on parsimony. That is, the nonsignificant χ^2 difference tests and high correlations between factors in the 2-factor models

TABLE 4

Model Comparison and Model Fit Statistics for Latent Models of Executive Tasks at Each Age

Model	Loglikelihood	Free Parameters	Scaling Factor	$\Delta\chi^{2\,a}$	Δdf	p	BIC	Δ BIC	AIC	RMSEA	RMSEA 90% CI	CFI
					3;0							
1-factor	−2,151.56	28	1.06	—	—	—	4,455.14	—	4,359.12	.06	[.04, .09]	.89
2-factor	−2,151.33	29	1.06	0.23	1	.514	4,460.10	4.97	4,360.65	.07	[.04, .09]	.89
3-factor[b]												
					3;9							
1-factor	−2,981.39	28	1.01	—	—	—	6,120.16	—	6,018.78	.04	[.00, .07]	.97
2-factor	−2,980.38	29	1.01	1.01	1	.172	6,123.75	3.60	6,018.76	.04	[.00, .07]	.97
3-factor[b]												
					4;6							
1-factor	−3,102.35	28	1.23	—	—	—	6,366.12	—	6,260.69	.04	[.01, .06]	.96
2-factor	−3,100.84	29	1.22	1.51	1	.082	6,368.87	2.75	6,259.68	.04	[.00, .06]	.96
3-factor[b]												
					5;3							
1-factor	−2,757.05	28	1.36	—	—	—	5,679.22	—	5,570.10	.00	[.00, .04]	1.00
2-factor[b]												
3-factor[b]												

Note. BIC = Bayesian information criterion; AIC = Akaike information criterion; RMSEA = root mean squared error of approximation; CI = confidence interval; CFI = Bentler's comparative fit index.
[a] χ^2 difference = −2*log likelihood difference/difference test scaling correction.
[b] Nonpositive definite latent variable covariance matrix.

TABLE 5

STANDARDIZED FACTOR LOADINGS FOR LATENT MODELS OF EXECUTIVE TASKS AT EACH AGE

Measure	3;0			3;9			4;6			5;3		
	1F	2F	3F[a]	1F	2F	3F[a]	1F	2F	3F[a]	1F	2F[a]	3F[a]
9B	.14*	.15*	—	.18*	.21*	—	.17*	.21*	—	.31*	—	—
DA	.27*	.27*	—	.28*	.31*	—	.34*	.37*	—	.25*	—	—
NB	.69*	.75*	—	.55*	.65*	—	.58*	.67*	—	.61*	—	—
BL	.48*	.48*	—	.65*	.65*	—	.49*	.49*	—	.57*	—	—
GNG	.31*	.31*	—	.51*	.51*	—	.50*	.50*	—	.49*	—	—
SSI	.54*	.55*	—	.66*	.67*	—	.40*	.41*	—	.26*	—	—
mSD	.42*	.43*	—	.38*	.38*	—	.50*	.49*	—	.41*	—	—
SSS	.68*	.67*	—	.75*	.75*	—	.72*	.74*	—	.47*	—	—
TRB	.47*	.48*	—	.31*	.31*	—	.36*	.36*	—	.33*	—	—

Note. 1F = 1 Factor; 2F = 2 Factor; 3F = 3 Factor; 9B = Nine Boxes; DA = Delayed Alternation; NB = Nebraska Barnyard; BL = Big-Little; GNG = Go/No-Go; SSI = Shape School–Inhibit; mSD = modified Snack Delay; SSS = Shape School–Switching; TRB = Trails–Switching.
[a]Nonpositive definite latent variable covariance matrix.
*p < .05.

suggest that the 1-factor model best represents EC structure at these ages (see Table 4). At age 5;3, the 1-factor EC model was the only model to estimate properly and thus was retained as the preferred model. Overall, the unitary EC structure emerged as the preferred model of executive task covariance at all time points across the preschool period. Note that an attempt to establish even partial measurement invariance in the unitary EC structure across the four ages failed, as it did in our previous work (Nelson, James, Chevalier et al., 2016) that did not include the two flexible shifting tasks included here.

EC-FCA Bifactor Models

After establishing that a unitary EC structure was preferred to represent the executive task battery at all four ages, the bifactor models incorporating measures of children's language, visual/spatial perception, and motor speed, in addition to the executive tasks, were employed to evaluate the relative contributions of EC and children's foundational cognitive abilities (FCA) to their observed task performance (see Figure 7 for factor loadings and R^2 values).

3 Years 0 Months

The EC-FCA bifactor model at age 3;0 fit the data well ($\chi^2(44) = 48.67$, $p = .291$, RMSEA = .02, CFI = .99). All of the executive tasks and the standardized Verbal Comprehension, Concept Formation, and Visual Matching subtests had significant positive loadings on the FCA latent factor. The majority of loadings were moderate to strong in magnitude. However,

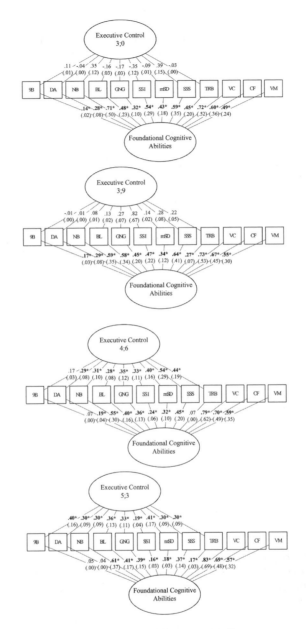

Figure 7.—EC-FCA bifactor model factor loadings and R^2 values at each age. R^2 values listed in parentheses. 9B = Nine Boxes; DA = Delayed Alternation; NB = Nebraska Barnyard; BL = Big-Little; GNG = Go/No-Go; SSI = Shape School–Inhibit; mSD = modified Snack Delay; SSS = Shape School–Switching; TRB = Trails–Switching; VC = Verbal Comprehension; CF = Concept Formation; VM = Visual Matching. $^*p < .05$.

none of the executive tasks loaded significantly on an EC factor at this age. By decomposing the R^2 associated with each executive task, more variance was explained by the FCA factor, compared to the EC factor, in all nine tasks. Latent FCA demonstrated significant variance ($\psi = .12$, $p < .001$), while latent EC did not ($\psi = .03$, $p = .461$). Therefore, at age 3;0, EC does not contribute significantly to performance on the executive tasks over and above children's foundational cognitive abilities.

3 Years 9 Months

The EC-FCA bifactor model at age 3;9 also fit the data well ($\chi^2(43) = 42.89$, $p = .476$, RMSEA $= .00$, CFI $= 1.00$). Like in the 3;0 model, all of the manifest indicators (the nine executive tasks and three standardized subtests—Verbal Comprehension, Concept Formation, and Visual Matching) had significant positive loadings on the FCA factor, most of moderate to strong magnitude, and latent FCA demonstrated significant variance ($\psi = .15$, $p < .001$). Again, none of the executive tasks loaded significantly on the EC factor, and as such, latent EC did not vary significantly ($\psi = .00$, $p = .787$). Based on the decomposed R^2 for the executive tasks, more variance was again explained by the FCA factor in eight of the nine tasks (with Shape School – Inhibit as the exception). Similar to at age 3, EC does not contribute to performance on the executive tasks in a manner that can be distinguished from the influence of children's foundational cognitive abilities at age 3;9.

4 Years 6 Months

The EC-FCA bifactor model at age 4;6 fit the data well ($\chi^2(44) = 67.16$, $p = .014$, RMSEA $= .04$, CFI $= .96$). The factor structure was markedly different from the bifactor models at ages 3;0 and 3;9. All but one of the executive tasks, Nine Boxes, had significant, positive, and moderate loadings on the EC factor. Furthermore, seven of the nine executive tasks also had positive, significant moderate loadings on the FCA factor (Nine Boxes and Trails did not). As anticipated, the Verbal Comprehension, Concept Formation, and Visual Matching subtests also loaded robustly on the FCA factor. Both latent EC and FCA demonstrated significant variance in the bifactor model at this age ($\psi = .07$, $p = .033$; $\psi = .20$, $p < .001$, respectively), and when decomposing the R^2 for the executive tasks, some variance explained in all tasks was attributable to EC, and more variance was explained by EC, compared to FCA, in six of the nine tasks. Overall, moderate loadings of the executive tasks on both the EC and FCA factors at this age are consistent with separable, dualistic contributions of both EC and FCA on observed task performance in preschoolers at age 4;6.

5 Years 3 Months

The bifactor model at 5;3 also fit the data well ($\chi^2(44) = 51.62$, $p = .201$, RMSEA $= .02$, CFI $= .99$). At this final age point, all nine of the executive tasks

57

had significant, positive loadings of moderate strength on the EC factor, while seven of the nine executive tasks also evidenced significant, positive loadings on the FCA factor (all except Nine Boxes and Delayed Alternation). The Verbal Comprehension, Concept Formation, and Visual Matching subtests again loaded strongly on the FCA factor as expected. Latent EC and FCA again each varied significantly ($\psi = .05$, $p = .011$; $\psi = .22$, $p < .001$, respectively), and based on the decomposed R^2 for the executive tasks, some variance in all tasks was again explained by EC, with more variance attributable to EC, compared to FCA, in five of the nine tasks. Similar to what was observed at age 4;6, a meaningful portion of the shared variance among the executive tasks formed a separable, cohesive EC factor at age 5;3, while at the same time children's foundational cognitive abilities contributed significantly to observed executive task performance.

Fractionated EC Structure With the EC-FCA Bifactor Model

Given our results revealing that the bifactor structure is a promising representation of EC and its overlap with, and distinction from, FCA at ages 4;6 and 5;3, we then specifically evaluated the comparative fit of a fractionated EC structure at these ages using the bifactor approach that also considers the influence of foundational cognitive abilities. We examined 1-, 2-, and 3-factor EC structures with the bifactor approach to determine whether EC was better-represented by a multiple-factor, correlated structure reflecting differentiation according to putative working memory, inhibition, and flexible shifting demands (see Figure 8).

Table 6 includes the likelihood difference tests and fit statistics for comparing the 1-, 2-, and 3-factor EC structures within the bifactor model at each age. Table 7 displays the factor loadings for each model. Indeed, in these bifactor models, the unitary EC structure remained preferred at both ages 4;6 and 5;3 (see Table 6). Further, the correlations between the components of EC were high in the 2-factor bifactor models ($r_{WM, INH} = .68$ at 4;6; $r_{WM, INH} = .89$ at 5;3; $p < .001$) and 3-factor bifactor models (at 4;6: $r_{WM, INH} = .97$, $p < .001$; $r_{WM, FS} = .57$, $p < .001$; and $r_{INH, FS} = .73$, $p < .001$; at 5;3: nonpositive definite latent covariance matrix and suggestion of correlations above 1 between some factors), indicating tight interrelations and a lack of fractionation among these EC subcomponents at ages 4;6 and 5;3 even when considered in the context of overlapping FCA.

Follow-Up Model: One-Factor FCA

In light of findings from the EC-FCA bifactor model that an EC-specific factor, distinct from FCA, was not evident at ages 3;0 or 3;9, we tested an alternative, post hoc model. Given that there were no significant factor

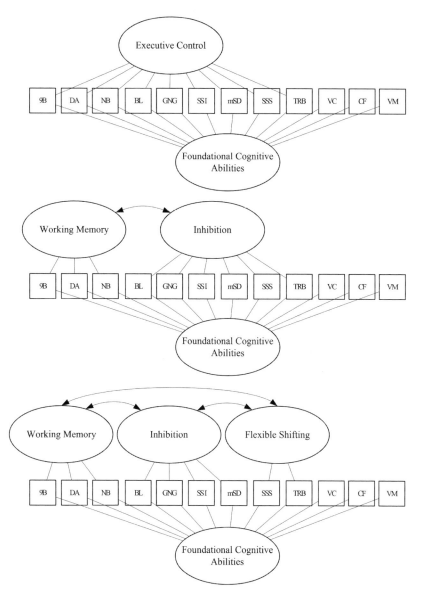

FIGURE 8.—Schematic representation of three EC structures within the EC-FCA bifactor models. 9B = Nine Boxes; DA = Delayed Alternation; NB = Nebraska Barnyard; BL = Big-Little; GNG = Go/No-Go; SSI = Shape School–Inhibit; mSD = modified Snack Delay; SSS = Shape School–Switching; TRB = Trails–Switching; VC = Verbal Comprehension; CF = Concept Formation; VM = Visual Matching.

TABLE 6

Model Comparison and Model Fit Statistics for EC Structures Within EC-FCA Bifactor Models at Ages 4;6 and 5;3

Model	Loglikelihood	Free Parameters	Scaling Factor	$\Delta\chi^{2a}$	Δdf	p	BIC	Δ BIC	AIC	RMSEA	RMSEA 90% CI	CFI
4;6												
1-factor EC	−6,570.62	46	1.18	—	—	—	13,407.02	—	13,233.25	.04	[.02, .06]	.96
2-factor EC	−6,568.53	47	1.18	2.09	1	.056	13,408.62	1.60	13,231.07	.04	[.01, .06]	.97
3-factor EC[b]												
5;3												
1-factor EC	−6,769.65	46	1.22	—	—	—	13,810.57	—	13,631.30	.02	[.00, .04]	.99
2-factor EC	−6,769.32	47	1.21	0.33	1	.433	13,815.80	5.24	13,632.64	.02	[.00, .04]	.99
3-factor EC	−6,767.64	49	1.21	2.01	3	.308	13,824.24	13.68	13,633.28	.02	[.00, .04]	.99

Note. BIC = Bayesian information criterion; AIC = Akaike information criterion; RMSEA = root mean squared error of approximation; CI = confidence interval; CFI = Bentler's comparative fit index.
[a] χ^2 difference = −2*loglikelihood difference/difference test scaling correction.
[b] Nonpositive definite latent variable covariance matrix.

TABLE 7

STANDARDIZED FACTOR LOADINGS FOR EC STRUCTURES WITHIN EC-FCA BIFACTOR MODELS AT 4;6 AND 5;3

| | 4;6 | | | | | | 5;3 | | | | | |
| | 1F EC | | 2F EC | | 3F EC[a] | | 1F EC | | 2F EC | | 3F EC | |
Measure	EC	FCA	EC	FCA	EC	FCA	EC	FCA	EC	FCA	EC	FCA
9B	.17	.07	.25*	.06	—	—	.40*	.05	.42*	.05	.43*	.05
DA	.29*	.19*	.35*	.18*	—	—	.30*	.04	.31*	.04	.31*	.04
NB	.31*	.55*	.42*	.55*	—	—	.30*	.61*	.32*	.61*	.32*	.61*
BL	.28*	.40*	.29*	.40*	—	—	.36*	.41*	.37*	.41*	.36*	.41*
GNG	.35*	.36*	.36*	.36*	—	—	.33*	.39*	.33*	.39*	.33*	.38*
SSI	.33*	.24*	.35*	.24*	—	—	.19*	.16*	.20*	.16*	.19	.16*
mSD	.40*	.32*	.39*	.32*	—	—	.41*	.18*	.41*	.18*	.41*	.18*
SSS	.54*	.45*	.57*	.45*	—	—	.30*	.37*	.31*	.36*	.41*	.37*
TRB	.44*	.07	.43*	.07	—	—	.30*	.17*	.30*	.17*	.39*	.16*
VC	@0	.79*	@0	.79*	—	—	@0	.83*	@0	.83*	@0	.83*
CF	@0	.70*	@0	.70*	—	—	@0	.69*	@0	.69*	@0	.69*
VM	@0	.59*	@0	.59*	—	—	@0	.57*	@0	.57*	@0	.57*

Note. 1F = 1 Factor; 2F = 2 Factor; 3F = 3 Factor; EC = Executive Control; FCA = Foundational Cognitive Abilities; 9B = Nine Boxes; DA = Delayed Alternation; NB = Nebraska Barnyard; BL = Big-Little; GNG = Go/No-Go; SSI = Shape School–Inhibit; mSD = modified Snack Delay; SSS = Shape School–Switching; TRB = Trails–Switching; VC = Verbal Comprehension; CF = Concept Formation; VM = Visual Matching.
[a]Nonpositive definite latent variable covariance matrix.
*$p < .05$.

loadings of the executive task indicators on an EC-specific factor at ages 3;0 and 3;9, we suspected that the bifactor model was overfitting the data (i.e., specifying a more complex model than is necessary to represent the true observed performance). To examine this question, we specified a model in which one factor was used to account for the common association among all 12 tasks; that is, all of the executive tasks and the standardized Verbal Comprehension, Concept Formation, and Visual Matching subtests were loaded on one single, integrated latent variable (see Figure 9). This specification conceptually represents a shared, or undifferentiated, foundational cognitive abilities construct that drives observed task performance regardless of the putative task type.

Table 8 shows the likelihood difference tests and fit statistics for comparing the alternative one-factor FCA model and the EC-FCA bifactor model across age, and in Table 9, the estimated factor loadings for these models are presented. Note that the substantially more complex bifactor models will likely provide better fit than the simpler alternative models due purely to the larger number of parameters estimated (i.e., larger number of *df*). Therefore, we relied here only on the fit statistic that corrects for the number of estimated parameters, the BIC, to evaluate comparative fit across

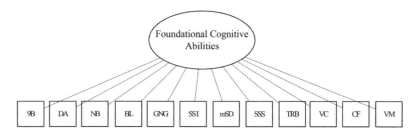

Figure 9.—Schematic representation of alternative one-factor FCA model. 9B = Nine Boxes; DA = Delayed Alternation; NB = Nebraska Barnyard; BL = Big-Little; GNG = Go/No-Go; SSI = Shape School–Inhibit; mSD = modified Snack Delay; SSS = Shape School–Switching; TRB = Trails–Switching; VC = Verbal Comprehension; CF = Concept Formation; VM = Visual Matching.

these two types of models (Schwarz, 1978). As we hypothesized, the one-factor FCA model fit the data well and evidenced a marked decrease in BIC compared to the EC-FCA bifactor model at ages 3;0 and 3;9 (see Table 8). All of the 12 indicators loaded significantly on this one undifferentiated factor at both ages (see Table 9).

Despite the obtained results for the bifactor model at ages 4;6 and 5;3, we proceeded to test this simple, one-factor FCA model to ensure the robustness of the results. This alternative model did *not* fit the data better than the bifactor model at ages 4;6 and 5;3 (see Table 8), indicating that the bifactor model with its co-occurring yet distinct EC-specific and FCA factors better represents the observed executive task performance at these ages, capturing the overlapping and distinct variance associated with these constructs that emerges later in the preschool period.

DISCUSSION

The purpose of this study was to improve understanding and statistical representation of the dynamic development of EC in preschool by considering the influence of foundational cognitive abilities in addition to EC, on observed executive task performance. The bifactor approach enabled determination of the degree to which children's performance on a battery of executive tasks was simultaneously driven by EC specifically and by foundational cognitive abilities more broadly. Using the pattern of loadings of observed task performance on the EC and foundational cognitive abilities constructs at four age points spanning the preschool period, a specific, qualitative developmental difference was revealed.

TABLE 8

Model Comparison and Model Fit Statistics for One-Factor FCA Model Compared to EC-FCA Bifactor Model at Each Age

Model	Loglikelihood	Free Parameters	Scaling Factor	$\Delta\chi^{2\,a}$	Δdf	p	BIC	Δ BIC	AIC	RMSEA	RMSEA 90% CI	CFI
3;0												
1-factor FCA	−4,575.43	37	1.02	—	—	—	9,351.74	—	9,224.85	.05	[.02, .07]	.94
Bifactor	−4,558.51	46	1.08	16.92	9	.003	9,366.77	15.04	9,209.02	.02	[.00, .05]	.99
3;9[b]												
1-factor FCA	−5,852.62	38	1.00	—	—	—	11,919.23	—	11,781.24	.03	[.00, .05]	.98
Bifactor	−5,838.82	47	1.09	13.80	9	.027	11,942.31	23.08	11,771.64	.00	[.00, .04]	1.00
4;6												
1-factor FCA	−6,607.34	37	1.20	—	—	—	13,428.45	—	13,288.68	.07	[.06, .09]	.86
Bifactor	−6,570.62	46	1.18	36.72	9	<.001	13,407.02	−21.43	13,233.25	.04	[.02, .06]	.96
5;3												
1-factor FCA	−6,807.62	37	1.25	—	—	—	13,833.43	—	13,689.24	.06	[.05, .08]	.89
Bifactor	−6,769.65	46	1.22	37.97	9	<.001	13,810.57	−22.87	13,631.30	.02	[.00, .04]	.99

Note. BIC = Bayesian information criterion; AIC = Akaike information criterion; RMSEA = root mean squared error of approximation; CI = confidence interval; CFI = Bentler's comparative fit index.
[a] χ^2 difference = −2*loglikelihood difference/difference test scaling correction.
[b] Models included a residual correlation between BL and SSS as model would not estimate properly without including this residual correlation.

TABLE 9

STANDARDIZED FACTOR LOADINGS FOR ONE-FACTOR FCA MODEL AT EACH AGE

Measure	3;0	3;9	4;6	5;3
9B	.15*	.17*	.14*	.17*
DA	.27*	.28*	.31*	.13*
NB	.69*	.59*	.64*	.68*
BL	.46*	.61*	.49*	.50*
GNG	.30*	.51*	.47*	.47*
SSI	.52*	.59*	.34*	.21*
mSD	.42*	.38*	.46*	.29*
SSS	.62*	.68*	.61*	.44*
TRB	.45*	.32*	.25*	.24*
VC	.73*	.70*	.67*	.74*
CF	.61*	.65*	.62*	.65*
VM	.50*	.54*	.58*	.57*

Note. 9B = Nine Boxes; DA = Delayed Alternation; NB = Nebraska Barnyard; BL = Big-Little; GNG = Go/No-Go; SSI = Shape School–Inhibit; mSD = modified Snack Delay; SSS = Shape School–Switching; TRB = Trails–Switching; VC = Verbal Comprehension; CF = Concept Formation; VM = Visual Matching.
*$p < .05$.

Results from the bifactor models indicated that EC, as a construct, uniquely and substantially contributes to children's manifest performance on an executive task battery at ages 4;6 and 5;3, the latter portion of the preschool period. Furthermore, the dualistic contribution of foundational cognitive abilities to executive task performance also was evident at these ages. In contrast, at the younger ages, 3;0 and 3;9, observed executive task performance was not related specifically to a distinct EC construct, but rather individual differences in executive task performance appeared to be driven predominantly by variation in foundational cognitive abilities. The demonstrated impact of foundational cognitive abilities on observed executive task performance has a number of important implications for how to approach the measurement of EC.

Findings revealed a difference in the relation between foundational cognitive abilities and EC as drivers of executive task performance over the course of the preschool period. At ages 3;0 and 3;9, the results were nearly identical. Nearly all of the executive tasks, as well as the standardized language, visual/spatial perception, and motor speed tasks, loaded significantly on the latent foundational cognitive abilities factor, meaning that a substantial portion of shared variance was common to all 12 tasks. The fact that the common variance across the executive tasks also was shared with measures of foundational cognitive abilities indicates that observed task performance was driven by a common, statistically inextricable set of abilities. The small and nonsignificant loadings of the executive tasks on the EC construct in turn indicated a lack of evidence for an EC-specific factor at ages

3;0 and 3;9. Taken together, these findings suggest that EC is not yet contributing substantial independent variance to executive task performance at these young ages, and may not yet have emerged early in the preschool period as a distinct, specialized construct that independently drives task performance beyond the contribution of individual variation in foundational cognitive abilities that are needed to process the task stimuli or make responses. Indeed, a unitary, undifferentiated foundational cognitive abilities factor best represented children's performance on all 12 tasks at these young ages. The relative contribution of these foundational cognitive processes should be considered within the overall context of the nature of EC, that is, in light of the dynamic interaction between stimulus- and response-driven demands related to foundational cognitive abilities and the executive component that orients and manages these abilities in accordance with changing goals. In this view, young preschool children's executive task performance appears to be more strongly related to individual differences in foundational processes involved in stimulus and response processing, such as language, visual/spatial perception, and motor speed. Although provocative, the pattern of results does not specifically answer whether EC is too immature at these ages to be separable from the foundational cognitive abilities it controls, or whether it is too intertwined with the variation in fundamental abilities to be distinguishable as a separable construct. Neurophysiological measures recorded during performance on multidimensional executive tasks may be useful to disentangle these alternative explanations.

In stark contrast, the bifactor model results at ages 4;6 and 5;3 were quite different. All of the executive tasks significantly loaded on the latent factor termed EC. At the same time, the majority of the executive tasks, as well as the standardized tasks assessing language, visual/spatial perception and motor speed, loaded on the foundational cognitive abilities factor. Overall, these findings suggest that at older ages in the preschool period, 4;6 and 5;3, manifest performance on the executive tasks is indeed driven by a discriminable, specific EC factor as well as by foundational cognitive abilities. At ages 4;6 and 5;3, children's performance on the executive tasks is made possible by roughly equivalent, yet unique, contributions from their EC abilities and their foundational cognitive abilities. In other words, by age 4;6, children are drawing both upon EC as well as the other basic abilities required to process the task stimulus and implement the needed response in a manner reflecting the dualistic nature of EC as a tertiary system that regulates fundamental cognitive abilities. Not surprisingly given the nature of EC and its endemic modulation of foundational cognitive abilities to achieve a goal or outcome, the majority of the executive tasks also loaded with the standardized language, visual/spatial perception, and motor speed subtests on the foundational cognitive abilities factor, likely reflecting the continued importance of these foundational abilities to basic stimulus and response processing of executive tasks as preschoolers mature. Importantly, the contrast between this dualistic nature of the EC and foundational cognitive abilities relation in older preschool children and the undifferentiated structure evident in younger preschool children reflects a structural change in EC within this developmental period that was not at all evident when examining children's behavior or responses at the individual task level. These findings also offer a potential explanation for the lack of measurement invariance noted in our previous longitudinal studies, where the properties of executive tasks may in part be changing due to underlying shifts in the relations between EC and foundational cognitive abilities that support performance.

Although the primary aim here was to better define the nature of the control process using the bifactor model, a secondary examination of the structure of EC independent from and in the context of foundational cognitive abilities was conducted. Traditional latent variable models of EC structure at each of our four preschool age points again revealed a unitary structure of EC throughout the preschool period, consistent with our previously published findings where we did not include tasks with greater flexible shifting demands. With the more sophisticated bifactor modeling approach that successfully distinguished EC as a distinct, unique construct independent from foundational cognitive abilities in driving executive task performance, a unitary structure of EC remained the preferred model compared to representations that parsed separate working memory, inhibition, and flexible shifting components. Notably, the latent correlations among the hypothesized EC components remained quite high in the two- and three-factor models, providing further support that EC cannot yet be discretely fractionated in the late preschool ages even when accounting for the influence of foundational cognitive abilities on observed task performance. The preschool period, then, can be characterized by the emergence of EC as a specific unitary latent construct. Perhaps, though, any further differentiation and specialization of EC by way of its more specific components observed in adulthood must occur beyond the preschool period, as children approach middle childhood and beyond. Nonetheless, modeling the dynamic interplay between EC and foundational cognitive abilities may offer substantial advantages in revealing further specialization of EC components with advancing age.

Although these findings are quite exciting, there are noted limitations. While the bifactor modeling approach helped to reveal the unique roles of both specific EC and foundational cognitive abilities that are the targets of EC modulation, the standardized language, visual/spatial perception, and motor speed tasks used to anchor the measurement of foundational cognitive abilities by no means fully represent all of the foundational mental processes that are controlled by the specific executive process. We chose these three tests as exemplars, in that they clearly map onto the stimulus and response processing demands of executive tasks and show known, measurable developmental gains in this age range. Furthermore, in light of the limitations of testing preschool children, including the short duration of time they are able to attend and persist with tasks, selecting three standardized tests covering a range of prototypic abilities is a reasonable choice, particularly given that such standardized tests in general are commonly accepted as measures that represent more global cognitive function. Future studies that build upon this work might consider different or additional measures of foundational cognitive abilities to test the robustness of these findings.

Note that upon identifying the best-fitting model of EC at each age point, taking into account foundational cognitive abilities, a next analytic step could ideally include evaluating the longitudinal relations among these EC and foundational abilities structures across the four age points. Given that dramatically different structures were identified at the younger compared to older ages (foundational cognitive abilities unitary compared to bifactor), it is not possible to test measurement invariance and subsequently model latent growth across time. However, autoregressive or cascade models would have some promise for determining the degree of relation in the structures longitudinally. Indeed, despite the lack of measurement variance in the unitary EC construct across our preschool age points, latent EC was highly correlated across the four measurement points (.73–.94), with higher correlations between adjacent ages, in a model that allowed some parameters to freely vary across time according to the results of invariance tests. This high degree of stability does suggest something is persisting across time. Unfortunately, the measures used to represent foundational cognitive abilities were not administered to all children at each 9-month data point. Therefore, it is not possible to conduct autoregressive models in this data set without introducing duplicated data at sequential age points. The present findings suggest such efforts as a useful future direction for the field.

The findings here have important implications both for the remaining research questions addressed in this monograph, as well as for future research and applied work more broadly. An important purpose of seeking to apply a sophisticated modeling approach to further specify the measurement of EC in preschool was to better equip the field to isolate potential effects of the early environment on the development of EC and to identify how variability in early EC affects risk for developing behaviors characteristic of emerging externalizing psychopathology, including ADHD symptomatology, as children approach school entry. In essence, we wanted to better understand the often hypothesized critical role of EC, as well as that of foundational cognitive abilities, in the landscape of early development. Overall, we can conclude from these results that EC is evident as a distinct and specialized cognitive construct that uniquely drives observed executive task performance at the later ages of 4;6 and 5;3, suggesting these later ages represent a particularly critical time for understanding the role of EC, and at the same time, consideration of the influence of foundational cognitive abilities in the control process is an important addition for precision of measurement.

IV. A NEW LOOK AT THE IMPLICATIONS OF THE SOCIO-FAMILIAL CONTEXT FOR YOUNG CHILDREN'S EXECUTIVE CONTROL: CLARIFYING THE MECHANISMS OF INDIVIDUAL DIFFERENCES

C. A. C. Clark, T. D. James, and K. A. Espy

This article is part of the issue "The Changing Nature of Executive Control in Preschool" Espy (Issue Editor). For a full listing of articles in this issue, see: http://onlinelibrary.wiley.com/doi/10.1111/mono. v81.4/issuetoc.

One in five children entering U.S. kindergarten classrooms today come from families with insufficient income to purchase even basic household necessities (Addy & Wight, 2012). Moreover, the rate of childhood poverty in the United States has increased steadily over recent years and is disproportionately high among children under 6 years of age. Even as they enter the classroom, children born into families with low socioeconomic status (SES) or low income are more likely than their peers to show delays in school readiness and the adverse consequences of poverty span the course of their lives (Lee & Burkham, 2002). On average, these children have lower IQ and reduced vocabulary, perform more poorly on measures of academic achievement, are more likely to drop out of school or repeat grades, and are more likely to experience unemployment and low SES in adulthood relative to children from higher SES backgrounds (Bradley et al., 1989; Duncan, Brooks-Gunn, & Klebanov, 1994; Duncan, Ziol-Guest, & Kalil, 2010; Hess & Shipman, 1965). Such marked achievement

Corresponding author: Caron Clark, email: caron.clark@unl.edu
DOI: 10.1111/mono.12271

disparities highlight a critical need for research that can inform preventative efforts to disrupt inter-generational cycles of social inequality.

DIMENSIONS OF SOCIO-FAMILIAL RISK

In the numerous studies that have examined the impact of poverty on children's development, SES typically has been measured with distal indicators, such as parent income or education. Despite the predictive power of these distal measures, they can only be viewed as proxies for a host of co-varying everyday risk and protective factors that cumulatively or interactively shape children's cognitive abilities and outcomes (Bronfenbrenner, 1979; Evans, 2003; Sameroff, Seifer, Baldwin, & Baldwin, 1993). Broadly, efforts to understand the proximal mechanisms through which SES exerts its effects on children's development have been driven by two, complementary theoretical perspectives (Yeung, Linver, & Brooks-Gunn, 2002). The first of these, the resource investment perspective, posits that higher SES enables parents to invest more educational resources and stimulating learning experiences in their children, which, in turn, foster learning and cognitive development. Not surprisingly, lower SES and household income are associated with more limited access to stimulating materials, including books, computers, good schools, or toys. The greater the length of time spent in poverty, the greater the paucity in these resources (National Research Council and Institute of Medicine, 2000; Yeung et al., 2002). Additionally, parents with higher education generally engage in more stimulating and complex conversational interactions with their children, including longer utterances, more contin-gent responses to children's speech and more elaborated labels (Hart & Risley, 1995; Hess & Shipman, 1965; Hoff, 2003). Mothers with higher education and occupational status also read more and model more learning-related behaviors for their children (Coley, 2002). Access to these learning resources mediates much of the relation between household income and child cognitive ability, providing strong support for the parental investment perspective in explaining SES-related achievement disparities (Guo & Harris, 2000; Linver, Brooks-Gunn, & Kohen, 2002; National Institute of Child Health and Human Development Early Child Care Research Network, 2005).

The second perspective on the SES-achievement link focuses on the detrimental impact of social stress (Barnett, 2008; McLoyd, 1998). Lower financial resources likely lead to increased daily concerns regarding food, shelter, and well-being. Lower SES is correlated with greater vulnerability to destabilizing events and chaos in the home (Evans, Gonnella, Marcynyszyn, Gentile, & Salpekar, 2005), a higher likelihood of maternal mental health problems (Petterson & Albers, 2001), increased daily hassles, and higher levels of conflict and violence exposure (McLoyd, 1998). Similarly, low SES has been related to diminished social capital and increased social discrimination (Brown & Lynn, 2010). These stressors are believed to deleteriously affect parents' emotional availability and their capacity to provide the warm, sensitive, and contingent responses associated with optimal self-regulatory skill development in children (McLoyd, 1990; Raikes & Thompson, 2005). In keeping with this theoretical perspective, higher levels of parent stress are associated with lower levels of nurturance, more harsh and restrictive disciplinary strategies, and less consistency during parent–child interactions (Anthony et al., 2005). Importantly, however, parents' level of access to social support networks such as friends and extended family has been shown to buffer the impact of stress on parenting behavior (Crnic & Greenberg, 1990).

EXECUTIVE CONTROL AND SOCIO-FAMILIAL RISK

New insights from genomics and neuroscience have renewed interest in these dimensions of socio-familial risk and their potential impact on childhood brain and cognitive development. Preclinical research with animals has revealed that neural synaptogenesis and pruning are experience-dependent and governed largely by variations in the richness of sensory input. Enriched environments lead to epigenetic modifications that silence or amplify gene expression (Szyf & Bick, 2013) to foster increased cortical thickness and glial cell numbers, as well as more dense dendritic elaboration (Greenough & Black, 1992; Greenough, Black, & Wallace, 1987; Halliwell, Comeau, Gibb, Frost, & Kolb, 2009; Roth & David Sweatt, 2011). These studies also highlight the importance of developmental timing, where the level of impact that the environment has on a particular cognitive ability varies with the maturational course of its underpinning neural systems. Some brain regions, such as the primary visual cortex, exhibit temporally confined sensitive periods during which the impact of environmental stimulation is amplified (Galván, 2010; Hubel & Wiesel, 1962; Knudsen, 2004). Given the prolonged course of synaptogenesis and myelination in prefrontal systems that subserve EC, some researchers have postulated a relatively protracted sensitive window of plasticity for EC relative to other cognitive abilities that are supported by earlier-maturing neural systems (Casey, 2000; Noble, Norman, & Farah, 2005). This extended window for prefrontal cortex maturation presumably allows individual experiences greater opportunity to affect EC development, both positively in the case of enrichment or intervention, and negatively in the case of socio-familial disadvantage. Coupled with this prolonged window of plasticity, the prefrontal system's involvement in the hormonal stress response system, as well as its dense connections to stress-sensitive hippocampal and limbic regions, may also enhance its vulnerability to the chronic stressors associated with socio-familial adversity (Blair, 2006; Cerqueira, Mailliet, Almeida, Jay, & Sousa, 2007).

Spurred by the tenet that EC may be particularly susceptible to environmental influence, several recent studies have focused specifically on the relation between socio-familial risk and EC, and have revealed positive correlations between relatively distal indicators of SES, such as parent income and education, and children's executive task performance. In general, effect sizes have been moderate to large, particularly when groups on the opposite ends of the SES scale have been compared (Allhusen et al., 2005; Ardila, Rosselli, Matute, & Guajardo, 2005; Hughes & Ensor, 2005; Lipina et al., 2013; Merz et al., 2014; Noble, McCandliss, & Farah, 2007; Raver, Blair, & Willoughby, 2012; Rhoades, Greenberg, Lanza, & Blair, 2011) (see Table 10 for a summary of several studies focusing on the relation of socio-familial experiences to children's EC; see also Lawson et al. (2015), for a review of existing research on this topic). In a group of children aged 11 years, Farah et al. (2006) examined the differential relation of SES to performance on tasks assessing a variety of neural systems. They suggested that SES has disproportionate rather than uniform effects on different cognitive systems, based on relatively stronger effect sizes for SES group differences in language ($d = .98$), working memory/executive control ($d = .4–.5$) and episodic memory ($d = .7$) relative to reward processing, spatial, and visual cognition. These findings are in keeping with suggestions that "the prefrontal/executive system is one of the primary cognitive systems associated with social inequalities in early experience" (Lipina et al., 2013, p. 697).

There is also accumulating evidence that these distal indicators of SES may be mediated by proximal household stressors and resources. Sarsour et al. (2011) demonstrated that observer ratings of factors such as household organization, learning resources, and parenting behavior mediated the link between global SES and school-aged children's performance on measures of inhibitory control. Effects were evident after statistical adjustment for performance on baseline, nonexecutive task conditions, providing support for the premise that EC is uniquely sensitive to variation in socio-familial experiences. Results from other studies show that maternal scaffolding during parent–child interactions, household organization and stability, and even measures of maternal EC, are related to children's executive task performance (Bernier, Carlson, Deschênes, & Matte-Gagné, 2012; Bernier, Carlson, & Whipple, 2010; Clark & Woodward, 2015; Hammond, Müller, Carpendale, Bibok, & Liebermann-Finestone, 2012; Hughes & Ensor, 2009; Landry, Miller-Loncar, Smith, & Swank, 2002). Notably, some dimensions of socio-familial risk may be more strongly related to EC than others: in Li-Grining (2007), demographic and neighborhood/residential risk factors were stronger predictors of children's EC than measures of parent stress and parent–child interactive synchrony.

72

TABLE 10

Summary of Studies Relating Socio-Familial Experiences to Children's Executive Control

Reference	Research Question	Country	Sample n	Age Group	Socio-Familial Measure	EF Measures	Effect Size	Findings
Aran-Filipetti & De Minzi (2012)	Do children with low SES have lower EC?	Argentina	129 low SES	7–12	Department of Education scale based on family income	Color-word stroop (Golden, 1978)	.66	• Group with low SES showed poorer performance on all EF measures.
	Is SES-EF link mediated by language or an impulsive response style?		125 middle SES		Family head profession	Wisconsin card sorting (Heaton, Chelune, Talley, Hay, & Curtiss, 1993)	1.47–1.99	• Maternal education was the strongest SES predictor.
					Source of family income	Digit span	2.49	• SES explained 9% of variance in latent EC and the relation was not mediated by K-BIT IQ performance.
					Housing conditions	Porteus Maze Test (Porteus, 1965)	1.75	
					Maternal education	Controlled Oral Word Association Task (Benton & Hamsher, 1978)	1.03	
Brown, Ackerman, & Moore (2013)	What are the relations between poverty, household chaos & inhibitory control	USA Pennsylvania	120	$M=4.17$ (6.5) years	Income to needs	Average score from:	$r=-.35$ to $-.57$ for adversity	• No correlation between income to needs and inhibitory control
					Adversity index from CHAOS scale and	Peg tapping (Diamond & Taylor, 1996)		• Moderate correlation of family chaos and instability with inhibitory control after

(Continued)

TABLE 10. (*Continued*)

Reference	Research Question	Country	Sample n	Age Group	Socio-Familial Measure	EF Measures	Effect Size	Findings
					family instability	Day/Night Stroop (Gerstadt et al., 1994) Bear/Dragon (Reed, Pien, & Rothbart, 1984)		accounting for verbal ability.
Lipina, Martelli, Vuelta, & Colombo (2005)	Do children with unsatisfied basic needs have lower EC?	Argentina	280	6–14 months	Unsatisfied vs. satisfied basic needs	A-not-B task	NA	• Children with unsatisfied basic needs made fewer consecutive correct responses and more perseverative errors.
						Consecutive correct responses Perseverative errors		
Lipina et al. (2013)	Do children with unsatisfied basic needs show lower nonverbal EC?	Argentina	14 satisfied basic needs, 98 unsatisfied basic needs	M = 4.87 (.59)	SES scale for basic needs	Corsi blocks	.72	• Children with unsatisfied basic needs showed lower performance on most tasks
	Are effects mediated by proximal risk factors				Perinatal risk, books in household, frequency of reading, computer use	Attention network test	.01–.59	• Large effects evident for baseline task conditions
						Butterfly/Frog stroop	.02–.51	• Reading and books in household mediated relation of SES to Corsi blocks performance.
						Self-ordered pointing	.11–.32	
						Tower of London	.35	
						K-BIT matrices	.51	

(*Continued*)

TABLE 10. (*Continued*)

Reference	Research Question	Country	Sample n	Age Group	Socio-Familial Measure	EF Measures	Effect Size	Findings
Raver, Blair & Willoughby (2012)	Do chronic poverty or spells of poverty relate to children's EF?	USA North Carolina & Pennsylvania	1,292	7 months, 15 months, 2, 3, and 4 years (EF assessed at 4)	Baseline income to needs	Flexible Item Selection Task (Jacques and Zelazo, 2001)	.22	• Chronic poverty exposure, maternal education and race explained 22% of EC variance
	Is effect of poverty moderated by child temperament or demographic profile?				Transitions below and above poverty line	Spatial conflict task (Gerardi-Caulton, 2000)		• Effects were stronger for children with high temperamental reactivity at age 7 months.
					Economic strain questionnaire	Animal working memory task		
					Observer-rated housing quality	Summarized into one EC score		
					Maternal education			
					Marital status			
Farah, Shera, Savage, Batancourt, Gianetta, Brodsky, Malmud, & Hurt (2006)	Does SES have broad or specific relations to cognition?	USA	30 low SES	$M = 11$ years		Anterior control: Go-/No-go	$d = .4$	• Highest effect size was for language, then WM and cognitive control
			30 middle-high SES			Number stroop	$d = .5$	
						Working memory:	$d = .1$	

(*Continued*)

TABLE 10. (*Continued*)

Reference	Research Question	Country	Sample n	Age Group	Socio-Familial Measure	EF Measures	Effect Size	Findings
						Two-back task CANTAB spatial WM Ventromedial reward processing Delay task Reversal learning Also assessed memory, spatial cognition, visual cognition & language		
Merz, Landry, Williams, et al., 2014	Does effortful control mediate relation of SES to academic achievement?	Texas and Florida, USA	308	2–4 years (middle, end, and one year after first preschool year)	Parent education HOME scale score	Composite measure of effortful control	Maternal education $r = .10$ $r = .19$ for HOME	• Maternal education and HOME scores predicted later effortful control
Noble et al. (2005)	Characterize correlations between SES and specific neurocognitive systems.	Philadelphia, USA	30 low SES 30 middle SES	Kindergarteners	Parent education, occupational status and income (Hollingshead scale)	Go/No-Go DCCS Spatial working memory	$d = 5.6$ $R^2 = .06$ $d = .31$	• Lower SES associated with lower performance. • Strongest predictor of composite EC was parent education • EC not related to SES after accounting for language performance.

(*Continued*)

TABLE 10. (Continued)

Reference	Research Question	Country	Sample n	Age Group	Socio-Familial Measure	EF Measures	Effect Size	Findings
Noble et al. (2007)	Characterize correlations between SES and specific neurocognitive systems.	New York, USA	50	First graders	Income to needs	Composite EF score Cognitive control composite from Go/No-Go	$d = .68$ $R^2 = .06$	• No relation between home environment and cognitive control composite
					Parent education	NEPSY auditory attention		• HOME scale score mediated relation of SES to working memory composite.
					Occupational status	Working memory composite from Spatial working memory task; Delayed nonmatch to sample	$R^2 = .06$	
					Home environment questionnaire			
Ardila, Roselli, Matute, & Guajardo (2004)	Determine relation of parent education to child EC	Colombia & Mexico	622	5–14	Parent education (public or private school)	Verbal fluency; Graphic fluency; Card sorting; Pyramid task; Matrices; Similarities	$r = .03–.46$	• Parent education predicted EC in MANOVA
Alloway, Alloway, & Wootan (2014	Characterize relations of SES to different cognitive skill	UK	264	Kindergartners	Residential neighborhood classification of SES	Backward digit span (working memory)	NS	• No significant differences between high and low SES groups
Sarsour,	Determine	California,	60	$M\ (SD) = 9.9$	MacArthur SES	Digit span	$r = .30$	• Lower SES related to lower EC

(Continued)

77

TABLE 10. (*Continued*)

Reference	Research Question	Country	Sample n	Age Group	Socio-Familial Measure	EF Measures	Effect Size	Findings
Sheridan, Jutte, Nuru-Jeter, Hinshaw, & Boyce (2011)	relation of SES, single parent status and home environment to EC	USA		(.96) years	scale			performance.
					Family income	Stroop color-word	$r = .40$	• HOME scales partially or fully mediated relation of SES to EC
					Hollingshead HOME scale	Trail-making test	$r = .41$	
Hughes & Ensor (2009)	Are associations between language and EC driven by common or distinct mechanisms?	UK	125	2 & 4 years	Maternal education	Aggregate EC score from:	$r = -.20$ to .32	• After accounting for EC at age 2 and language ability, occupational status, household chaos, inconsistent parenting, and maternal scaffolding correlated with EC.
					Occupational status	Spin the pots (working memory)		
					Parent–child interaction coding	Baby stroop		
					Family chaos questionnaire	Trucks sorting task		
					Arnold parenting questionnaire	Stanford–Binet beads		
						Detour reaching box (age 2 only) Tower of London (age 4 only)		
Hughes & Ensor (2005)	Examine relations between distal and proximal family factors and EC	UK	140	2 years	Cumulative social disadvantage score	Aggregate EC score from: Spin the pots (working memory)	$r = -.22$ for SES and EC	• Social disadvantage explained 8% of variance in EC

(*Continued*)

TABLE 10. (Continued)

Reference	Research Question	Country	Sample n	Age Group	Socio-Familial Measure	EF Measures	Effect Size	Findings
					Ratings of parent positive control, responsiveness, and talk	Baby stroop; Trucks sorting task; Stanford–Binet beads; Detour reaching box	$r = .27$ for parenting and EC	• No significant relation after accounting for language ability
Hughes, Ensor, Wilson, & Graham (2010)	Model growth in EC from 4 to 6 years	UK	191	4–6 years	Family income, maternal education and occupation	Factor score from: Day/Night stroop; Stanford-Binet beads; Tower of London	NA	• Family income correlated with EC intercept, not slope of latent EC growth.
Bernier, Carlson, Deschenes, & Matte-Gagne (2011)	Determine relation of toddler attachment security to later EC	Canada	62	12, 15, 18 months, 2 years, 3 years	Parent education; Parent income; Attachment behavior Q-sort	Average "conflict-EF" score derived from: Spin the pots; Shape stroop	$r = .34$–$.44$ for SES measures; $R^2 = .06$–$.12$ for parenting and attachment	• SES (education and income average) correlated with EC; • Parenting and attachment status predicted conflict EF scores at 3 after accounting for SES, verbal ability and EC at 2. • No relation of parenting to delay of gratification.

(Continued)

TABLE 10. (*Continued*)

Reference	Research Question	Country	Sample n	Age Group	Socio-Familial Measure	EF Measures	Effect Size	Findings
					Parent support factor score	Baby stroop at 2 years		
						Bear/dragon		
						Day/night stroop DCCS at 3 years		
						Delay of gratification at 2 and 3 years		

80

THE CURRENT STUDY

In summary, there is an extensive corpus of literature demonstrating the profound negative implications of socio-familial risk for children's cognitive development, with particularly pervasive effects noted on vocabulary and language proficiency (Hoff, 2003), although nonverbal skills are not spared (e.g., Espy, Molfese, & DiLalla, 2001). Critically, the utility of the new research focus on socio-familial risk and EC for applied practice and social policy hinges on its specificity. If EC is relatively more vulnerable than other cognitive systems, then intervention is best targeted directly at EC, as exemplified in the approach of extant working memory training packages (Klingberg, Forssberg, & Westerberg, 2002). Alternatively, a lack of specificity in the relation of socio-familial experiences to EC would suggest that EC and other cognitive abilities are affected by socio-familial risk to the same degree and that focusing specifically on EC may not be the best approach to early intervention for children at risk.

To effectively determine whether there is specificity in the relation of socio-familial risk to EC, a richer conceptualization of EC needs to be modeled, one that includes both the control process as well as the foundational cognitive abilities that together facilitate performance on executive tasks. Historically, covariate approaches that adjust statistically for potential confounds, such as performance on language or IQ tests, have been employed to determine the unique relation of socio-familial risk to EC. The covariate approach does reduce extraneous variance, but does not capture the dualistic contributions of EC and foundational cognitive abilities (as shown in Chapter I, this volume). Perhaps not surprisingly then, the covariate approach has produced mixed findings. In some studies, the correlations between socio-familial characteristics and EC remained statistically robust after controlling for confounds, whereas results from other studies support a mediational model, where relations between social risk and EC are attenuated after controlling for children's language abilities (Bernier et al., 2010; Hammond et al., 2012; Hughes & Ensor, 2005; Noble et al., 2005; Sarsour et al., 2011). Moreover, as shown in Table 10, the majority of studies to date have employed individual or summed scores from manifest tasks to measure EC. As highlighted in Chapter I of this volume, this approach rests on a flawed assumption that observed executive task performance fully represents the latent construct of interest, in this case EC. In preschoolers particularly, the demands on EC processes per se cannot easily be parsed from other foundational cognitive abilities that also drive observed executive task performance. These issues of measurement impurity, coupled with a potentially high degree of measurement error associated with the use of manifest executive task scores, likely increase the chances for misspecification in covariate models. For example, a single receptive vocabulary score entered into a linear regression model likely will not properly account for all of the overlap in variance between a social risk indicator and a summed or composite-dependent measure from an executive task. This commonly used, simple model does not sufficiently account for the range of individual differences in foundational cognitive abilities that children draw upon to perform manifest executive tasks, let alone adequately capture the specific variance related to EC. Given these limitations, covariate models cannot effectively address the specificity of the relation between socio-familial risk and EC.

Here, we address the methodological issues of previous studies with the goal of better characterizing the link between important dimensions of children's socio-familial environment and their early EC. As shown in Chapter III, this volume, the bifactor approach is particularly well-suited to examine the specificity issue because it allows for direct modeling of the multidimensional demands of executive tasks. Foundational cognitive abilities that also drive performance on executive tasks can be segregated with the bifactor approach to provide a purer representation of the processes that are unique to executive tasks. In keeping with an ecological, multidimensional approach to social risk, this study characterized individual differences in socio-familial experiences using both proximal and distal indicators. Drawing on theoretical perspectives such as the resource investment and social stress models outlined above, we first examined the relation of distal financial stressors, proximal household resources, and social network stressors to EC as modeled using a traditional, unitary approach at age points spanning the preschool period. Then, we used the bifactor representation of EC that was found to best fit the data at ages 4;6 and 5;3 to determine whether there is a unique, specific relation of social risk to EC over and above its relation to foundational cognitive abilities that also are engaged in executive tasks.

METHOD

There were 228 children included in analyses at age 3, 285 at age 3;9; 323 at age 4;6, and 364 at age 5;3. Details regarding the subjects, measures, and procedures are provided in Chapter II, this volume, with additional measures used to characterize children's socio-familial settings described below.

Measures of Socio-Familial Risk

Measures of socio-familial risk included questionnaires and interviews, as well as a direct observational measure of children's home and neighborhood environments. All of these socio-familial measures were collected during the initial home visit at study entry or during the child's first laboratory-based assessment.

Background Interview Measures

As part of the comprehensive background interview administered at study entry, caregivers reported their household income from various sources, highest level of education, the number of rooms and the number of residents in the child's home, and the frequency with which they read to their child (0 = Every night, 1 = At least once per week, 2 = Never). An index of household crowding was derived by calculating the number of people relative to rooms in the house (Gove, Hughes, & Galle, 1979). The family's income to needs ratio also was calculated by dividing the total household income by the federal poverty threshold for a family of that size. Thus, a score of 1 indicates a household income equal to the poverty threshold, with the degree of difference from 1 representing the degree of distance from the poverty threshold (Brooks-Gunn, Klebanov, & Duncan, 1996). The income to needs ratio was log transformed to obtain a normal distribution for analyses.

The Life Stressors and Social Resources Inventory (LISRES; Moos & Moos, 1994)

The LISRES was completed by caregivers during the initial lab session to provide a detailed survey of personal and familial stressors encountered on a daily basis. The scale includes 200 items that vary in response format. Scales assess financial stressors and resources; positive and negative life events; home and neighborhood stressors; physical health stressors; work and employment stress; spousal or partner relationship stressors and resources; family and extended family stressors and resources; and friend and social stressors and resources. As the spouse/partner and work-related scales were not applicable for a number of participating families, these scales were not considered further. The LISRES scales have high internal reliability ($\alpha = .83–.84$) and adequate ($r = .67–.70$) test-retest reliability (Moos, 1995).

The Early Childhood HOME Observation for Measurement of the Environment (EC-HOME; Caldwell & Bradley, 1984)

The EC-HOME provided a direct observational and interview-based assessment of the child's home environment and was administered during the home visit at study entry. The eight scales of the EC-HOME assess the availability of learning materials, such as books and toys; language stimulation, such as exposure to the alphabet; the physical and aesthetic quality of the residence and neighborhood setting; the level of maternal responsiveness to children's questions and interests; the academic stimulation provided to the child, including direct teaching of numbers, shapes, and patterns; appropriate modeling of behaviors such as manners; the variety of exposure to new places and activities; and finally, the acceptance that the parent shows for the child, a scale that focuses particularly on the use of harsh discipline strategies. The EC-HOME has been used widely in developmental science and is correlated with cognitive and behavioral outcomes (Bradley, 1993). To maintain administration fidelity, research assistants were individually trained and regularly monitored by a senior staff member, and unclear items were resolved by consensus during weekly supervision meetings. Inter-rater reliability for the EC-HOME in our studies is consistently high (Cohen's $\kappa = .85$–1.00), and internal reliability for this sample was .77.

The Satisfaction With Parenting Scale (SWPS)

The SWPS from the Inventory of Parent Experiences (Ragozin, Basham, Crnic, Greenberg, & Robinson, 1982) is a 17-item checklist assessing caregivers' subjective levels of parental stress and satisfaction with their parenting role, as well as their available levels of social and professional support. The SWPS was completed by mothers at the initial lab visit. Items such as, "If you were having a minor problem with your child, how many people (friends and family) could you talk to, whose advice you trust," are rated on a 5-point scale. Internal consistencies for the SWPS range from .70 to .77 and the questionnaire correlates with observer ratings of parenting behavior (Crnic & Greenberg, 1990; Crnic et al., 1983).

Data Analysis

Data analysis was conducted in four major steps. First, we conducted an exploratory factor analysis of all scales from the socio-familial measures to reduce the data and distill underlying dimensions of risk that these measures might reflect. Prior to conducting exploratory factor analysis, all scales were standardized and reversed where appropriate so that high values reflected greater levels of stress or adversity. Multiple imputation with expectation maximization was used before performing the exploratory factor analysis to handle the very few instances of missing data so that data from all children could be included in this preliminary part of the analyses. Note that this method was only applied for the exploratory factor analysis to maximize available data. For all other models, the approach was to use full maximum likelihood estimation in MPLUS. To determine the number of social risk factors, Kaiser's criterion (i.e., eigenvalues greater than 1.0), the scree-plot, and interpretability were considered. Given that we expected dimensions of socio-familial risk to correlate, we used promax rotation to obtain an oblique factor structure. In the second phase of analyses, we regressed the unitary foundational cognitive abilities factor identified as the best fitting model of foundational cognitive abilities and EC at ages 3 and 3;9, on each of the socio-familial factors identified in the exploratory factor analysis. Third, we regressed EC at ages 4 and 5;3, modeled using a more

84

traditional, unitary construct without language, visuo/spatial and motor speed subtests, on the socio-familial risk factors. This step was intended to frame our research relative to existing literature that has used this more traditional approach. It also allowed for a descriptive comparison against the bifactor approach, which considers the role of foundational cognitive abilities. Finally, we re-estimated these latter models, replacing the unitary EC latent with the bifactor parameterization identified as the best model of EC for ages 4;6 and 5;3.

RESULTS

Dimensions of Socio-Familial Risk

Table 11 shows the correlations between socio-familial measures, most of which were of low to moderate magnitude. Exceptions included the Positive Life Events and Physical Health scales from the LISRES and the Acceptance scale from the EC-HOME, which showed few significant correlations with other measures. Consistent with these correlations, the Positive Life Events and Physical Health scales from the LISRES and the Acceptance and Physical Environment scales from the EC-HOME did not load clearly on any identified factors in an initial exploratory factor analysis and little of their variance was explained. Similarly, the Negative Life Events Scale did not show a clear and conceptually relevant loading on any factor. Thus, these scales were dropped and the exploratory analysis was repeated. Kaiser's criterion and the scree-plot indicated that three factors provided the most meaningful characterization of the remaining socio-familial risk indicators. Table 12 presents the loading pattern for the rotated solution. The first factor, labeled *distal financial stress*, included household income, maternal education, crowding in the home and the Home and Neighborhood Stressor scale from the LISRES. All of the EC-HOME scales, as well as a question from the background interview regarding the number of times that the child was read to each week, comprised the second factor, labeled *proximal household stress*. The third factor, *social network stress*, was composed of the Family and Friend Stress and Resources scales from the LISRES, as well as the SWPS. The variance of the various individual scales explained by the EFA ranged from .20 to .77. Factors were moderately correlated ($r = .33-.49$). Findings from the EFA are in keeping with a multidimensional model of socio-familial risk (Yeung et al., 2002), incorporating the distal economic stress indicators commonly used to measure SES, the proximal learning resources that the child is exposed to on a daily basis and the social stressors faced by caregivers. Descriptive statistics for the scales included in the three factors are presented in Table 13.

TABLE 11

Correlations Between Indicators of Children's Socio-Familial Background

	1.	2.	3.	4.	5.	6.	7.	8.	9.	10.	11.	12.	13.	14.	15.	16.	17.	18.	19.	20.	21.
1. IN																					
2. M Ed	.48*																				
3. Crowd	−.44*	−.27*																			
4. Read	−.18*	−.23*	.05																		
5. Fi S	−.60*	−.34*	.30*	.24*																	
6. Fi R	.83*	.49*	−.33*	−.21*	−.60*																
7. HN	−.37*	−.19*	.28*	.20*	.45*	−.36*															
8. Fam S	−.19*	−.11*	.07	.10	.24*	−.19*	.24*														
9. Fam R	.17*	.12*	−.12*	−.27	−.25*	.14*	−.21*	−.55*													
10. Fr S	−.07	−.03	−.03	.03	.13*	−.11*	.25*	.41*	−.20*												
11. Fr R	.25*	.19*	−.20*	−.14*	−.32*	.27*	−.28*	−.22*	.43*	−.24*											
12. NLE	−.36*	−.19*	.16*	.12*	.40*	−.36*	.19*	.23*	−.23*	.15*	−.28*										
13. PLE	−.07	−.14*	.03	.05	.04	−.12*	−.03	.04	.07	−.01	.06	.17*									
14. Lear	.31*	.35*	−.24*	−.40*	−.32*	.38*	−.24*	−.10	.19*	−.04	.21*	−.21*	−.14*								
15. Lang	.15*	.13*	−.10	−.23*	−.20*	.17*	−.11	−.17*	.15*	−.03	.08	−.09	−.09	.40*							
16. PhyE	.32*	.28*	−.30*	−.20*	−.31*	.34*	−.31*	−.09	.08	−.05	.19*	−.19*	−.02	.29*	.31*						
17. Resp	.17*	.06	−.05	−.16*	−.15*	.19*	−.14*	−.17*	.08	−.10	.04	.00	−.08	.25*	.31*	.25*					
18. Acad	.18*	.21*	−.15*	−.15*	−.18*	.25*	−.16*	−.11*	.10	.00	.17*	−.16*	.01	.42*	.37*	.25*	.20*				
19. Mod	.17*	.20*	−.06	−.29*	−.19*	.21*	−.23*	−.14*	.11*	−.08	.13*	−.11*	.04	.23*	.24*	.23*	.25*	.26*			
20. Var	.34*	.27*	−.15*	−.32*	−.35*	.37*	−.23*	−.19*	.20*	−.07	.18*	−.27*	−.12*	.51*	.30*	.23*	.26*	.31*	.34*		
21. Acc	.06	.12*	−.07	−.11*	−.05	.13*	−.12*	−.11*	.05	−.17*	−.01	−.03	−.04	.11*	.12*	.12*	.11*	.07	.26*	.11*	
22. SWP	.10	.00	−.02	−.13*	−.26*	.07	−.22*	−.31*	.31*	−.23*	.31*	−.20	.10	.12*	.14*	.06	−.05	.09	.09	.19*	.10

Note. IN = Income to needs; M Ed = Maternal Education; Crowd = Number of residents to rooms; Read = Frequency of reading; Fi S = Lisres Financial stressor; Fi R = Lisres Financial Resources; HN = Lisres Home and Neighborhood Stressors; Fam S = Lisres Family Stressors; Fa R = Lisres Family Resources; Fr R = Lisres Family Resources; NLE = Lisres Negative Life Events; PLE = Lisres Positive Life Events; Lear = EC-HOME Learning; Lang = EC-HOME Language Stimulation; PhyE = EC-HOME Physical Environment; Resp = EC-HOME Responsivity; Acad = EC-HOME Academic Stimulation; Mod = EC-HOME Modeling; Var = EC-HOME Variety; Acc = EC-HOME Acceptance; SWP = Satisfaction with Parenting Scale.
*$p < .05$.

TABLE 12

FACTOR LOADINGS FOR MEASURES OF CHILDREN'S SOCIO-FAMILIAL ENVIRONMENT

	Factor 1 *Distal Financial Stress*	Factor 2 *Proximal Household Stress*	Factor 3 *Social Network Stress*
Income to needs ratio	**.93**	−.09	−.02
LISRES financial resources	**.88**	.02	−.06
LISRES financial stressors	**.60**	.03	.19
Maternal education	**.51**	.15	−.09
Household crowding	**.49**	−.03	−.02
LISRES home and neighborhood stressors	**.34**	.04	.29
EC-HOME learning materials	.15	**.65**	−.06
EC-HOME language stimulation	−.11	**.60**	.03
EC-HOME academic stimulation	.02	**.54**	−.05
EC-HOME variety	.1	**.54**	.05
EC-HOME responsivity	−.04	**.46**	−.01
EC-HOME modeling	.01	**.46**	.02
Frequency of reading	.01	**.46**	.08
LISRES family stressors	−.03	.02	**.68**
LISRES family resources	−.03	.06	**.66**
Satisfaction with parenting scale	−.04	.02	**.51**
LISRES friend stressors	−.02	−.07	**.51**
LISRES friend resources	.21	−.02	**.45**

Note. Bolded values loaded > .3 and were retained as indicators of the factor in subsequent analyses.

Relation of Socio-Familial Risk to Foundational Cognitive Abilities at Ages 3 and 3;9

Findings from Chapter III indicated that the variance shared by executive tasks administered at 3 and 3;9 years could not be parsed from the variance of tasks designed to measure other foundational cognitive abilities. We, therefore, regressed the general foundational cognitive abilities factor at ages 3 and 3;9 on each of the socio-familial factors identified in the exploratory factor analysis. Figures 10 and 11 describe the results of these analyses. As shown, both distal and proximal household stress predicted lower foundational cognitive abilities at the 3-year age point and the socio-familial risk factors collectively explained 31% of the variance in the foundational cognitive abilities factor, $\chi^2(348) = 509.99$, $p < .001$; RMSEA = .05, CFI = .91. Similar findings emerged at age 3;9, with social risk explaining 28% of the variance in children's foundational cognitive abilities, $\chi^2(348) = 512.95$ $p < .001$; RMSEA = .04, CFI = .92. These analyses confirm the relation between socio-familial risk and early cognitive abilities that has been shown in numerous other studies.

TABLE 13

DESCRIPTIVE STATISTICS FOR MEASURES OF CHILDREN'S SOCIO-FAMILIAL ENVIRONMENTS

Measure/Scale	N	M	SD	Range Low	Range High
Factor 1: Distal financial stress					
Income to needs ratio[a]	383	2.54	1.86	0	18.65
LISRES financial stressors	386	52.66	9.34	40	80
LISRES financial resources	386	51.82	7.94	42	61
Maternal education	388	14.97	2.37	11	20
Household crowding	386	0.67	0.25	0.17	2
LISRES neighborhood/home stressors	387	49.48	10.00	38	99
Factor 2: Proximal household stress					
EC-HOME learning materials	388	57.08	4.94	31.14	62.57
EC-HOME language stimulation	388	55.00	4.64	21.42	57.14
EC-HOME academic stimulation	388	58.39	6.45	24.61	63.07
EC-HOME variety	388	49.28	5.81	25.50	55.50
EC-HOME modeling	388	58.87	8.58	31.53	70
Frequency of reading	388	0.34	0.35	0	2
Factor 3: Parent social stress					
LISRES family stressors	387	51.28	9.12	36	91
LISRES family resources	387	50.97	9.09	24	67
Satisfaction with parenting scale	388	36.04	4.44	21	46
LISRES friend stressors	383	48.78	9.99	35	92
LISRES friend resources	383	55.65	9.20	21	70

[a]Unlogged variable presented for interpretability, although the variable was log transformed for analysis.

Dimensions of Socio-Familial Risk in Relation to Children's Executive Control

Next, we turned to EC at ages 4;6 and 5;3. We first describe the relation of socio-familial risk to EC when modeled in the traditional way as a unitary construct without consideration of foundational cognitive abilities. In a model regressing unitary EC at 4;6 on the three dimensions of socio-familial risk, proximal household stress was the only significant predictor, β $(SE) = -.34$ (.10), $p < .05$; $\chi^2(270) = 407.73$, $p < .001$; RMSEA $= .04$, CFI $= .93$, explaining 17% of the variance in EC. Neither distal financial risk (β $(SE) = -.08$ (.10), $p = .46$) nor parent social stress (β $(SE) = -.07$ (.13), $p = .61$) were related to EC after accounting for proximal household stress. In a similar model regressing the unitary EC factor from age 5;3 on all risk factors, the strongest predictor was the distal financial stress factor, where children with higher risk scores had lower latent EC scores, β $(SE) = -.25$ (.09), $p < .05$; χ^2 $(270) = 407.69$, $p < .001$; RMSEA $= .04$, CFI $= .93$. The proximal household stress score also showed a marginally significant negative relation to EC at age 5 (β $(SE) = -.22$ (.11), $p = .053$), whereas parent social stress was not related, (β $(SE) = .03$ (.13), $p = .85$; $R^2 = .16$. These results

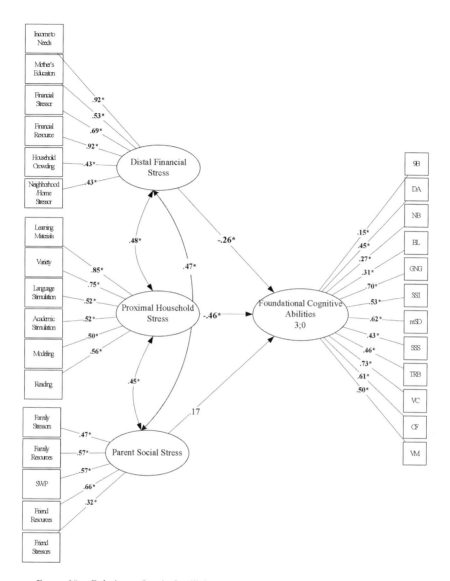

FIGURE 10.—Relations of socio-familial stress to children's foundational cognitive abilities at age 3 years. 9B = Nine Boxes; DA = Delayed Alternation; NB = Nebraska Barnyard; BL = Big-Little; GNG = Go/No-Go; SSI = Shape School–Inhibit; mSD = modified Snack Delay; SSS = Shape School–Switching; TRB = Trails–Switching; VC = Verbal Comprehension; CF = Concept Formation; VM = Visual Matching.

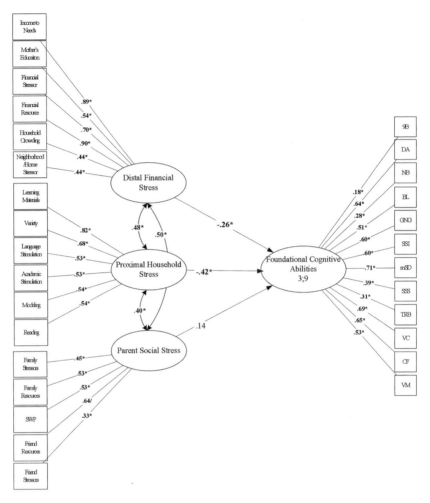

FIGURE 11.—Relations of socio-familial stress to children's foundational cognitive abilities at age 3;9. 9B = Nine Boxes; DA = Delayed Alternation; NB = Nebraska Barnyard; BL = Big-Little; GNG = Go/No-Go; SSI = Shape School–Inhibit; mSD = modified Snack Delay; SSS = Shape School–Switching; TRB = Trails–Switching; VC = Verbal Comprehension; CF = Concept Formation; VM = Visual Matching.

demonstrate a correlation between social risk and EC, captured using a traditional, unitary factor in this sample.

Relations of Socio-Familial Risk to Children's Executive Control in the Bifactor Model

In the next set of analyses, EC was modeled using the bifactor method. The EC and foundational cognitive abilities latents for ages 4;6 and 5;3 each

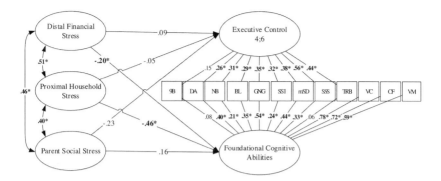

FIGURE 12.—Relations of socio-familial stress to the bifactor model of children's EC and foundational cognitive abilities at age 4;6. Full model with loadings for socio-familial factors available from the authors. 9B = Nine Boxes; DA = Delayed Alternation; NB = Nebraska Barnyard; BL = Big-Little; GNG = Go/No-Go; SSI = Shape School–Inhibit; mSD = modified Snack Delay; SSS = Shape School–Switching; TRB = Trails–Switching; VC = Verbal Comprehension; CF = Concept Formation; VM = Visual Matching.

were regressed on the three dimensions of socio-familial risk. Figure 12 describes the findings for age 4;6. Although distal financial stress and proximal household stress each predicted foundational cognitive abilities, they did not directly predict EC when modeled using the bifactor approach, $\chi^2(336) = 491.53$, $p < .001$; RMSEA = .04, CFI = .93; R^2 for foundational cognitive abilities = .29; R^2 for EC = .05. Figure 13 shows a similar model for age 5;3. Again, proximal household stress predicted foundational cognitive abilities, but was not significantly associated with EC in this age 5;3 bifactor

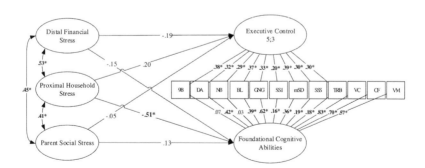

FIGURE 13.—Relations of socio-familial stress to the bifactor model of children's EC and foundational cognitive abilities at age 5;3. Full model with loadings for socio-familial factors available from the authors. 9B = Nine Boxes; DA = Delayed Alternation; NB = Nebraska Barnyard; BL = Big-Little; GNG = Go/No-Go; SSI = Shape School–Inhibit; mSD = modified Snack Delay; SSS = Shape School–Switching; TRB = Trails–Switching; VC = Verbal Comprehension; CF = Concept Formation; VM = Visual Matching.

model. Distal financial stress also correlated with lower EC and foundational cognitive abilities at age 5;3, although these paths did not quite reach significance, $p = .051$ and $.059$, respectively. Collectively, socio-familial risk accounted for 31% of the variance in foundational cognitive abilities and only 4% of the variance in EC in this age 5;3 bifactor model.

DISCUSSION

Socio-familial adversity is a well-known risk factor for disparities in cognition, achievement, and behavior. With new neuroscientific and genomic evidence, developmental science is revisiting questions regarding the influences of socio-familial risk through the lifespan, grounded in a growing recognition of the importance of EC for children's school achievement and other key outcomes. Studies documenting relations between socio-familial risk and EC suggest that EC may be a productive target for intervention efforts. Research to date, however, has not fully considered the interrelation between EC and foundational cognitive abilities that is fundamental to higher-order cognitive control. The present study provides a more nuanced characterization of the relation between socio-familial risk and executive task performance using the bifactor approach to segregate the respective specific EC and foundational cognitive ability constructs. Findings indicate that the mechanism by which socio-familial adversity relates to executive task performance at ages 4;6 and 5;3 is through its relation to foundational cognitive abilities, the substrates upon which the EC processes act to enable well-regulated, goal-directed thoughts and behaviors. More specifically, distal and proximal aspects of children's socio-familial environments explained variance that was common to both EC and foundational cognitive tasks during the late preschool period but showed little to no independent relation to EC-specific variance in the bifactor models. Thus, children's access to concrete learning supports and stimulation appears to foster the development of foundational cognitive abilities that are drawn upon by EC in the dynamic context of performing executive tasks and yet show no identifiably distinctive relation to the construct engaged specifically in EC tasks. Such findings have important theoretical and applied implications.

Findings were substantively different when EC was modeled using a bifactor approach as opposed to more traditional approach incorporating only the executive tasks. Results from the traditional, unitary models correspond with several studies reporting decrements in EC performance among children exposed to socio-familial adversity, with effect sizes being quite substantial (socio-familial factors explained 15–17% of the variance in latent EC). However, results from the bifactor models argue against the

92

notion that EC is uniquely or specifically vulnerable, with effect sizes dropping to <6%. The benefits of the bifactor approach are immediately apparent, as the approach identifies potential mechanisms of socio-familial effects within executive task performance itself. Specifically, it is the general skills that are brought to bear when performing any cognitive task, rather than more discrete control processes per se, that are most related to social risk in this age group.

The notion that EC may be particularly vulnerable to socio-familial risk rests on the protracted course of development of prefrontal connections. While neuroimaging research does suggest a hierarchical pattern of brain development, with sensory and motor regions maturing prior to prefrontal regions, this notion assumes a disconnection between the development of these systems. During sensitive periods, the architecture of neural circuitry supporting basic perceptual and cognitive processes is forged, with the organization of these circuits becoming less plastic thereafter (Knudsen, 2004). With each closure of a sensitive period, neural development becomes progressively canalized, a process termed entrenchment (Fox, Levitt, & Nelson, 2010). Socio-familial disadvantage is likely to have widespread implications even for the establishment of basic sensory, attentional, and semantic networks. Indeed, recent ERP studies indicate that brain electrophysiological responses during basic attention tasks differ in children of low SES backgrounds in contrast to those who are more advantaged (Kishiyama, Boyce, Jimenez, Perry, & Knight, 2009; Stevens, Lauinger, & Neville, 2009). Recent work also has shown that prior exposure to visual inputs enhances perceptual identification of the stimuli, allowing children to identify visual stimuli at lower thresholds relative to stimuli that they have not had prior exposure to. Therefore, richer semantic representations gained through exposure to rich environmental inputs benefit even early perceptual processing (Giganti & Viggiano, 2014). Individual differences in these foundational cognitive abilities likely bias the cognitive system along a particular trajectory, canalizing or limiting the development of higher-order cognitive processes. Essentially, if the foundational cognitive skills are deleteriously affected, then EC cannot properly integrate the weaker representations, which will result in poorer observed performance on executive tasks.

Prior research lends support to the idea that early learning experiences contribute to individual variation in foundational cognitive abilities, which in turn affect executive task performance in a bottom-up manner. In functional neuroimaging studies with adults, working memory maintenance involves sustained activity in sensory regions of the brain (e.g., primary visual cortex) that encode stimuli. Even perceptual processes traditionally thought to be relatively automatic (e.g., color constancy) have now been linked to working memory (Allen, Beilock, & Shevell, 2011; Ester, Serences, & Awh, 2009). The proficiency of children's basic perceptual encoding of stimuli likely is integral to their ability to hold representations on line in the service of executive task performance. Similarly, individual experience with the stimulus or response demands involved in executive tasks can have a significant impact on performance. For instance, an EEG study indicated that expert pianists showed greater neural efficiency during a working memory task involving hand movements than did novices (Calmels, Foutren, & Stam, 2011; Scolari, Vogel, & Awh, 2008). Children who have greater knowledge and experience identifying patterns, colors and shapes, gained through their access to resources that teach and reinforce these concepts, therefore, are likely to be advantaged on executive tasks incorporating these types of stimuli by richer representations of these concepts that then are able to be held in mind, inhibited, or switched with fewer demands on cognitive processing resources.

Although language abilities were modeled generally as a part of foundational cognitive abilities and not teased apart as an independent construct in the current study, the role of language warrants special mention in light of theory and research suggesting that language may mediate the relation between maternal scaffolding and EC (Hammond et al., 2012). Given strong loadings of the verbal comprehension subtest on the foundational abilities factor at age 4;6 ($\gamma = .78$) and age 5;3 ($\gamma = .83$), it is likely that language makes up at least some of the variance in this factor. Even in young children, language likely is tied to conceptual abilities and also provides an integrative symbolic code to support goal maintenance and information manipulation, particularly as language moves toward increasing automaticity with advancing development. Developmental theory posits that language supports EC by allowing the child to exercise internal dialog or rehearsal (Brocki & Bohlin, 2004; Vygotsky, 1978).

It is worth noting that social stressors did not emerge as a significant predictor of either EC or foundational cognitive abilities in any of the models. Instead, proximal stressors consistently emerged as the strongest predictor of early foundational cognitive processes, although there was evidence that these household stressors did not completely mediate the role of distal financial indicators, as distal financial stress showed independent significant effects. Certainly, then, it appears that children's concrete access to books, toys, and stimulating learning experiences is particularly important for cognitive development in this early childhood period. The independent contribution of distal financial stress above and beyond these household resources may reflect unmeasured influences or perhaps even biological transmission processes. It is also important to acknowledge, however, that parent social stress is perhaps more difficult to measure objectively, which may explain the nonsignificant findings for this factor.

The findings have interesting implications for applied intervention efforts. In line with the idea that the prefrontal cortex and associated executive processes are particularly vulnerable to socio-familial risk, interest in training specific EC abilities has burgeoned, with commercial working memory training packages now available. Although these packages show some promise, to date the training effects appear to be largely task-specific, with limited transfer to related cognitive domains or to key outcomes, such as academic achievement or externalizing behavior (Melby-Lervåg & Hulme, 2012; Shipstead, Redick, & Engle, 2012). In contrast to this focus on discrete EC skills, our data suggest that cognitive skills may be more diffusely organized and more generally susceptible to environmental influence, at least in this early age range. These findings are encouraging, as they suggest that there may be a wider scope for intervening at various entry points in the developing cognitive system of young children. Broad-based interventions that support semantic representations and language may have cascading implications for developing EC. As such, the study only serves to highlight the importance of early childhood as a period of particular opportunity for the provision of stimulating learning experiences that can help to set all children on optimal developmental trajectories.

V. ELUCIDATING NEW PATHWAYS TO DIMENSIONS OF ADHD SYMPTOMS IN PRESCHOOL BY JOINTLY MODELING EXECUTIVE CONTROL AND FOUNDATIONAL COGNITIVE ABILITIES

J. M. Nelson, T. D. James, and K. A. Espy

This article is part of the issue "The Changing Nature of Executive Control in Preschool" Espy (Issue Editor). For a full listing of articles in this issue, see: http://onlinelibrary.wiley.com/doi/10.1111/mono. v81.4/issuetoc.

Poorer executive control (EC) in childhood relates to, and in some cases precedes, a variety of difficulties with behavior regulation, including problems with hyperactivity, impulsivity, and inattention. In the developmental psychopathology literature, these dimensions of dysregulated behavior coincide with the domains of Attention-Deficit/Hyperactivity Disorder (ADHD) symptoms (American Psychiatric Association, 2013). Indeed, deficits in EC among youth displaying symptoms of ADHD are well-documented in both clinical and community samples (see Pauli-Pott & Becker, 2011; Willcutt, Doyle, Nigg, Faraone, & Pennington, 2005 for meta-analyses of studies in preschool and older children and adolescents, respectively), and EC has been implicated as one of the core neuropsychological deficits that precede the onset of ADHD among affected children and adolescents (Barkley, 1997; Sonuga-Barke, Sergeant, Nigg, & Willcutt, 2008). Given the novel model of preschool EC central to this monograph, the goals of this chapter were to review the literature linking EC to commonly associated behavior difficulties (i.e., hyperactivity, impulsivity, and inattention), particularly at preschool age,

Corresponding author: Jennifer Nelson, email: jnelson18@unl.edu
DOI: 10.1111/mono.12272

and to examine the relation of EC to these difficulties using the bifactor model of EC in order to evaluate the predictive utility of this specification. At the same time, we aimed to advance the field in understanding of how EC relates to behavior dysregulation at a young age, by applying more refined methodological characterization of the key constructs. After all, rapid development of EC during the preschool period (Garon et al., 2008) may mean EC deficits that contribute to the development of behavior problems are first identifiable at this age, making this age range critical for study.

Executive Task Performance and Hyperactivity, Impulsivity, and Inattention

The majority of research that has examined relations between EC and ADHD symptoms has focused on single executive tasks or particular "components" of EC in isolation, such as inhibition, and has not examined relations to an empirically derived latent EC construct per se (see Pauli-Pott & Becker, 2011; Willcutt et al., 2005). Results consistently reveal deficits in response inhibition among children displaying symptoms of ADHD, including during preschool specifically (e.g., Berlin & Bohlin, 2002; Berlin, Bohlin, & Rydell, 2003; Brocki, Nyberg, Thorell, & Bohlin, 2007; Hughes et al., 1998; Sonuga-Barke, Dalen, Daley, & Remington, 2002; Sonuga-Barke, Dalen, & Remington, 2003; Thorell & Wåhlstedt, 2006). In the few studies that have examined relations to tasks considered to measure working memory, some studies have documented similar deficits in working memory in preschool (e.g., Mariani & Barkley, 1997; Sonuga-Barke et al., 2003; Thorell & Wåhlstedt, 2006), while others have not (e.g., Brocki et al., 2007; Sonuga-Barke et al., 2002). Finally, there has been a paucity of research examining flexible shifting in relation to ADHD symptoms (Nigg, 2006; Pauli-Pott & Becker, 2011).

When considering how hyperactivity, impulsivity, and inattention each relate to executive task performance, there appear to be significant age-related differences. At school age, when the majority of this research has been conducted, deficits on executive tasks appear to be prevalent at similar levels among children with inattentive or combined symptoms (hyperactivity and impulsivity with inattention; see Willcutt et al., 2005). However, only a few studies have examined these deficits among school-aged children in relation to hyperactivity and impulsivity specifically, and none of them show much of a link between deficits on executive measures and symptoms in these domains (e.g., Chhabildas, Pennington, & Willcutt, 2001). These findings suggest that EC deficits in school-age children seem to underpin inattention problems and not problems with hyperactivity and impulsivity (Willcutt et al., 2005).

Of importance, though, the few studies among preschool children do show unique relations between executive task performance and hyperactivity and impulsivity (Brocki & Bohlin, 2006; Brocki et al., 2007). These findings align with reports of the instability of the types of ADHD symptoms prevalent in preschool age versus in older children. Hyperactivity and impulsivity symptoms are typically endorsed more frequently and are more sensitive to clinical disorder than inattention symptoms at ages 4–5 years (Curchack-Lichtin, Chacko, & Halperin, 2014). Additionally, children diagnosed exclusively with ADHD symptoms in the hyperactivity and impulsivity domains, and showing no significant inattention symptoms, were nearly all preschool age (4–6 years) in DSM-IV field trials (Lahey et al., 1994). However, in an 8-year longitudinal study, the majority of children displaying difficulties exclusively with hyperactivity and impulsivity in preschool went on to show equally significant problems with hyperactivity, impulsivity, and inattention by elementary school, while some children showed symptom remittance (Lahey, 2005; see also Curchack-Lichtin et al., 2014). These findings suggest difficulties with hyperactivity and impulsivity in preschool may presage more widespread problems that include attention deficits at school age, perhaps highlighted by increasing demands for attention in the formal school setting. In the clinical literature, some suggest that the Predominantly Hyperactive-Impulsive Presentation of ADHD in preschool may often be a precursor to the Combined Presentation, which also includes inattentive symptoms, in school age (Riley et al., 2008). These developmental changes when children display difficulties across the hyperactivity, impulsivity, and inattention dimensions are critical to hypotheses about their relation to early EC deficits. In line with the few studies linking these problems in younger children (Brocki & Bohlin, 2006; Brocki et al., 2007), it seems likely that poorer EC may relate to hyperactivity and impulsivity in preschool, despite theory that EC deficits are most prevalent among children specifically with attention problems at school age.

Linking a New Model of Latent EC With Current Models of Dysregulated Behavior

In moving from single executive task performance to latent models of EC, we and others have documented the unitary structure of EC across the preschool period, at least in typically developing or nonclinically identified samples (Chapter III, this volume; Fuhs & Day, 2011; Nelson, James, Chevalier et al., 2016; Wiebe et al., 2008, 2011; Willoughby et al., 2010; Willoughby, Blair, et al., 2012). Much more limited, emerging work has begun to examine the relation of latent EC to behavior difficulties. We are aware of only a handful of studies that have specifically evaluated the relation between latent EC and the symptom dimensions characteristic of ADHD, including studies among community and clinical samples. Willoughby and colleagues (2012) found poorer EC to be correlated with higher levels of ADHD symptoms represented as a single latent factor in a community sample of 3-year-olds. Among a community sample of 3- to 5-year-olds, Espy and colleagues (2011) found lower EC to be related to broad dimensions of parent-reported problem behaviors, including hyperactive behaviors, attention problems, and disinhibition behaviors, and these relations were robust when IQ was controlled. Further, in a clinically defined sample of preschoolers specifically diagnosed with ADHD only, ADHD and Disruptive Behavior Disorders (DBD), or DBD only, compared to a typically developing sample, Schoemaker and colleagues (2012) found that a two-factor (labeled "Inhibition" and "Working Memory") latent EC structure best fit the data. Children with an ADHD diagnosis (ADHD only or ADHD + DBD) showed deficits on the Inhibition composite score, but not on Working Memory.

In the current study, we aimed to take a further step beyond utilizing traditional latent models of EC and employ the bifactor modeling approach described earlier in this volume. Using the bifactor to parse the contributions of latent EC and foundational cognitive abilities to executive task performance allowed us to evaluate the more unique relation of EC to dysregulated behavior in the latter preschool period. Nigg (2006) underscored the importance of incorporating children's other cognitive abilities, in addition to EC, when evaluating the etiology of ADHD but called for moving beyond simple covariate models to seek a more sophisticated understanding of the roles of EC and other cognitive abilities. Accordingly, delineating the relation of EC to behavior difficulties here, using the bifactor to segregate the respective influences of EC and foundational cognitive abilities, allowed us to evaluate whether a purer EC construct relates to hyperactivity, impulsivity, and inattention at this critical age.

Of note, an increasingly substantial literature in both community and clinical samples, including the current sample of preschool children (Nelson, James, & Espy, 2016), supports the use of a hierarchical latent model to best represent the simultaneous overlap and separability of hyperactivity, impulsivity, and inattention difficulties (see Figure 14; Dumenci,

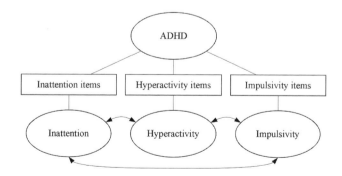

FIGURE 14.—Hierarchical latent model of ADHD symptoms.

99

McConaughy, & Achenbach, 2004; Martel, Von Eye, & Nigg, 2010; Martel, von Eye, & Nigg, 2012; Normand, Flora, Toplak, & Tannock, 2012; Toplak et al., 2009, 2012). Therefore, this model was applied here to represent the relevant dimensions of dysregulated behavior in this age range. Of importance conceptually, the model includes a general factor, which represents the common variance among all hyperactivity, impulsivity, and inattention symptoms, and separate, specific hyperactivity, impulsivity, and inattention factors that each represent the unique variance shared only among the symptoms associated with each dimension (Martel et al., 2010; Toplak et al., 2009). Proponents of this model in the clinical literature suggest the general factor aligns with the Combined Presentation of ADHD (including difficulties with inattention and hyperactivity/impulsivity), whereas the specific factors align with the Predominantly Hyperactive-Impulsive and Predominantly Inattentive Presentations (e.g., Martel, Roberts, Gremillion, Eye, & Nigg, 2011). Note that in our preschool data, unique rather than combined hyperactivity and impulsivity specific factors best fit the data, a finding supported by other studies at this age (e.g., Bauermeister, Canino, Polanczyk, & Rohde, 2010; Hardy et al., 2007; Willoughby, Pek, et al., 2012) and perhaps related to developmental differences in when difficulties emerge in the two dimensions and in etiological pathways (e.g., Sagvolden, Johansen, Aase, & Russell, 2005).

In addition to the empirical suggestion that this hierarchical symptom model is preferred, it also has a number of applied benefits. The manner in which the hierarchical model captures the interaction among the symptom dimensions of interest theoretically allows for representing the heterogeneity in ADHD expression (Martel et al., 2010, 2011; Nigg, 2006; Sonuga-Barke, 2005; Sonuga-Barke et al., 2008; Toplak et al., 2009, 2012). In turn, such representation of the general versus specific liabilities across the symptom dimensions allows for identification of general and unique genetic and environmental influences on each (Martel et al., 2010, 2011; Normand et al., 2012). Additionally, the dimensional approach that underlies the hierarchical model is most appropriate for studies with nonclinically referred community samples like ours in which children display the full range of dysregulated behaviors and do not necessarily meet criteria for diagnosis. Furthermore, there is emerging support for the validity of these models in relation to neurocognitive constructs, such as EC. Martel and colleagues (2011) found that higher levels of symptoms on the latent general factor and latent hyperactivity/impulsivity specific factor were associated with lower response inhibition, increased response variability, and poorer flexible shifting, where no relation was found between the latent inattention specific factor and these EC scores. These findings are in contrast to those from more traditional studies at school age in which the use of ADHD symptom counts and subtype diagnoses suggest EC is most related to inattention problems. The more recent findings suggest the hierarchical model of symptoms may be productive to better explicate the relation of EC to difficulties with behavior dysregulation in preschool children as well.

The Current Study

The aim of the study presented in this chapter was to elucidate the relation between EC and behavior difficulties associated with ADHD at ages 4;6 and 5;3. The bifactor model parsing EC from foundational cognitive abilities and the hierarchical model of ADHD symptoms were applied in line with the novel representation of EC central to this monograph, and current dimensional models of ADHD symptoms in the literature. These research questions were examined at the two later measurement points in the preschool period, given these were the age points at which the relative influences of both EC and foundational cognitive abilities were distinguishable, and thus the specific consideration of links between EC and behavior difficulties possible. Individual variation in EC was hypothesized to predict higher ratings on the general ADHD symptom factor and on the hyperactivity and impulsivity specific factors, and not the inattention factor, consistent with the higher prevalence and sensitivity of hyperactivity and impulsivity difficulties in preschool (Curchack-Lichtin et al., 2014) and the findings of Martel and colleagues (2011) applying the hierarchical model of ADHD in school age children.

METHOD

Participants and Procedure

Information concerning the participants, procedures, and measures consistent across the studies in this volume can be found in Chapter II, while information specific to this chapter is described below. ADHD symptom ratings were provided by parents (most often mothers) for a total sample of 364 children at their final study lab visit. Of this sample, 323 children belonged to the cohorts represented at the 4;6 measurement point and were, therefore, included in analyses evaluating the relation of EC at age 4;6 to ADHD symptoms at study exit. The full sample with symptom ratings ($N = 364$) was included in analyses of the relation of EC at the 5;3 age point to ADHD symptoms.

Measures of ADHD Symptoms

Child Behavior Checklist for Ages 1½–5 (CBCL/1½–5; Achenbach & Rescorla, 2000)

The CBCL/1½–5 is a standardized rating form for obtaining parents' reports of young children's symptoms of behavioral and emotional difficulties. Parents completed all 99 items of the full measure; however, for the purposes of the present study, only items loading on the Attention Problems syndrome scale and Attention Deficit/Hyperactivity Problems DSM-oriented scale were included (total of eight items). Parents rated how well each item described their child at present or within the prior 2 months using a 3-point scale (0 = *Not True (as far as you know)*, 1 = *Somewhat or Sometimes True*, 2 = *Very True or Often True*). The scales from which items were used for this study demonstrated strong test–retest reliability ($r=.78$ and $.74$, respectively), and the items and scales both significantly distinguished between clinically referred and nonreferred children in the original validation sample (Achenbach & Rescorla, 2000).

SNAP-IV Rating Scale (Revision of the Swanson, Nolan, and Pelham (SNAP) Questionnaire; Swanson et al., 1983)

The SNAP-IV is a standardized rating scale for obtaining caregiver reports of children's DSM-IV symptoms (American Psychiatric Association, 1994). Parents completed the full 90-item measure, yet only those items on the ADHD-Inattention and ADHD-Hyperactivity/Impulsivity subscales were included in the present study (total of 18 items). Parents used a 4-item scale to indicate the degree to which each symptom described their child (0 = *Not at All*, 1 = *Just a Little*, 2 = *Quite a Bit*, 3 = *Very Much*). The SNAP-IV has been used widely in ADHD research, including in evaluations of clinical trials (e.g., Multimodal Treatment Study of Children with ADHD; Swanson et al., 2001).

Data Analysis

Items drawn from the two measures of dysregulated behavior described above were included in a hierarchical model of ADHD symptoms with a general symptom factor and three, specific Hyperactivity, Impulsivity, and Inattention factors (see Figure 14). This hierarchical model with three specific factors was determined to best represent the structure of ADHD symptoms in the present preschool-aged community sample, when compared to a one-factor model; correlated two- and three- factor models; two- and three-factor higher-order models; and a hierarchical model with two specific factors (see Nelson, James, & Espy, 2016). Table 14 details which items represented each of the three specific, symptom dimensions.

After setting up the hierarchical model to represent ADHD symptoms, two structural models were estimated to determine the relation between EC at ages 4;6 and 5;3 and parent-rated child ADHD symptoms at study exit, using the EC bifactor model at each age. Note that these models were implemented using the robust maximum likelihood (MLR) estimator, and given the manifest symptom items were treated as categorical, as opposed to

TABLE 14

CBCL/1½–5 AND SNAP-IV ITEMS BY SPECIFIC SYMPTOM DIMENSIONS

Item
Inattention

Makes a lot of careless mistakes (SNAP1)
Difficulty sustaining attention on tasks (SNAP2)
Does not listen (SNAP3)
Difficulty following instructions (SNAP4)
Difficulty organizing tasks (SNAP5)
Avoids tasks requiring attention (SNAP6)
Loses things (SNAP7)
Easily distracted (SNAP8)
Forgetful in daily activities (SNAP9)
Cannot pay attention (CBCL5)
Quickly shifts between activities (CBCL59)
Wanders off (CBCL95)

Hyperactivity

Fidgets (SNAP11)
Difficulty remaining seated (SNAP12)
Runs or climbs excessively (SNAP13)
Difficulty playing quietly (SNAP14)
On the go/acts like driven by a motor (SNAP15)
Talks excessively (SNAP16)
Cannot sit still (CBCL6)
Gets into lots of things (CBCL36)
Clumsy (CBCL56)

Impulsivity

Blurts out answers (SNAP17)
Difficulty waiting turn (SNAP18)
Interrupts (SNAP19)
Cannot stand waiting (CBCL8)
Wants demands met immediately (CBCL16)

Note. Items are paraphrased or shortened from the original measures for the purposes of presentation here.

continuous, numerical integration was required. All ADHD items were deemed categorical due to their response options and the overall pattern of parents' responses (see Nelson, James, & Espy, 2016). Models using the MLR estimator with numerical integration do not yield the same conventional fit statistics as models estimated without numerical integration. However, the fit of the EC bifactor and ADHD symptom hierarchical models was previously deemed good (see Chapter III, this volume; and Nelson, James, & Espy, 2016, respectively). Of most interest here was the strength of the structural paths linking EC to the symptom dimensions.

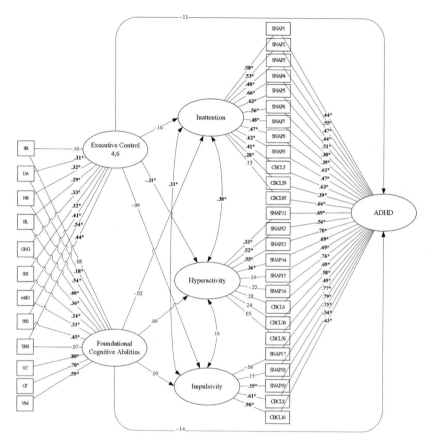

FIGURE 15.—Structural model relating the EC and foundational cognitive abilities bifactor at 4 years 6 months to ADHD symptoms. 9B = Nine Boxes; DA = Delayed Alternation; NB = Nebraska Barnyard; BL = Big-Little; GNG = Go/No-Go; SSI = Shape School–Inhibit; mSD = modified Snack Delay; SSS = Shape School–Switching; TRB = Trails–Switching; VC = Verbal Comprehension; CF = Concept Formation; VM = Visual Matching. *$p < .05$.

RESULTS

The structural models in which the EC bifactor models at ages 4;6 and 5;3 were estimated as predictors of ADHD symptoms at study exit are shown in Figures 15 and 16. In the 4;6 model, EC predicted the Hyperactivity specific factor in the expected direction ($\beta = -.31$, $p < .05$), such that children displaying lower EC were reported by their parents as showing higher levels of hyperactivity-specific symptoms. No other directed paths between either EC or foundational cognitive abilities and any of the other factors in the ADHD

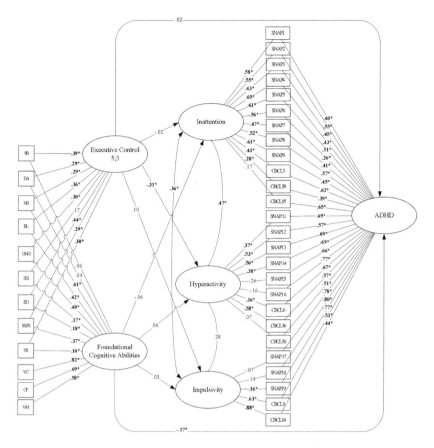

FIGURE 16.—Structural model relating the EC and foundational cognitive abilities bifactor at 5 years 3 months to ADHD symptoms. 9B = Nine Boxes; DA = Delayed Alternation; NB = Nebraska Barnyard; BL = Big-Little; GNG = Go/No-Go; SSI = Shape School–Inhibit; mSD = modified Snack Delay; SSS = Shape School–Switching; TRB = Trails–Switching; VC = Verbal Comprehension; CF = Concept Formation; VM = Visual Matching. *$p < .05$.

hierarchical model were significant (neither the general ADHD, Inattention specific, nor Impulsivity specific factors).

In the 5;3 model, EC again negatively predicted the Hyperactivity specific latent factor ($\beta = -.31$, $p < .05$). In addition, a negative relation between foundational cognitive abilities and the general ADHD factor emerged ($\beta = -.17$, $p < .05$), such that children displaying lower foundational cognitive abilities at study exit were reported by their parents as showing higher levels of general ADHD symptoms. No other directed paths in the model were significant.

105

DISCUSSION

Preschool represents a period of rapid and dynamic development of executive control (EC), which as demonstrated in this volume, involves differentiation of EC as unique from children's foundational cognitive abilities in its contribution to executive task performance. This emergence of EC as a particularly unique set of abilities in the latter half of preschool coincides with a developmental period marked by a high degree of individual heterogeneity in behavior observed by parents and others. During this period, children transition from normative expectations of "in the moment" behavior to increased self-regulated behavior, with emerging behavior dysregulation possibly signaling the unfolding of clinically significant problems. Against the backdrop of literature linking EC to behavior difficulties, the current study further examined the relation of EC to hyperactivity, impulsivity, and inattention late in the preschool period, utilizing the novel bifactor model of latent EC central to this monograph. This model offered improved precision and developmental sensitivity beyond traditional modeling approaches in evaluating how EC relates to dysregulated behavior during this critical time in early childhood. At both ages 4;6 and 5;3, EC was related to hyperactivity-specific symptoms, within a hierarchical model of ADHD symptom dimensions that also included specific impulsivity and inattention factors, and a general symptom factor. Children with lower EC were rated as displaying more hyperactivity. At neither age was EC related to the specific impulsivity or inattention factors, or to the general factor. These findings underscore the predictive utility of the EC bifactor model in delineating discriminative relations to behavioral dimensions.

Overall, the findings relating EC to behavior difficulties were identical for both age points at which executive task performance was measured and were mixed with respect to our hypotheses. Turning first to the null findings for inattention-specific difficulties, EC was, as posited, unrelated to the inattention-specific factor, which was comprised of the unique aspects of inattention not shared across the other ADHD symptom dimensions. At first glance, these results seem to contradict a wealth of previous research at school age suggesting EC deficits predominantly underlie the attention deficits characteristic of ADHD, as opposed to problems with hyperactivity or impulsivity (Chhabildas et al., 2001; Willcutt et al., 2005). However, we believe the developmental context of the current study is critical in interpreting the findings. Studies have long highlighted that inattention symptom ratings are less sensitive to clinical disorder at preschool age (e.g., Curchack-Lichtin et al., 2014), and almost no children are diagnosed with the Predominantly Inattentive Presentation of ADHD in this age range (Egger, Kondo, & Angold, 2006; Lahey et al., 1998; Nolan, Gadow, & Sprafkin, 2001). Even if a sizeable number of parents report that their preschool children are distracted or quickly shift between activities, for example, these behaviors are less likely to be viewed as problematic, but rather age-appropriate, making such inattention symptoms less clinically meaningful than at later ages. In turn, such behaviors may be less likely to relate to other difficulties, such as poorer EC, in preschool. Instead, impairment related to inattention is typically detected later in the course of the disorder (Barkley, 1997), postulated in part due to the far fewer situational demands for focused or sustained attention in school and at home placed on preschool children that would bring to the fore overt difficulties in this domain. Furthermore, the manner in which children display inattention earlier in preschool may be to engage in other more salient behaviors, such as motor hyperactivity or an inability to sit quietly, which are reflected in ratings of hyperactivity or impulsivity. In sum, these features render it more challenging to capture inattentive problems at preschool age, which may obfuscate the role of EC as a contributor to inattention as rated by informants in young children.

As also hypothesized, a different story emerged with respect to the relation of EC to early difficulties with hyperactivity. Preschool children with lower EC, when parsed from their foundational cognitive abilities both at ages 4;6 and 5;3, were rated as displaying more significant problems with the unique aspects of hyperactivity not shared across the other ADHD symptom dimensions. Closer examination of the items that contributed to the hyperactivity-specific factor (e.g., "often leaves seat in situations when remaining seated is unexpected," "often runs or climbs excessively in situations in which inappropriate") indicates these difficulties are specific to physical body control, as opposed to excessive talking. Therefore, preschool children with poorer EC appear to have particular difficulty maintaining control of their physical bodies and suppressing extraneous movement (e.g., sitting still and refraining from running and climbing about when not appropriate). These findings are somewhat in line with a recent study among older children that used the ADHD hierarchical model and documented poorer executive task performance on response inhibition and flexible shifting measures in particular among children with higher levels of hyperactivity-impulsivity specific symptoms (Martel et al., 2011), with the caveat that our preschool findings are limited to the hyperactivity-specific dimension only.

Developmentally, despite findings at school age that EC does not uniquely relate to hyperactivity (e.g., Chhabildas et al., 2001; Willcutt et al., 2005), the current findings may align with the relative frequency with which hyperactivity, versus inattention, is rated by parent informants as problematic at preschool age (Applegate et al., 1997; Curchack-Lichtin et al., 2014; Egger & Angold, 2006; Lahey et al., 1994). After all, self-regulation in the motor domain is a hallmark achievement of preschool, with problems with

107

hyperactivity by nature demanding increased parent attention and intervention. Perhaps the early significant relation between EC deficits and hyperactivity symptoms, in particular, reflects the close relation between cognitive and motor development in this age range, as well as the linked functionality between the dorsolateral prefrontal cortex and neocerebellum in cognitively demanding tasks or activities (Diamond, 2000). When apparent at this young age, gross motor overactivity is among the most predictive characteristics of children who go on to develop externalizing behavior problems (Campbell, 1995), and early hyperactivity has been found to persist and lead to future diagnoses of ADHD and even other psychological disorders (Lahey et al., 2004). Overall, the predictive relation between EC and hyperactivity-specific difficulties likely reflects a developmentally specific manifestation core to the ontogeny of ADHD.

Note that in our preschool sample, impulsivity-specific difficulties emerged as indicative of a unique latent factor separate from and uncorrelated with the hyperactivity-specific factor in the hierarchical symptom model (Nelson, James, & Espy, 2016), despite findings that the two are not distinct in school age (Dumenci et al., 2004; Martel et al., 2010; Toplak et al., 2009). Given that the items loading on the impulsivity-specific factor were most characteristic of demanding interpersonal conduct (e.g., "can't stand waiting," "demands must be met immediately") compared to those indicating a lack of inhibition (e.g., "blurting out answers"), the null relation between EC and impulsivity is not surprising, though initially not expected. In fact, in clinically diagnosed preschool children with disruptive behavior disorders, executive task performance is not substantially impaired, after controlling for comorbid ADHD symptoms (Schoemaker et al., 2012). Perhaps the more demanding (as opposed to inhibitory) nature of the items representing this impulsivity-specific factor in our preschool sample also makes the items simply less reflective of any deficits in EC.

The methodological advancement of the use of the EC bifactor model in relation to the ADHD hierarchical model revealed interesting insights into the core, general domain of ADHD symptoms in preschool children. Simply put, as EC became more differentiated from children's foundational cognitive abilities later in the preschool period, the relation of foundational abilities to the general symptom factor was evident. Given that diagnosed children with ADHD symptoms are found, on average, to have lower measured general intellectual abilities (Frazier, Demaree, & Youngstrom, 2004; Lahey et al., 2004; Rapport, Scanlan, & Denney, 1999), it was not unexpected to find this path to be significant, as this may represent the relation between general abilities and the core of what is shared across the symptoms of hyperactivity, impulsivity, and inattention. Further, the EC bifactor model effectively reduces the confounding influences of foundational cognitive abilities when relating EC to the general symptom factor, which may in turn also lead to weaker relations between EC and the general factor, given the known overlap between foundational abilities and inattention in particular (Castellanos, Sonuga-Barke, Milham, & Tannock, 2006).

The community nature of the present sample was both a strength and a limitation in the current study. The interpretation of our results is particularly meaningful for characterizing how EC relates to behavior dysregulation in the hyperactivity, impulsivity, and inattention domains among broadly defined typically developing preschool children, some of whom may be at risk for developing ADHD. However, future work targeting a clinical sample of diagnosed preschool children will be important to evaluate the generalizability of our findings to this end of the spectrum and may or may not yield a different pattern of results. Longitudinal follow-up of the current research beyond the preschool period will be important to characterize the dynamic unfolding of behavior difficulties across development. We began here to see differential relations between precursors and behavioral outcomes, such as between EC and hyperactivity-specific versus inattention-specific symptoms, as a function of developmentally salient demands placed on young children. In a similar vein then, continued differential relations may be expected with the further development of behavior difficulties defined by the changing demands of elementary school. Furthermore, person-centered analyses that classify children according to the degree of their EC deficits may help inform etiological heterogeneity of ADHD symptoms as they unfold among different children. This analytic approach would allow for determining whether pathways to symptomatology between children with and without EC deficits differ (e.g., relations between EC and ADHD may be strengthened when evaluated only among children with known EC deficits; Nigg, Willcutt, Doyle, & Sonuga-Barke, 2005).

In conclusion, this study evaluated how EC development relates to ratings of hyperactivity, impulsivity, and inattention in a preschool-aged community sample, made possible, in part, by carefully selected and newly applied measurement approaches. The EC bifactor model parsed the overlap of foundational cognitive abilities and EC in driving executive task performance in a more sophisticated fashion than previously used covariate models, which afforded a more precise evaluation of the relations between EC and ADHD symptom dimensions (Nigg, 2006). Additionally, the application of an ADHD hierarchical model that best fit the symptom rating data in preschool allowed for a more developmentally sensitive representation of the symptom dimensions under study. In the end, we can conclude that EC, as distinguished from foundational cognitive abilities, is related to hyperactivity-specific difficulties in preschool. Because EC has been suggested as an important component of ADHD intervention, particularly among children with underlying EC deficits (Sonuga-Barke, 2005; Sonuga-Barke & Halperin, 2010), it may be that EC is perhaps best targeted for this purpose near the time children enter the latter half of the preschool period, when EC can be discriminated from other foundational cognitive abilities. However, given the lack of EC training effects on more distal outcomes found to date (Thorell, Lindqvist, Bergman, Bohlin, & Klingberg, 2009), there is much to be learned about how the dualistic EC and foundational cognitive ability subcomponents contribute to the dynamic unfolding of ADHD symptoms across development and among individuals before rushing to quick application.

VI. EXECUTIVE CONTROL IN PRESCHOOLERS: NEW MODELS, NEW RESULTS, NEW IMPLICATIONS

K. A. Espy, C. A. C. Clark, J. P. Garza, J. M. Nelson, T. D. James, and H.-J. Choi

This article is part of the issue "The Changing Nature of Executive Control in Preschool" Espy (Issue Editor). For a full listing of articles in this issue, see: http://onlinelibrary.wiley.com/doi/10.1111/mono. v81.4/issuetoc.

Executive control (EC) has gained increasing acceptance in developmental science as a central construct that helps to explain both normative age-related change and individual variation in learning and behavior. This popularity is not unfounded, given the utility of executive tasks in predicting individual differences across a range of important developmental domains, including internalizing and externalizing behavior; theory of mind; academic achievement; emotion regulation; and creativity, often over extended time intervals (Carlson & Moses, 2001; Carlson & Wang, 2007; Clark et al., 2010; Riggs, Jolley, & Simpson, 2013; Welsh et al., 2010). Despite these ubiquitous associations, consensus on the definition of EC continues to elude the field. This lack of clarity is especially evident for early childhood, where theoretical models derived from adult literature may not adequately reflect the dynamic nature of rapidly maturing neural and cognitive systems.

In this volume, we tackled these challenges through the unique application of the bifactor model to data collected across the preschool age range. The bifactor approach provided an innovative means to address a central measurement issue in EC research: the inherent conflation of the specific control processes of interest with the foundational stimulus- and

Corresponding author: Kimberly Espy, email: kespy@email.arizona.edu
DOI: 10.1111/mono.12273

response-processing demands of executive tasks. In the past, these measurement concerns have been addressed using experimental manipulation, statistical covariation, and traditional latent variable models. None of these methods completely address the problem of measurement impurity or provide an accurate characterization of EC in early development, a time when individual differences in foundational cognitive abilities are particularly pronounced and likely substantially contribute to varying performance on executive tasks. Our use of the bifactor model at different age points is an important methodological advancement, allowing for a clearer segregation of the variance associated with the EC construct of interest from that more closely tied to the other, subordinate foundational abilities that form the "targets" of EC. Use of the bifactor model improved our ability to address three key questions that have predominated in the early childhood EC literature: (i) How is EC organized in early childhood and how might its nature change over the course of this developmental period? (ii) How specific is the relation of the child's socio-familial context to EC independent of the relation of foundational cognitive abilities that underlie the various stimulus- and response-processing demands of executive tasks? (iii) What are the manifestations of individual differences in early EC that relate to the emergence of observable dimensions of dysregulated, hyperactive, impulsive, inattentive, behaviors, referred to in the clinical/developmental psychopathology literature as ADHD symptoms?

Findings afford novel insights into the fundamental structure and importance of EC in young children. First, the relative contributions of EC and foundational cognitive abilities to executive task performance differed with age. As children matured through the latter half of the preschool period, specific EC was evident and distinguishable from the subordinate foundational cognitive abilities that also influence executive task performance. In addition to this evidence for a separable control process, the latent EC factor was modeled most parsimoniously as a unitary, and not a fractionated, construct throughout the preschool period. That is, separate working memory, inhibitory control, and flexible shifting components of EC were not evident even at later preschool age points when the influence of foundational cognitive abilities could be segregated. Second, variations in socio-familial background factors, and particularly children's access to proximal learning resources, did not contribute to executive task performance via EC, but instead related to variations in foundational cognitive abilities that also are engaged when children perform executive tasks. In contrast, hyperactive symptoms in this preschool period were predicted by individual differences in EC specifically, and not by children's foundational cognitive abilities, when these two components of executive task performance were considered in tandem using the bifactor model. Below, we discuss these findings in relation to existing views on EC and begin to formulate a new approach that recognizes its dynamic relation to other neural systems and grounds it firmly within the developmental literature.

A MORE REFINED CONCEPTUALIZATION OF EXECUTIVE CONTROL DEVELOPMENT OVER THE COURSE OF THE PRESCHOOL PERIOD

Werner's orthogenetic principle states that "wherever development occurs, it occurs from a state of relative globality and lack of differentiation to a state of increasing differentiation, articulation and hierarchic integration" (Werner, 1957, p. 126). Systems become more specialized, but also more flexible in response to the environment (Wapner & Demick, 2000). Accordingly, as children grow and mature, they develop a greater "arsenal" of abilities that are progressively honed in order to navigate experiences in increasingly complex environments (Werner, 1957). This movement from a global, undifferentiated state to one that is more specialized and modularized is evident in many realms of development. For instance, phoneme perception gradually becomes more specialized for the unique sounds of the child's language over the course of infancy (Polka & Werker, 1994). Similarly, Siegler's (1983) overlapping waves model suggests that children initially use multiple, varied strategies to approach cognitive problems with similar demands but progressively tune these strategies to particular problems so that they become increasingly precise and efficient over time.

Findings from the first study in this volume suggest that the same pattern of progressive differentiation and fractionation characterizes the early ontogeny of EC. Using the bifactor approach, EC did not emerge as a unique factor, independent of a foundational cognitive abilities factor, at ages 3 years or 3 years 9 months. Substantively, the contribution that EC makes to executive task performance could not be distinguished from subordinate foundational cognitive abilities at these young ages. In fact, prior to age 4, the empirically preferred model of the variance shared among the different executive tasks was a simple, undifferentiated, unitary one, where all tasks, and correspondingly all of the processes underlying performance of the tasks—executive, language, visual/spatial perception, and motor—loaded onto one factor. At age 4 years 6 months, two constructs drove performance on executive tasks, an EC-specific factor, as well as one we termed "foundational cognitive abilities," reflecting the overall processing demands of the task stimuli and responses modeled by inclusion of cardinal language, visual/spatial perception, and motor speed tasks. Therefore, the present results suggest that the specific cognitive control system that enables adaptive prioritization and pursuit of abstract goals becomes evident, and thus perhaps differentiated and more discretely organized, over the course of early childhood.

The notion that foundational cognitive abilities and EC may be more diffusely organized and interdependent in early childhood to together drive executive task performance is in keeping with Johnson's (2011) notion of interactive specialization. In Johnson's model, cortical functions are organized in a more diffuse fashion in early development. With development, these brain regions compete for more specialized functional roles. However, their organization is dependent on interaction, such that changes in the organization of one system will have cascading implications for the development of other functions. Here, the gradual honing of semantic representations (e.g., the color red) through repeated experiences in the environment likely has cascading implications for the ability of control processes to act on these representations through differential biasing that reflects goals and contingencies. This co-dependence would then make it very difficult to measure a separate EC factor in this very young age group.

There are at least two possible explanations for the lack of evidence for a specific EC component of executive task performance in children younger than 4 years. The first possibility is that a discrete, separable, EC construct is not present in younger preschoolers below this age, and the underlying drivers of executive task performance actually are the stimulus and response demands that are processed with the cardinal language, visual/spatial perception, and motor abilities. Taking this explanation to the extreme, one could argue that executive tasks, at least in children under 4 years of age, could be considered "executive" erroneously. This account harkens back to views that the prefrontal system inexplicably "turns on" late in childhood and that the relevance of EC in young children therefore is negligible (Chelune & Baer, 1986). This interpretation seems unlikely. Even infants can engage in purposeful, goal-directed behavior, inhibit prepotent looking or reaching tendencies and voluntarily engage and disengage attention to salient stimuli, at least in a rudimentary manner (Diamond, 1985; Johnson, 1995). Furthermore, neuroimaging studies with infants reveal activation profiles that include the ventral and dorsal medial prefrontal cortex (Gao et al., 2009). Based on the substantial body of research characterizing these rudimentary executive abilities in infants and toddlers, it is doubtful that the failure here to identify a separate EC factor that uniquely contributes to executive task performance at age 3 years reflects a complete absence of a tertiary control process in these very young preschoolers.

A second more plausible, but nuanced, explanation is that EC is more tightly entwined and integrated with foundational cognitive abilities that are invoked by the processing of stimuli and response requirements at this young age, as these foundational abilities also are developing rapidly and differ widely among children. For instance, a child who has a larger vocabulary, a richer linguistic context, or more practiced associations between the verbal label and its referent typically will achieve a higher score on executive tasks compared to a child who struggles with language or has an impoverished language environment, regardless of each child's "true" level of executive ability. Thus, the faint signal of EC in very young children under 4 years of age likely is overwhelmed by the noise of individual variability in foundational cognitive abilities that are used in varying degrees to process task stimulus and response demands in the course of maintaining, inhibiting, and shifting among these representations as required by the specific executive task. With advancing age, the majority of older preschool children reach a reasonable level of proficiency in processing the basic linguistic, semantic, or visual information and the motor abilities demanded by executive tasks, rendering these processes to be relatively more automatic and allowing for better detection of the individually varying EC signals. Most developmental executive tasks include stimuli that are selected on the supposition that they represent cardinal exemplars for which most children will have reasonably robust associations, such that their impact on performance will be less pronounced with advancing maturation. The findings here suggest that there are meaningful individual differences in proficiency that account for substantive variance in executive task performance in younger and older preschool children.

What are these two components that drive executive task performance in preschool children? The application of the bifactor model to this problem is new, the answer is not yet clear, and thus our interpretation has not strayed far from what indicators were included in the model: one component is specific to the executive tasks, and another reflects shared variation across the executive tasks and cardinal cognitive processes. In some ways, the two factors identified with the bifactor modeling approach are similar in concept to Braver's (2012) proactive and reactive components of control. In his dual mechanism model, proactive control is the "sustained and anticipatory maintenance of goal relevant information within lateral prefrontal cortex to enable optimal cognitive performance, whereas reactive control reflects transient stimulus-driven goal reactivation that recruits lateral prefrontal cortex (plus a wider brain network) based on interference demands or episodic associations" (Braver, 2012, p. 106). Using this framework for broad interpretation, the identification of the specific EC factor after age 4 years may represent the emergent ability of the older preschooler to carry forward information in a future-oriented way that is necessary to shape thought and action toward an internalized goal. In like fashion, the stimulus-driven reactive control that is invoked by task-specific interference demands in Braver's model seems similar to our foundational cognitive abilities factor. Integrating the model with our results would suggest that reactive control, the stimulus driven process that resolves interference among stimulus- or response-specific attributes, predominates earlier in development, and is a key component that drives executive task performance in both younger and older preschool children. In contrast, the identification of the specific EC factor in older preschoolers suggests that only after age 4 years does young children's ability to effectively extrapolate beyond the specific stimulus and response demands to represent and maintain information to proactively guide thought and action toward an internalized goal begin to meaningfully impact performance. Interestingly, this cascading pattern of development of these dual control mechanisms does explain the qualitative jump in the observed accuracy at this age on many executive measures in the battery. Alternatively, the foundational cognitive abilities factor instead may represent other common variance, such as that attributable to sustained attention or motivation required across all tasks. This generic explanation is less tenable, however, as the variance from these influences also would contribute substantively to EC. Our interpretation is speculative, and is intended to generate directions for additional research, not definitive answers at this time.

Regardless of the explanation, the novelty of our findings is that they provide evidence for a qualitative shift in the organization of EC relative to foundational cognitive abilities during this critical preschool period, and this shift has implications for the measurement of EC in the early childhood period. This statistical finding of a difference in the relation of EC to foundational cognitive abilities, which together drive observed performance on executive tasks, sheds new light on studies that have examined growth trajectories for manifest executive tasks across the preschool age range. These studies reveal relatively sudden and rapid gains in accuracy on manifest inhibitory control and cognitive flexibility tasks between the ages of 3 and 4 years (Carlson, 2005; Clark et al., 2013; Jones, Rothbart, & Posner, 2003; Wiebe et al., 2012). Such abrupt increases in task accuracy, sometimes from rates of less than 30% to rates of almost perfect accuracy in the span of a year, suggest an underlying, fundamental change in children's conceptualization and approach to executive tasks, where children are less influenced by the specific and concrete task attributes and are more able to process at an effortful, executive level with age. Coupled with these group-level gains in accuracy are more nuanced age-related changes in children's approach to executive tasks. Between 3 and 4.5 years, individual children show a relative slowing of reaction time to preserve accuracy on executive tasks, suggesting that they are implementing different strategies to achieve increasing competence in task performance (Espy et al., 2006; Wiebe et al., 2012). Although this previous longitudinal work has provided tantalizing intimations that the underlying mechanisms of executive task performance change between 3 and 4 years, findings from the present volume provide compelling evidence that the spurt in executive task accuracy between these ages may reflect an unfolding differentiation of specific EC from the task-bound processing associated with foundational cognitive abilities.

The progressive shift in children's reliance on less differentiated, global cognitive abilities to the joint recruitment of more modularized cognitive systems is evident in broad assessments of cognition from preschool to postadolescence (Mungas et al., 2013), as well as assessments focused specifically on EC (Brydges et al., 2014). This pattern in behavioral performance is consistent with brain imaging studies demonstrating cyclic rearrangements in neural connectivity and increasing functional specialization of neural systems through the course of childhood (Bell et al., 2007; Durston et al., 2006; Rubia et al., 2006). For instance, electrophysiological activity in the brain becomes increasingly coherent and synchronized over the course of early childhood, particularly with respect to short-range neural connections (Bell & Wolfe, 2007; Thatcher, North, & Biver, 2008). Neural circuits involved in executive task performance also progressively dissociate over time, with the development and myelination of long-range connections between distal brain regions likely enabling greater efficiency of communication between distributed neural systems (Fair et al., 2007; Margulies et al., 2007). Adults show more focal functional activation of neural regions associated with better executive task performance relative to children, who often show more extensive, distributed activation, including activation of neural regions associated with language and visual/spatial processing, when completing executive tasks (Bunge et al., 2002; Durston et al., 2006; Tamm, Menon, & Reiss, 2002). Collectively, these neuroimaging studies suggest a honing, specialization, and modularization of neural systems over the course of childhood, where cognitive skills become more discretely organized in segregated neural regions and connectivity between these regions enables more effective integration.

Based on neurological and behavioral research such as that reviewed above, Posner, Rothbart, Sheese, and Voelker (2012) contend that the attention systems modulating self-regulation change during the preschool period (see also Colombo & Cheatham, 2006). In their model, infant self-regulation is subserved by the orienting system. This system is driven by external events and stimuli and is modulated by parietal and orbito-frontal regions. In other words, younger children are governed by a reactive, exogenous form of cognitive control as opposed to a proactive, self-modulated, endogenous form of control (Munakata et al., 2012). As more long-range neural connections develop, areas such as the anterior cingulate gradually differentiate and are able to wield greater control over distal neural circuits (Posner et al., 2012). Thus, the executive network gradually gains precedence over the orienting network such that, by age 3–4 years, children are better able to resolve conflict between competing stimuli in a voluntary, proactive manner. Although Posner et al.'s work is centered on attention, the overlap between their work and our findings from the bifactor model suggests an emerging consensus that the transition from age 3–4 years is one of

117

fundamental reorganization of the structure of EC relative to foundational cognitive abilities in order to enable goal-directed thought and action.

THE UNITARY STRUCTURE OF EXECUTIVE CONTROL IN EARLY CHILDHOOD

The bifactor model not only elucidates differences in the relation of EC to foundational cognitive abilities in 3-year-olds compared to older, 4- and 5-year-olds, but it also provides more concrete evidence that EC is best conceptualized as a global, unitary system in typically developing children during this early developmental period. The one-factor structure of EC that emerged using the bifactor approach mirrors the unitary models identified when the impact of foundational cognitive abilities was not modeled, both in this volume and in previous studies (Wiebe et al., 2008; Willoughby et al., 2010). However, the bifactor model provides a more sophisticated evaluation of the structure of EC, as it directly addresses the task impurity problem in the identification of the EC construct. Of course, support for a unitary EC structure even when the bifactor approach is used contrasts markedly with fractionated theoretical models of EC derived from the adult literature, as well as with findings using latent variable modeling with older children and adult samples, where two- or three-factor models most often have been identified (Brydges et al., 2014; Lehto et al., 2003; Miyake et al., 2000). Indeed, studies with older participants show that different components of EC identified using latent variable modeling are differentially related to important outcomes. In one study, for example, working memory, but not inhibitory control, predicted word reading and comprehension in children aged 8–16 years (Christopher et al., 2012). Again, these findings highlight the importance of a developmental approach to EC, which acknowledges its changing nature through the lifespan.

One explanation for these noted differences in EC structure at different ages may relate, at least in part, to the nature of the tasks that can be employed. Adults and school-aged children are able to perform working memory tasks that draw heavily on updating and mental manipulation and thus studies generally utilize N-back tasks, reading span tasks, or counting span tasks to measure working memory (Friedman et al., 2008; Miyake et al., 2000; St Clair-Thompson & Gathercole, 2006). Given that N-back and complex span tasks generally are too difficult for preschool and early elementary school-aged children, forward or backward span tasks are often used in studies with preschoolers (e.g., Wiebe et al., 2008; although see Miller et al. [2012], who specifically tried to address this issue by including multiple performance measures from the same tasks and found support for a two-factor model in preschoolers). Although working memory span tasks do evoke patterns of dorsolateral prefrontal and anterior cingulate activation

(Gerton et al., 2004), how these ability differences relate to measurement changes across developmental periods remains unstudied. If the ability to update information in working memory is not a more advanced representation of simple working memory maintenance observed in preschoolers, but rather reflects a qualitatively different, separable working memory subcomponent of EC, it would indeed be expected to be distinct from other EC components in adolescents and adults.

Another difference between the measurement approach in adults versus children is the nature of the stimuli used to assess different EC components. In older children and adults, there often is a tighter coherence in stimulus demands among executive task conditions designed to assess working memory, inhibitory control, and cognitive flexibility (e.g., numbers with an added shifting demand or numbers with an added inhibition demand, as in van der Sluis et al., 2004). This controlled experimental variation in EC demand from a common baseline stimulus set may mean that it is easier to extract fine-grained, specific variance components using latent variable modeling. In contrast, tasks designed for youngsters need to vary widely in their stimulus features and demands in order to maintain the interest and persistence of the very young child. Perhaps the core EC construct pulled from the tasks, then, will inevitably be a unitary dimension that all tasks share, especially once the variance from foundational cognitive skills also has been segregated.

Relatedly, the capacity to detect greater levels of granularity for the proposed subcomponents of EC necessarily is limited with young children due to limits in persistence, which are a barrier to administration of a large number of tasks. For instance, Friedman and Miyake (2004) found evidence for two distinct and uncorrelated types of inhibitory control—(i) the ability to resist distraction and override prepotent responses and (ii) the ability to resist interference from previous memory representations. The proper specification of different dimensions of inhibition like those identified in the Friedman study requires the administration of at least two tasks to assess each putative dimension. For example, by administering only a battery of inhibition tasks, Gandolfi et al. (2014) identified two inhibitory factors, response inhibition and interference suppression, in 3–4 year olds, but a single undifferentiated inhibition factor in 2-year-olds. Because preschoolers cannot tolerate large batteries of tasks, there are limits to the feasibility of detecting fine-grained subcomponents of EC in this manner.

It also is possible that the unitary structure of EC consistently found in early childhood reflects a more diffuse organization of EC, which perhaps becomes even more specialized and fractionated into different EC components during middle childhood. This differentiation of unitary EC into more specific EC subcomponents with age complements the progressive differentiation of EC from foundational cognitive abilities demonstrated here using the bifactor model. It also is in keeping with other studies using latent modeling to determine the structure of EC at different age points. For instance, Shing et al. (2010) showed that working memory maintenance and inhibition are not separable until relatively late in childhood, around 9.5 years of age. Similarly, in Lee et al. (2013) a two-factor solution provided the most parsimonious model of EC at age 6 years and inconsistently provided a better solution at each subsequent longitudinal follow-up point through 15 years. Only in late adolescence (age 16) did a stable, three-factor model incorporating the working memory, inhibition, and shifting components found in adults emerge, even though the tasks employed were identical at each age. Even in adults, studies indicate that executive tasks to some extent tap a universal, common EC construct while also placing distinct demands on separate updating and switching factors (Friedman et al., 2008). Miyake and Friedman (2012) have argued that the more general, global EC factor reflects goal maintenance. Integrating these findings with those of this monograph, it may be that the universal EC construct observed in adults is the core substrate for EC, evident in preschool children with the unitary structure. Note also that the core EC factor identified in these adult studies shows the strongest relation with self-restraint measured in early childhood (Friedman et al., 2011) is strongly genetically determined (Friedman et al., 2008) and is more highly correlated with general cognitive ability (Friedman et al., 2006) than distinct updating or switching factors, further suggesting that there may be a unitary, core substrate for EC, which differentiates and becomes more modularized over time.

Taken together, the evidence for a unitary configural model for EC simultaneous with a progressive differentiation of this tertiary component from foundational abilities provides a viable explanation for the lack of longitudinal measurement invariance of our executive task battery (Nelson, James, Chevalier et al., 2016). Specifically, we are unable to constrain the factor loadings or intercepts of our executive tasks to be equal across different age points, despite the fact that the same tasks were administered in our study at each age. Practically, our inability to demonstrate longitudinal measurement invariance indicates that the tasks do not assess EC in the same way over time. Admittedly, our findings contrast with those of Willoughby, Wirth, and Blair (2012) who showed that the one-factor model of EC was partially invariant for their longitudinal data spanning the 3–5 year age range. In contrast to our approach, Willoughby et al. used tasks that were more similar in their stimulus and response demands (e.g., all flip book pictures, mainly verbal response). Nonetheless, only two of their five EC tasks showed strong longitudinal invariance, suggesting that the measurement properties for most tasks in their battery did differ with age. Our results with the bifactor model suggest that this lack of invariance does not represent measurement "failure," but rather reflects a shift in the organization of the cognitive systems that subserve executive task performance. Younger children thus are drawing on a less specialized ability set related more to the foundational abilities to resolve interference among task attributes to complete executive tasks, whereas older children are able to proactively abstract more generalized rule-based information that is then deployed across particular tasks. Given these results, it is not surprising that our EC construct is noninvariant, as the fundamental relation between EC and foundational cognitive abilities differs in younger versus older preschoolers. In fact, this noninvariance probably provides a truer empirical reflection of the underlying developmental processes at work in this age range.

RELATION OF SOCIO-FAMILIAL BACKGROUND TO EXECUTIVE CONTROL IN THE CONTEXT OF THE BIFACTOR MODEL

Findings in Chapter IV indicate that the socio-familial environment does relate to children's executive task performance, although the relation may not be as specific in early childhood. Dimensions of socio-familial risk were more robustly associated with early foundational cognitive abilities than with the specific EC process. These findings once again highlight the importance of acknowledging the dynamic interactions of cognitive systems that coalesce to enable proficient executive performance. The contributions of foundational cognitive abilities are evident even in adult neuroimaging studies, where working memory maintenance appears to be modulated in large part by the co-occurring activation of specific regions in the brain that encode sensory information in addition to prefrontal regions associated with EC (Ester et al., 2009). The prefrontal cortex modulates these sensory representations by manipulating levels of excitation and counteracting levels of lateral inhibition in the sensory regions so that adults are able to maintain representations in working memory (Edin et al., 2009; Zanto, Rubens, Thangavel, & Gazzaley, 2011). In other words, the role of the prefrontal cortex is to exert control over levels of activation and inhibition in distal neural regions that are responsible for foundational processing so that this processing is biased in accordance with task demands or goals (Miller & Cohen, 2001; Munakata et al., 2011). Essentially then, there is an ongoing interaction between sensory-perceptual, semantic, motor output and control networks and the proficiency of these other cognitive systems likely has cascading consequences for EC's ability to exert hierarchical control.

In a recent monograph, Buss and Spencer (2014) developed a neurocomputational "dynamic field theory" (DFT) model of EC and evaluated it using the DCCS task. Critically, one of the major changes that allows the model to overcome conflict is a boost to the strength of the color or shape inputs, which theoretically reflects increasing long-range connectivity between posterior and anterior neural systems and a more refined concept of shape in the "older" or "more mature" model. Like our findings, the model suggests that children's ability to successfully accomplish an executive task is critically tied to their representations of key concepts like color or shape, representations that are built up through experiences in the socio-familial environment.

In early childhood, children's diverse learning experiences and associated mastery of concepts such as shape or color leads to substantial individual variation in the semantic networks that children can activate to support neural representations required for maintenance, inhibition, or switching. For instance, children with more advanced language skills will have more salient conceptualizations of the task goal sets and more elaborated abstract concepts like "square." More advanced representations of these abstract concepts in turn will facilitate performance on executive tasks (Snyder & Munakata, 2010). Thus, the relation between children's socio-familial environments and their performance on executive tasks is likely to depend on these representational abilities, modeled as foundational cognitive abilities in our bifactor model.

Like almost all studies that have examined the impact of the socio-familial environment on children's EC, our design was not set up to evaluate the role of genetic factors. Results from the Colorado twin study indicate that EC is highly heritable (Friedman et al., 2008), at least in adolescents, making it likely that the apparent relations of the child's environment also reflect genetic variation and gene-environment interactions to some unknown degree. The use of the bifactor approach may help to further clarify the mechanisms by which genetic influences shape these relations at different points in development. Notwithstanding this limitation, the findings suggest that broad interventions and early education programs that support motor, language, and visuo-spatial perception development may benefit children's EC development in this critical preschool period.

THE SPECIFIC LINK OF EXECUTIVE CONTROL TO EARLY PROBLEM BEHAVIORS

One consequence of this tight interconnectedness of EC and foundational cognitive processes is that impairments in different foundational abilities associated with disparate neural systems may manifest as similar performance decrements on executive tasks (i.e., different mechanisms may lead to the same behavioral or clinical end point observed in the child, an example of developmental equifinality). Accordingly, while many developmental disorders are associated with an array of performance deficits on executive tasks, weaknesses in the control processes that we conceptualize as EC may not necessarily be the cause of these deficits.

Instead, deficits in task performance may be driven by impairments in other foundational cognitive abilities such as language or motor skills that are drawn upon as part of the control process in order for the child to perform the executive task. In this volume, we used the bifactor approach to address this issue by examining the integrated relation of foundational cognitive abilities and EC components that drive executive task performance to empirically derived dimensions of dysregulated behavior. The precise characterization of EC and ADHD symptoms using separate bifactor, or hierarchical, models yielded new insights into the specificity of the relation of EC to different ADHD symptom dimensions. The EC-specific variance at both ages 4;6 and 5;3 correlated with hyperactivity symptoms measured late in the preschool period. In contrast, the foundational cognitive abilities demanded by executive tasks correlated with the general ADHD factor in the age 5;3 bifactor model.

The link between the foundational cognitive abilities component of executive task performance and the general ADHD symptoms in the age 5;3 model suggests that a common trait-like dimension may underlie children's behavior across contexts and tasks. In general, children who do more poorly on tasks that assess language, visuo-spatial perception, and motor speed, including the discrete portion of performance on executive tasks that is related to these foundational cognitive abilities, also are rated by their parents as having higher global levels of externalizing behavior. Notably, the fact that foundational cognitive abilities and ADHD symptoms were measured in different formats and across different contexts argues against the notion that their relation simply reflects extraneous method variance. That is, the general ADHD construct in our hierarchical symptom model is unlikely to reflect a general tendency of the parent to endorse the higher or lower ends of the scale because this general ADHD symptom construct was predicted by foundational cognitive abilities assessed in vivo by an independent examiner in a structured laboratory setting.

In contrast to the relation between foundational cognitive abilities and general ADHD symptoms, specific hyperactivity symptoms showed a distinct and unique relation to EC. When we consider what it is that discriminates EC from the foundational cognitive abilities components of executive task performance at a broad theoretical level, EC is posited to enable proactive goal-directed, purposeful behavior by reducing attention to irrelevant stimuli and allowing the child to evaluate response options (Calkins & Marcovitch, 2010). In adults, the inhibition of incipient motor behavior relies on a cortical circuit including the right inferior frontal cortex, the presupplementary motor area, and the subthalamic nucleus, which collectively operate as a braking system, allowing the prefrontal cortex to evaluate competing response options (Aron, 2008). Perhaps the overlap between specific EC and hyperactive behavior reflects a failure to exert this brake or temporal buffer, which simultaneously contributes to elevated and dysfunctional levels of motor activity as well as difficulties overcoming automatic response tendencies elicited by executive tasks (similar to the model proposed by Barkley, 1997). Of course, the impact of this "braking system" failure also may vary developmentally, where the early manifestations are perhaps more likely to be noticeable by the parent in the form of "acting out," motor-driven behavior (i.e., the hyperactive dimensions of ADHD symptomatology), and not in the form of interrupting, blurting out, or intruding on others (i.e., the impulsive dimensions of ADHD symptomatology). Given that the prominence of different ADHD symptoms appears to change over the course of development (Willoughby, 2002), the relation of the EC and foundational cognitive abilities components of executive task performance may differ later in development and the bifactor model provides a rich approach to better explicate varying symptom trajectories.

EXECUTIVE CONTROL AS A VALID DEVELOPMENTAL CONSTRUCT

The bifactor model also offers greater scope for the psychometric evaluation of executive tasks designed for young children. Much of the popularity of executive measures in developmental research derives from their strong ability to predict a broad array of outcomes. However, this predictive validity may be due, at least in part, to the fact that executive tasks tap both EC and foundational cognitive abilities and therefore are likely to relate to multiple outcome measures (Pennington, Bennetto, McAleer, & Roberts, 1996). Indeed, it could be argued that strong evidence for the predictive validity of executive tasks simultaneously detracts from their discriminant validity, as performance deficits on executive tasks are evident in varying degrees in almost all developmental disorders (see Diamond, 2013, for examples). The bifactor approach offers a stringent evaluation of the discriminant validity of EC by determining whether the pooled variance of executive tasks overlaps completely with tasks designed to assess nonexecutive, subordinate cognitive processes directly, or whether there is some distinct and meaningful specific EC component that drives, at least in part, executive task performance. Findings from the model offer cause for optimism, suggesting that executive tasks do indeed measure a discrete, separate construct that is distinct from more general foundational cognitive abilities at least by age 4 years. Moreover, this discrete, specific EC construct demonstrates a unique, discriminative relation with hyperactive symptomatology at the transition to formal schooling.

The demonstration of EC construct validity is critical if executive tasks are to be applied in prevention settings. Our findings suggest that executive tasks administered after 4 years of age can provide clinically meaningful information above and beyond the administration of measures assessing basic stimulus and response processing abilities. Unfortunately, the added utility of executive tasks in 3-year-old children is less clear, as a separable EC construct could not be distilled from the other foundational cognitive processes at this young age. Moreover, even after the age of 4 years, where the dualistic contributions of specific EC and foundational cognitive abilities were evident in executive task performance, meaningful distinctions between inhibitory control and working memory subcomponents were not evident in these typically developing children. This pattern of results suggests that individual sub-components of EC are difficult to parse in this young age group.

MOVING TOWARD A GENERAL MODEL FOR THE EARLY DEVELOPMENT OF EXECUTIVE CONTROL

Taken together, findings from this volume ground the EC construct more firmly in the developmental literature, which incorporates the dynamic temporal, maturational, and social contexts in the understanding of cognitive processes. Figure 17 integrates the various findings summarized above into a conceptual schematic to guide future developmental theory and research on EC. As shown, EC and foundational cognitive processes are tightly bound in early development to the extent that their contribution to executive task performance cannot be differentiated prior to age 4. The foundational

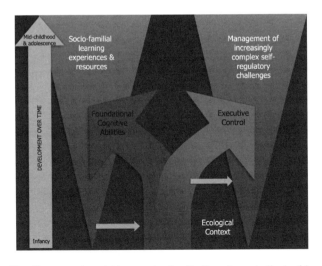

FIGURE 17.—Conceptual model integrating key findings from studies in this monograph.

125

cognitive systems are embedded in the child's socio-familial context, where proximal learning experiences, including parent–child interactions, toys and other learning materials, shape the child's acquisition of language, the degree of elaboration of their semantic representations, and the child's expertise with various concepts and symbols, for example, represented in our bifactor model as foundational cognitive abilities. In turn, these elaborated representations provide the substrate with which specific EC works, perhaps boosting the representational salience of rules, and affording children access to more efficient symbolic codes (e.g., words, colors) to represent these attribute-general rules and deploy them in new contexts with greater proficiency. The result is that children gradually become better able to mentally manipulate, organize, inhibit, and sequence these sensory and semantic inputs in an effortful, volitional way. Over time, children's social contexts expand and widen and demands for self-regulation within these increasingly complex social contexts increase. Operating on increasingly specialized foundational cognitive abilities, simultaneously developing EC processes gradually allow the child to master increasingly complex self-regulatory challenges, from the need for basic motor control to contextually appropriate social behavior. Ultimately, these more specialized EC capacities determine how well the child is able to manage his/her behavior in everyday contexts, and distinguish children with more clinically relevant difficulties that may warrant intervention.

What are the implications of this model for the scientific understanding of EC? First, the fact that EC is so tightly bound to preschool children's foundational cognitive abilities, which in turn are tied to the social ecology and experiences of the child, means that children's performance on executive tasks is more likely to be context-bound in early childhood. Given that the foundational cognitive abilities of young children are rapidly developing and as a consequence differ markedly among individual children, even relatively minor changes to the stimuli used in tasks may alter the level of executive demand, according to the individual child's experience with the stimuli. For instance, subtle changes to the stimuli used in variations of the A-not-B type paradigm are known to dramatically affect infants' ability to pass the performance criterion, and increased experience with the test apparatus itself can lead to improved accuracy (Smith, 2005). Having children label stimuli repeatedly has been shown to improve performance on card sorting tasks, again highlighting the importance of semantic associations in the control process (Doebel & Zelazo, 2013; Müller, Zelazo, Hood, Leone, & Rohrer, 2004). Moreover, the provision of salient cues can boost executive task performance likely by dampening demands on foundational cognitive abilities and thus facilitating EC deployment (Chevalier & Blaye, 2009).

A clear next step is to determine how this model might extend into middle childhood and whether the relations between EC and foundational cognitive abilities change through childhood in a way that helps to understand key outcomes. There is evidence that spurts in EC growth occur through the course of childhood (Anderson, Anderson, Northam, Jacobs, & Catroppa, 2001). For instance, adolescence is another period characterized by dramatic physiological changes and shifts in neural organization (Blakemore & Choudhury, 2006). Bifactor modeling approaches may yield novel insight into the dynamic interactions between emotion and EC systems during the adolescent period.

There are also several aspects of this model that basic behavioral research, even with advanced statistical modeling, cannot address. Although the dualistic EC and foundational cognitive ability components that drive executive task performance were segregated, the complex neurophysiology that subserves this distinction is not known and merits investigation. A productive path would be to integrate these types of statistical approaches with neuroimaging measures or neurocomputational models to determine whether the differentiation of ability components that we identified here have unique neural signatures that also vary with individual child characteristics (e.g., socio-familial background; ADHD symptoms). Similarly, a well-planned intervention study could tease apart specific mechanisms of impact. For instance, an intervention focused on boosting foundational concepts (e.g., colors, shapes, vocabulary) could be pitted against a specific intervention for EC at different ages to determine whether either or both produced differential changes in executive task performance. Given our findings from this volume, it is possible that additional EC training may help to bolster the impact of training in more general cognitive skills, but may be less impactful in very young children.

CONCLUSIONS

Developmental science inherently relies on reductionist models or concepts to understand human behavior in the most parsimonious way. The concept of EC is no exception, historically arising from a need to efficiently describe the diverse collection of symptoms of individuals with damage to the prefrontal cortex. Executive tasks (or test items) were developed explicitly to capture specific symptoms associated with disruption to modular neurocognitive systems. However, as pointed out by Golden (1982) the earliest neuropsychologists understood that these tasks were not tapping an isolated construct: "the concept of 'pure' items reflects localizationist presuppositions that Luria would reject. Luria's notion of functional systems, the theory that any behavior requires the integration of a number of elementary skills mediated by different brain areas, would preclude the existence of completely 'pure' test items affected by one and only one area of the brain" (p. 294). In this volume, we have targeted this issue of construct impurity from a developmental perspective. Ultimately, our findings support theoretical ideas (e.g., Durston et al., 2006; Johnson, 2011) that EC development reflects the increasing specialization, differentiation, and sharpening of connected systems over time. In early childhood, executive task performance is even more closely tied to basic language, visual, spatial representation, and motor processing—all of which are developed in the context of the child's unique learning experiences. Our findings draw attention to the necessity of considering the brain as a dynamic system whose regions may interact in different ways through the lifespan. By combining advanced statistical techniques with a developmentally nuanced perspective, we captured the complex and simultaneous contributions of different cognitive processes that collectively enable goal-directed, regulated behavior in everyday contexts.

REFERENCES

This article is part of the issue "The Changing Nature of Executive Control in Preschool" Espy (Issue Editor). For a full listing of articles in this issue, see: http://onlinelibrary.wiley.com/doi/10.1111/mono. v81.4/issuetoc.

Achenbach, T., & Rescorla, L. (2000). *Manual for the ASEBA preschool forms and profiles*. Burlington: University of Vermont.

Addy, S., & Wight, V. R. (2012). Basic facts about low-income children, 2010 *National Center for Children in Poverty*. Retrieved from http://www.nccp.org/publications/pub_1049.html

Akaike, H. (1987). Factor analysis and AIC. *Psychometrika,* **52**(3), 317–332. doi: 10.1007/BF02294359

Allen, E. C., Beilock, S. L., & Shevell, S. K. (2011). Working memory is related to perceptual processing: A case from color perception. *Journal of Experimental Psychology: Learning, Memory and Cognition*, 37, 1014–1021. doi: 10.1037/a0023257

Allhusen, V., Belsky, J., Kersey, H. B., Booth-Laforce, C., Bradley, R., Brownell, C. A., & Weintraub, M. (2005). Predicting individual differences in attention, memory, and planning in first graders from experiences at home, child care, and school. *Developmental Psychology*, **41**(1), 99–114. doi: 10.1037/0012-1649.41.1.99

American Psychiatric Association (1994). *Diagnostic and statistical manual of mental disorders* (4th ed.). Washington, DC: Author.

American Psychiatric Association (2013). *Diagnostic and statistical manual of mental disorders* (5th ed.). Washington, DC: Author.

Anderson, P. J. (2008). Towards a developmental model of executive function. In V. Anderson, R. Jacobs, & P. J. Anderson (Eds.), *Executive functions and the frontal lobes: A lifespan perspective* (pp. 3–21). New York, NY: Psychology Press.

Anderson, V. A., Anderson, P. J., Northam, E., Jacobs, R., & Catroppa, C. (2001). Development of executive functions through late childhood and adolescence in an Australian sample. *Developmental Neuropsychology*, **20**(1), 385–406. doi: 10.1207/S15326942DN2001_5

DOI: 10.1111/mono.12274

Ansari, D. (2010). Neurocognitive approaches to developmental disorders of numerical, mathematical cognition: The perils of neglecting the role of development. *Learning, Individual Differences, 202*, 123–129. doi: 10.1016/j.lindif.2009.06.001

Applegate, B., Lahey, B. B., Hart, E. L., Biederman, J., Hynd, G. W., Barkley, R. A., et al. (1997). Validity of the age-of-onset criterion for ADHD: A report from the DSM-IV field trials. *Journal of the American Academy of Child & Adolescent Psychiatry, 36*(9), 1211–1221. doi: 10.1097/00004583-199709000-00013

Ardila, A., Rosselli, M., Matute, E., & Guajardo, S. (2005). The influence of the parents' educational level on the development of executive functions. *Developmental Neuropsychology, 28* (1), 539–560. doi: 10.1207/s15326942dn2801_5

Aron, A. R. (2008). Progress in executive-function research: From tasks to functions to regions to networks. *Current Directions in Psychological Science, 17*(2), 124–129. doi: 10.1111/j.1467-8721.2008.00561.x

Aron, A. R., & Poldrack, R. A. (2006). Cortical and subcortical contributions to stop signal response inhibition: Role of the subthalamic nucleus. *The Journal of Neuroscience, 26*(9), 2424–2433. doi: 10.1523/JNEUROSCI.4682-05.2006

Baddeley, A. D. (1986). *Working memory.* Oxford, Oxfordshire: Clarendon Press.

Baddeley, A. D., & Hitch, G. J. (1974). Working memory. In G. H. Bower (Ed.), *The psychology of learning and motivation: Advances in research and theory* (Vol. 8, pp. 47–89). New York, NY: Academic Press.

Barkley, R. A. (1997). Behavioral inhibition, sustained attention, and executive functions: Constructing a unifying theory of ADHD. *Psychological Bulletin, 121*(1), 65–94. doi: 10.1037/0033-2909.121.1.65

Barnett, M. A. (2008). Economic disadvantage in complex family systems: Expansion of family stress models. *Clinical Child and Family Psychology Review, 11*(3), 145–161. doi: 10.1007/s10567-008-0034-z

Bauermeister, J. J., Canino, G., Polanczyk, G., & Rohde, L. A. (2010). ADHD across cultures: Is there evidence for a bidimensional organization of symptoms? *Journal of Clinical Child and Adolescent Psychology, 39*(3), 362–372. doi: 10.1080/15374411003691743

Bell, M. A., & Wolfe, C. D. (2007). Changes in brain functioning from infancy to early childhood: Evidence from EEG power and coherence during working memory tasks. *Developmental Neuropsychology, 31*(1), 21–38. doi: 10.1207/s15326942dn3101_2

Bell, M. A., Wolfe, C. D., & Adkins, D. R. (2007). Frontal lobe development during infancy and childhood. In D. Coch, G. Dawson, & K. W. Fischer (Eds.), *Human behavior, learning, and the developing brain: Typical development* (pp. 247–276). New York, NY: Guilford Press.

Bentler, P. M. (1990). Comparative fit indexes in structural models. *Psychological Bulletin, 107*(2), 238–246. doi: 10.1037/0033-2909.107.2.238

Berlin, L., & Bohlin, G. (2002). Response inhibition, hyperactivity, and conduct problems among preschool children. *Journal of Clinical Child Psychology, 31*(2), 242–251. doi: 10.1207/S15374424JCCP3102_09

Berlin, L., Bohlin, G., & Rydell, A. (2003). Relations between inhibition, executive functioning, and ADHD symptoms: A longitudinal study from age 5 to 8 1/2 years. *Child Neuropsychology, 9*(4), 255–266. doi: 10.1076/chin.9.4.255.23519

Bernier, A., Carlson, S. M., Deschênes, M., & Matte-Gagné, C. (2012). Social factors in the development of early executive functioning: A closer look at the caregiving environment. *Developmental Science, 15*(1), 12–24. doi: 10.1111/j.1467-7687.2011.01093.x

Bernier, A., Carlson, S. M., & Whipple, N. (2010). From external regulation to self-regulation: Early parenting precursors of young children's executive functioning. *Child Development*, **81**(1), 326–339. doi: 10.1111/j.1467-8624.2009.01397.x

Best, J. R., Miller, P. H., & Jones, L. L. (2009). Executive functions after age 5: Changes and correlates. *Developmental Review*, **29**(3), 180–200. doi: 10.1016/j.dr.2009.05.002

Blair, C. (2006). How similar are fluid cognition and general intelligence? A developmental neuroscience perspective on fluid cognition as an aspect of human cognitive ability. *Behavioral and Brain Sciences*, **29**(02), 109–125. doi: 10.1017/S0140525X06009034

Blair, C., & Razza, R. P. (2007). Relating effortful control, executive function, and false belief understanding to emerging math and literacy ability in kindergarten. *Child Development*, **78**(2), 647–663. doi: 10.1111/j.1467-8624.2007.01019.x

Blakemore, S.-J., & Choudhury, S. (2006). Development of the adolescent brain: Implications for executive function and social cognition. *Journal of Child Psychology and Psychiatry*, **47**(3–4), 296–312. doi: 10.1111/j.1469-7610.2006.01611.x

Boersma, M., Smit, D. J. A., de Bie, H. M. A., Van Baal, G. C. M., Boomsma, D. I., de Geus, E. J. C., et al. (2011). Network analysis of resting state EEG in the developing young brain: Structure comes with maturation. *Human Brain Mapping*, **32**(3), 413–425. doi: 10.1002/hbm.21030

Bollen, K. A. (1989). *Structural equations with latent variables*. New York, NY: Wiley.

Bradley, R. H. (1993). Children's home environments, health, behavior, and intervention efforts: A review using the HOME inventory as a marker measure. *Genetic, Social and General Psychology Monographs*, **119**(4), 439–490.

Bradley, R. H., Caldwell, B. M., Rock, S. L., Ramey, C. T., Barnard, K. E., Gray, C., et al. (1989). Home environment and cognitive development in the first 3 years of life: A collaborative study involving six sites and three ethnic groups in North America. *Developmental Psychology*, **25**(2), 217–235. doi: 10.1037/0012-1649.25.2.217

Braver, T. S. (2012). The variable nature of cognitive control: A dual mechanisms framework. *Trends in Cognitive Sciences*, **16**(2), 106–113. doi: 10.1016/j.tics.2011.12.010

Brocki, K. C., & Bohlin, G. (2004). Executive functions in children aged 6 to 13: A dimensional and developmental study. *Developmental Neuropsychology*, **26**(2), 571–593. doi: 10.1207/s15326942dn2602_3

Brocki, K. C., & Bohlin, G. (2006). Developmental change in the relation between executive functions and symptoms of ADHD and co-occurring behaviour problems. *Infant and Child Development*, **15**(1), 19–40. doi: 10.1002/icd.413

Brocki, K. C., Nyberg, L., Thorell, L. B., & Bohlin, G. (2007). Early concurrent and longitudinal symptoms of ADHD and ODD: Relations to different types of inhibitory control and working memory. *Journal of Child Psychology and Psychiatry*, **48**(10), 1033–1041. doi: 10.1111/j.1469-7610.2007.01811.x

Bronfenbrenner, U. (1979). *The ecology of human development*. Cambridge, MA: Harvard University Press.

Brooks-Gunn, J., Klebanov, P. K., & Duncan, G. J. (1996). Ethnic differences in children's intelligence test scores: Role of economic deprivation, home environment, and maternal characteristics. *Child Development*, **67**(2), 396–408. doi: 10.1111/j.1467-8624.1996.tb01741.x

Brown, E., & Lynn, T. K. (2010). Daily poverty-related stress and mood for low-income parents, as a function of the presence of a cohabiting partner relationship. *Individual Differences Research*, **8**(4), 204–213.

Brydges, C. R., Fox, A. M., Reid, C. L., & Anderson, M. (2014). The differentiation of executive functions in middle and late childhood: A longitudinal latent-variable analysis. *Intelligence*, **47**, 34–43. doi: 10.1016/j.intell.2014.08.010

Bull, R., Espy, K. A., & Wiebe, S. A. (2008). Short-term memory, working memory, and executive functioning in preschoolers: Longitudinal predictors of mathematical achievement at age 7 years. *Developmental Neuropsychology*, **33**(3), 205–228. doi: 10.1080/87565640801982312

Bull, R., Espy, K. A., Wiebe, S. A., Sheffield, T. D., & Nelson, J. M. (2011). Using confirmatory factor analysis to understand executive control in preschool children: Sources of variation in emergent mathematic achievement. *Developmental Science*, **14**(4), 679–692. doi: 10.1111/j.1467-7687.2010.01012.x

Bull, R., & Scerif, G. (2001). Executive functioning as a predictor of children's mathematics ability: Inhibition, switching, and working memory. *Developmental Neuropsychology*, **19**(3), 273–293. doi: 10.1207/S15326942DN1903_3

Bunge, S. A., Dudukovic, N. M., Thomason, M. E., Vaidya, C. J., & Gabrieli, J. D. E. (2002). Immature frontal lobe contributions to cognitive control in children: Evidence from fMRI. *Neuron*, **33**(2), 301–311. doi: 10.1016/S0896-6273(01)00583-9

Buss, A. T., & Spencer, J. P. (2014). The emergent executive: A dynamic field theory of the development of executive function. *Monographs of the Society for Research in Child Development*, **79**(2), 1–132.

Byrne, B. M. (1998). *Structural equation modeling with LISREL, PRELIS, and SIMPLIS: Basic concepts, applications, and programming*. Mahwah, NJ: Lawrence Erlbaum.

Caldwell, B. M., & Bradley, R. H. (1984). *HOME observation for measurement of the environment*. Little Rock: University of Arkansas at Little Rock.

Calkins, S. D., & Marcovitch, S. (2010). Emotion regulation and executive functioning in early development: Integrated mechanisms of control supporting adaptive functioning. In S. D. Calkins & M. A. Bell (Eds.), *Child development at the intersection of emotion and cognition* (pp. 37–57). Washington, DC: American Psychological Association.

Calmels, C., Foutren, M., & Stam, C. J. (2011). Influence of instructions and expertise on the mechanisms involved during a working memory task: An EEG study. *Journal of Psychophysiology*, **25**, 105–115. doi: 10.1027/0269-8803/a000046

Campbell, S. B. (1995). Behavior problems in preschool children: A review of recent research. *Journal of Child Psychology and Psychiatry*, **36**(1), 113–149. doi: 10.1111/j.1469-7610.1995.tb01657.x

Carlson, S. M. (2005). Developmentally sensitive measures of executive function in preschool children. *Developmental Neuropsychology*, **28**(2), 595–616. doi: 10.1207/s15326942dn2802_3

Carlson, S. M., Mandell, D. J., & Williams, L. (2004). Executive function and theory of mind: Stability and prediction from ages 2 to 3. *Developmental Psychology*, **40**(6), 1105–1122. doi: 10.1037/0012-1649.40.6.1105

Carlson, S. M., & Moses, L. J. (2001). Individual differences in inhibitory control and children's theory of mind. *Child Development*, **72**(4), 1032–1053. doi: 10.1111/1467-8624.00333

Carlson, S. M., & Wang, T. S. (2007). Inhibitory control and emotion regulation in preschool children. *Cognitive Development*, **22** (4), 489–510. doi: 10.1016/j.cogdev.2007.08.002

Carpenter, P., Just, A. M., & Reichle, E. D. (2000). Working memory and executive function: Evidence from neuroimaging. *Current Opinion in Neurobiology*, **10**, 195–199.

Carter, C. S., & Van Veen, V. (2007). Anterior cingulate cortex and conflict detection: An update of theory and data. *Cognitive, Affective and Behavioral Neuroscience*, **7**(4), 367–379. doi: 10.3758/CABN.7.4.367

Casey, B. J. (2000). Structural and functional brain development and its relation to cognitive development. *Biological Psychiatry*, **54**, 241–257.

Casey, B. J., Trainor, R. J., Orendi, J. L., Schubert, A. B., Nystrom, L. E., Giedd, J. N., et al. (1997). A developmental functional MRI study of prefrontal activation during performance of a go-no-go task. *Journal of Cognitive Neuroscience*, **9**(6), 835–847.

Castellanos, F. X., Sonuga-Barke, E. J. S., Milham, M. P., & Tannock, R. (2006). Characterizing cognition in ADHD: Beyond executive dysfunction. *Trends in Cognitive Sciences*, **10**(3), 117–123. doi: 10.1016/j.tics.2006.01.011

Cepeda, N. J., Kramer, A. F., & Gonzalez de Sather, J. C. M. (2001). Changes in executive control across the life span: Examination of task-switching performance. *Developmental Psychology*, **37**(5), 715–730. doi: 10.1037/0012-1649.37.5.715

Cerqueira, J. J., Mailliet, F., Almeida, O. F., Jay, T. M., & Sousa, N. (2007). The prefrontal cortex as a key target of the maladaptive response to stress. *The Journal of Neuroscience*, **27**(11), 2781–2787. doi: 10.1523/jneurosci.4372-06.2007

Chambers, C. D., Garavan, H., & Bellgrove, M. A. (2009). Insights into the neural basis of response inhibition from cognitive and clinical neuroscience. *Neuroscience and Biobehavioral Reviews*, **33**(5), 631–646. doi: 10.1016/j.neubiorev.2008.08.016

Chatham, C. H., Frank, M. J., & Munakata, Y. (2009). Pupillometric and behavioral markers of a developmental shift in the temporal dynamics of cognitive control. *PNAS Proceedings of the National Academy of Sciences of the United States of America*, **106**(14), 5529–5533. doi: 10.1073/pnas.0810002106

Chelune, G. J., & Baer, R. A. (1986). Developmental norms for the Wisconsin Card Sorting Test. *Journal of Clinical and Experimental Neuropsychology*, **8**, 219–228.

Chevalier, N., & Blaye, A. (2009). Setting goals to switch between tasks: Effect of cue transparency on children's cognitive flexibility. *Developmental Psychology*, **45**(3), 782–797. doi: 10.1037/a0015409

Chevalier, N., Huber, K. L., Wiebe, S. A., & Espy, K. A. (2013). Qualitative change in executive control during childhood and adulthood. *Cognition*, **128**, 1–12. doi: 10.1016/j.cognition.2013.02.012

Chevalier, N., Sheffield, T. D., Nelson, J. M., Clark, C. A. C., Wiebe, S. A., & Espy, K. A. (2012). Underpinnings of the costs of flexibility in preschool children: The roles of inhibition and working memory. *Developmental Neuropsychology*, **37**(2), 99–118. doi: 10.1080/87565641.2011.632458

Chhabildas, N., Pennington, B. F., & Willcutt, E. G. (2001). A comparison of the neuropsychological profiles of the DSM-IV subtypes of ADHD. *Journal of Abnormal Child Psychology*, **29**(6), 529–540. doi: 10.1023/A:1012281226028

Christopher, M. E., Miyake, A., Keenan, J. M., Pennington, B., deFries, J. C., Wadsworth, S. J., et al. (2012). Predicting word reading and comprehension with executive function and speed measures across development: A latent variable analysis. *Journal of Experimental Psychology: General*, **141**(3), 470–488. doi: 10.1037/a0027375

Clark, C. A. C., Pritchard, V. E., & Woodward, L. J. (2010). Preschool executive functioning abilities predict early mathematics achievement. *Developmental Psychology*, **46**(5), 1176–1191. doi: 10.1037/a0019672

Clark, C. A. C., Sheffield, T. D., Chevalier, N., Nelson, J. M., Wiebe, S. A., & Espy, K. A. (2013). Charting early trajectories of executive control with the shape school. *Developmental Psychology*, **49**(8), 1481–1493. doi: 10.1037/a0030578

Clark, C. A. C., & Woodward, L. J. (2015). Relation of perinatal risk and early parenting to executive control at the transition to school. *Developmental Science*, **18**(4), 525–542. doi: 10.1111/desc.12232

Coley, R. J. (2002). *An uneven start: Indicators of inequality in school readiness*. Princeton, NJ: Educational Testing Services.

Colombo, J., & Cheatham, C. L. (2006). The emergence and basis of endogenous attention in infancy and early childhood. In R. Kail (Ed.), *Advances in child development and behavior* (pp. 283–322). London: Elsevier.

Crnic, K. A., & Greenberg, M. T. (1990). Minor parenting stresses with young children. *Child Development*, **61**(5), 1628–1637. doi: 10.2307/1130770

Crnic, K. A., Greenberg, M. T., Ragozin, A. S., Robinson, N. M., & Basham, R. B. (1983). Effects of stress and social support on mothers and premature and full-term infants. *Child Development*, **54**(1), 209–217. doi: 10.2307/1129878

Crone, E. A., & Ridderinkhof, K. R. (2011). The developing brain: From theory to neuroimaging and back. *Developmental Cognitive Neuroscience*, **1**(2), 101–109. doi: 10.1016/j.dcn.2010.12.001

Cuevas, K., & Bell, M. A. (2014). Infant attention and early childhood executive function. *Child Development*, **85**(2), 397–404. doi: 10.1111/cdev.12126

Curchack-Lichtin, J. T., Chacko, A., & Halperin, J. M. (2014). Changes in ADHD symptom endorsement: Preschool to school age. *Journal of Abnormal Child Psychology*, **42**(6), 993–1004. doi: 10.1007/s10802-013-9834-9

D'Souza, D., & Karmiloff-Smith, A. (2011). When modularization fails to occur: A developmental perspective. *Cognitive Neuropsychology*, **28**(3–4), 276–287. doi: 10.1080/02643294.2011.614939

Damasio, A. (1979). *The frontal lobes*. New York, NY: Oxford University Press.

Davidson, M. C., Amso, D., Anderson, L. C., & Diamond, A. (2006). Development of cognitive control and executive functions from 4 to 13 years: Evidence from manipulations of memory, inhibition, and task switching. *Neuropsychologia*, **44**(11), 2037–2078. doi: 10.1016/j.neuropsychologia.2006.02.006

DeMars, C. E. (2006). Application of the bi-factor multidimensional item response theory model to testlet-based tests. *Journal of Educational Measurement*, **43**(2), 145–168. doi: 10.1111/j.1745-3984.2006.00010.x

Diamond, A. (1985). Development of the ability to use recall to guide action, as indicated by infants' performance on AB. *Child Development*, **56**(4), 868–883. doi: 10.1111/1467-8624.ep7251346

Diamond, A. (1990). Developmental time course in human infants and infant monkeys, and the neural bases of, inhibitory control in reaching. *Annals of the New York Academy of Sciences*, **608**(1), 637–676. doi: 10.1111/j.1749-6632.1990.tb48913.x

Diamond, A. (2000). Close interrelation of motor development and cognitive development and of the cerebellum and prefrontal cortex. *Child Development*, **71**(1), 44–56. doi: 10.1111/1467-8624.00117

Diamond, A. (2001). Prefrontal cortex development and development of cognitive functions. In N. J. Smelser & P. B. Baltes (Eds.), *International encyclopedia of the social and behavioral sciences* (pp. 11976–11982). Oxford, UK: Pergamon.

Diamond, A. (2013). Executive functions. *Annual Reviews in Psychology*, **64**, 135–168. doi: 10.1146/annurev-psych-113011-143750

Diamond, A., & Goldman-Rakic, P. S. (1986). Comparative development in human infants and infant rhesus monkeys of cognitive functions that depend on prefrontal cortex. *Society for Neuroscience Abstracts*, **12**, 742–742.

Diamond, A., Kirkman, N., & Amso, D. (2002). Conditions under which young children can hold two rules in mind and inhibit a prepotent response. *Developmental Psychology*, **38**(3), 352–362.

Diamond, A., Prevor, M. B., Callender, G., & Druin, D. P. (1997). Prefrontal cortex cognitive deficits in children treated early and continuously for PKU. *Monographs of the Society for Research in Child Development*, **62**(4), i–206. doi: 10.2307/1166208

Diamond, A., & Taylor, C. (1996). Development of an aspect of executive control: Development of the abilities to remember what I said and to "Do as I say, not as I do." *Developmental Psychobiology*, **29**(4), 315–334. doi: 10.1002/(SICI)1098-2302(199605)29:4

Doebel, S., & Zelazo, P. D. (2013). Bottom-up and top-down dynamics in young children's executive function: Labels aid 3-year-olds' performance on the Dimensional Change Card Sort. *Cognitive Development*, **28**(3), 222–232. doi: 10.1016/j.cogdev.2012.12.001

Dumenci, L., McConaughy, S. H., & Achenbach, T. M. (2004). A hierarchical three-factor model of inattention-hyperactivity-impulsivity derived from the attention problems syndrome of the teacher's report form. *School Psychology Review*, **33**(2), 287–301.

Duncan, G. J., Brooks-Gunn, J., & Klebanov, P. K. (1994). Economic deprivation and early childhood development. *Child Development*, **65**(2), 296–318. doi: 10.1111/j.1467-8624.1994.tb00752.x

Duncan, G. J., Ziol-Guest, K. M., & Kalil, A. (2010). Early-childhood poverty and adult attainment, behavior, and health. *Child Development*, **81**(1), 306–325. doi: 10.1111/j.1467-8624.2009.01396.x

Durston, S., Davidson, M. C., Tottenham, N., Galvan, A., Spicer, J., Fossella, J. A., & Casey, B. J. (2006). A shift from diffuse to focal cortical activity with development. *Developmental Science*, **9**(1), 1–8. doi: 10.1111/j.1467-7687.2005.00454.x

Edin, F., Klingberg, T., Johansson, P., McNab, F., Tegnér, J., & Compte, A. (2009). Mechanism for top-down control of working memory capacity. *PNAS Proceedings of the National Academy of Sciences of the United States of America*, **106**(16), 6802–6807. doi: 10.1073/pnas.0901894106

Edin, F., Macoveanu, J., Olesen, P., Tegnér, J., & Klingberg, T. (2007). Stronger synaptic connectivity as a mechanism behind development of working memory-related brain activity during childhood. *Journal of Cognitive Neuroscience*, **19**(5), 750–760. doi: 10.1162/jocn.2007.19.5.750

Egger, H. L., & Angold, A. (2006). Common emotional and behavioral disorders in preschool children: Presentation, nosology, and epidemiology. *Journal of Child Psychology and Psychiatry*, **47**(3–4), 313–337. doi: 10.1111/j.1469-7610.2006.01618.x

Egger, H. L., Kondo, D., & Angold, A. (2006). The epidemiology and diagnostic issues in preschool attention-deficit/hyperactivity disorder: A review. *Infants and Young Children*, **19**(2), 109–122. doi: 10.1097/00001163-200604000-00004

Ellis, A. E., & Oakes, L. M. (2006). Infants flexibly use different dimensions to categorize objects. *Developmental Psychology*, **42**(6), 1000–1011. doi: 10.1037/0012-1649.42.6.1000

Espy, K. A. (1997). The shape school: Assessing executive function in preschool children. *Developmental Neuropsychology*, **13**(4), 495–499. doi: 10.1080/87565649709540690

Espy, K. A., Bull, R., Martin, J., & Stroup, W. (2006). Measuring the development of executive control with the shape school. *Psychological Assessment*, **18**(4), 373–381. doi: 10.1037/1040-3590.18.4.373

Espy, K. A., & Cwik, M. F. (2004). The development of a trial making test in young children: The TRAILS-P. *The Clinical Neuropsychologist*, **18**(3), 411–422. doi: 10.1080/138540409052416

Espy, K. A., Kaufmann, P. M., McDiarmid, M. D., & Glisky, M. L. (1999). Executive functioning in preschool children: Performance on A-not-B and other delayed response format tasks. *Brain and Cognition*, **41**(2), 178–199. doi: 10.1006/brcg.1999.1117

Espy, K. A., McDiarmid, M. M., Cwik, M. F., Stalets, M. M., Hamby, A., & Senn, T. E. (2004). The contribution of executive functions to emergent mathematic skills in preschool children. *Developmental Neuropsychology*, **26**(1), 465–486. doi: 10.1207/s15326942dn2601_6

Espy, K. A., Molfese, V. J., & DiLalla, L. F. (2001). Effects of environmental measures on intelligence in young children: Growth curve modeling of longitudinal data. *Merril-Palmer Quarterly*, **47**, 42–73.

Espy, K. A., Sheffield, T. D., Wiebe, S. A., Clark, C. A. C., & Moehr, M. J. (2011). Executive control and dimensions of problem behaviors in preschool children. *Journal of Child Psychology and Psychiatry*, **52**(1), 33–46. doi: 10.1111/j.1469-7610.2010.02265.x

Ester, E. F., Serences, J. T., & Awh, E. (2009). Spatially global representations in human primary visual cortex during working memory maintenance. *The Journal of Neuroscience*, **29**(48), 15258–15265. doi: 10.1523/jneurosci.4388-09.2009

Evans, G. W. (2003). A multimethodological analysis of cumulative risk and allostatic load among rural children. *Developmental Psychology*, **39**(5), 924–933. doi: 10.1037/0012-1649.39.5.924

Evans, G. W., Gonnella, C., Marcynyszyn, L. A., Gentile, L., & Salpekar, N. (2005). The role of chaos in poverty and children's socioemotional adjustment. *Psychological Science*, **16**(7), 560–565. doi: 10.1111/j.0956-7976.2005.01575.x

Fair, D. A., Dosenbach, N. U. F., Church, J. A., Cohen, A. L., Brahmbhatt, S., Miezin, F. M., et al. (2007). Development of distinct control networks through segregation and integration. *PNAS Proceedings of the National Academy of Sciences of the United States of America*, **104**(33), 13507–13512. doi: 10.1073/pnas.0705843104

Farah, M. J., Shera, D. M., Savage, J. H., Betancourt, L., Giannetta, J. M., Brodsky, N. L., et al. (2006). Childhood poverty: Specific associations with neurocognitive development. *Brain Research*, **1110**(1), 166–174. doi: 10.1016/j.brainres.2006.06.072

Fisher, R. A. (1922). On the mathematical foundations of theoretical statistics. *Philosophical Transactions of the Royal Society of London. Series A, Containing Papers of a Mathematical or Physical Character*, **222**(594–604), 309–368. doi: 10.1098/rsta.1922.0009

Fox, S. E., Levitt, P., & Nelson, C. A., III. (2010). How the timing and quality of early experiences influence the development of brain architecture. *Child Development*, **81**(1), 28–40. doi: 10.1111/j.1467-8624.2009.01380.x

Frazier, T. W., Demaree, H. A., & Youngstrom, E. A. (2004). Meta-analysis of intellectual and neuropsychological test performance in attention-deficit/hyperactivity disorder. *Neuropsychology*, **18**(3), 543–555. doi: 10.1037/0894-4105.18.3.543

Friedman, N. P., Haberstick, B. C., Willcutt, E. G., Miyake, A., Young, S. E., Corley, R. P., et al. (2007). Greater attention problems during childhood predict poorer executive functioning in late adolescence. *Psychological Science*, **18**(10), 893–900. doi: 10.1111/j.1467-9280.2007.01997.x

Friedman, N. P., & Miyake, A. (2004). The relations among inhibition and interference control functions: A latent-variable analysis. *Journal of Experimental Psychology: General*, **133**(1), 101–135. doi: 10.1037/0096-3445.133.1.101

Friedman, N. P., Miyake, A., Corley, R. P., Young, S. E., DeFries, J. C., & Hewitt, J. K. (2006). Not all executive functions are related to intelligence. *Psychological Science*, **17**(2), 172–179. doi: 10.1111/j.1467-9280.2006.01681.x

Friedman, N. P., Miyake, A., Robinson, J. L., & Hewitt, J. K. (2011). Developmental trajectories in toddlers' self-restraint predict individual differences in executive functions 14 years later: A behavioral genetic analysis. *Developmental Psychology*, **47**(5), 1410–1430. doi: 10.1037/a0023750

Friedman, N. P., Miyake, A., Young, S. E., Defries, J. C., Corley, R. P., & Hewitt, J. K. (2008). Individual differences in executive functions are almost entirely genetic in origin. *Journal of Experimental Psychology: General*, **137**(2), 201–225. doi: 10.1037/0096-3445.137.2.201

Frye, D., Zelazo, P. D., & Palfai, T. (1995). Theory of mind and rule-based reasoning. *Cognitive Development*, **10**(4), 483–527. doi: 10.1016/0885-2014(95)90024-1

Fuhs, M. W., & Day, J. D. (2011). Verbal ability and executive functioning development in preschoolers at head start. *Developmental Psychology*, **47**(2), 404–416. doi: 10.1037/a0021065

Galván, A. (2010). Neural plasticity of development and learning. *Human Brain Mapping*, **31**(6), 879–890. doi: 10.1002/hbm.21029

Gandolfi, E., Viterbori, P., Traverso, L., & Usai, M. C. (2014). Inhibitory processes in toddlers: A latent-variable approach. *Frontiers in Psychology*, **5**(Article 381), 1–11. doi: 10.3389/fpsyg.2014.00381

Gao, W., Zhu, H., Giovanello, K. S., Smith, J. K., Shen, D., Gilmore, J. H., et al. (2009). Evidence on the emergence of the brain's default network from 2-week-old to 2-year-old healthy pediatric subjects. *PNAS Proceedings of the National Academy of Sciences of the United States of America*, **106**, 6790–6795. doi: 10.1073pnas.0811221106

Garon, N., Bryson, S. E., & Smith, I. M. (2008). Executive function in preschoolers: A review using an integrative framework. *Psychological Bulletin*, **134**(1), 31–60. doi: 10.1037/0033-2909.134.1.31

Gerton, B. K., Meyer-Lindenberg, A., Kohn, P., Holt, J. L., Olsen, R., & Berman, K. F. (2004). Shared and distinct neurophysiological components of digit span forward and backward tasks as revealed by functional neuroimaging. *Neuropsychologia*, **42**(13), 1781–1787. doi: 1016/j.neuropsychologia.2004.04.023

Gibbons, R. D., Rush, A. J., & Immekus, J. C. (2009). On the psychometric validity of the domains of the PDSQ: An illustration of the bi-factor item response theory model. *Journal of Psychiatric Research*, **43**(4), 401–410. doi: 10.1016/j.jpsychires.2008.04.013

Giedd, J. N., & Rapoport, J. L. (2010). Structural MRI of pediatric brain development: What have we learned and where are we going? *Neuron*, **67**(5), 728–734. doi: 10.1016/j.neuron.2010.08.040

Giganti, F., & Viggiano, M. P. (2014). How semantic category modulates preschool children's visual memory. *Child Neuropsycholy*, **21**(6) 845–855. doi: 10.1080/09297049.2014.945406

Golden, C. J. (1982). *The Luria-Nebraska neuropsychological battery*. Los Angeles, CA: Western Psychological Services.

Goldman, P. S., Rosvold, H. E., Vest, B., & Galkin, T. W. (1971). Analysis of the delayed-alternation deficit produced by dorsolateral prefrontal lesions in the rhesus monkey. *Journal of Comparative and Physiological Psychology*, **77**(2), 212–220. doi: 10.1037/h0031649

Gove, W. R., Hughes, M., & Galle, O. R. (1979). Overcrowding in the home: An empirical investigation of its possible pathological consequences. *American Sociological Review*, **44**(1), 59–80. doi: 10.2307/2094818

Greenough, W. T., & Black, J. E. (1992). Induction of brain structure by experience: Substrates for cognitive development. In M. R. Gunnar & C. A. Nelson (Eds.), *Developmental behavioral neuroscience* (pp. 155–200). Hillsdale, NJ: Lawrence Erlbaum.

Greenough, W. T., Black, J. E., & Wallace, C. S. (1987). Experience and brain development. *Child Development*, **58**(3), 539–559. doi: 10.2307/1130197

Guo, G., & Harris, K. M. (2000). The mechanisms mediating the effects of poverty on children's intellectual development. *Demography*, **37**(4), 431–447. doi: 10.1353/dem.2000.0005

Gutermuth Anthony, L., Anthony, B. J., Glanville, D. N., Naiman, D. Q., Waanders, C., & Shaffer, S. (2005). The relationships between parenting stress, parenting behaviour and preschoolers' social competence and behaviour problems in the classroom. *Infant and Child Development*, **14**(2), 133–154. doi: 10.1002/icd.385

Hagmann, P., Sporns, O., Madan, N., Cammoun, L., Pienaar, R., Wedeen, V. J., et al. (2010). White matter maturation reshapes structural connectivity in the late developing human brain. *PNAS Proceedings of the National Academy of Sciences of the United States of America*, **107**(44), 19067–19072. doi: 10.1073/pnas.1009073107

Halliwell, C., Comeau, W., Gibb, R., Frost, D. O., & Kolb, B. (2009). Factors influencing frontal cortex development and recovery from early frontal injury. *Developmental Neurorehabilitation*, **12**(5), 269–278. doi: 10.3109/17518420903087715

Hammond, S. I., Müller, U., Carpendale, J. I. M., Bibok, M. B., & Liebermann-Finestone, D. P. (2012). The effects of parental scaffolding on preschoolers' executive function. *Developmental Psychology*, **48**(1), 271–281. doi: 10.1037/00025519

Hardy, K. K., Kollins, S. H., Murray, D. W., Riddle, M. A., Greenhill, L., Cunningham, C., et al. (2007). Factor structure of parent- and teacher-rated attention-deficit/hyperactivity disorder symptoms in the preschoolers with attention-deficit/hyperactivity disorder treatment study (PATS). *Journal of Child and Adolescent Psychopharmacology*, **17**(5). doi: 10.1089/cap.2007.0073

Harlow, J. M. (1848). Passage of an iron rod through the head. *The Boston Medical and Surgical Journal*, **39**(20), 389–393. doi: doi:10.1056/NEJM184812130392001

Harlow, J. M. (1993). Recovery from the passage of an iron bar through the head. *History of Psychiatry*, **4**(14, Pt 2), 271–281. doi: 10.1177/0957154X9300401406

Hart, B., & Risley, T. R. (1995). *Meaningful differences in the everyday experience of young American children*. Baltimore, MD: Brookes Publishing.

Hazy, T. E., Frank, Michael, J., & O'Reilly, Randall C. (2007). Towards an executive without a homunculus: Computational models of the prefrontal cortex/basal ganglia system. *Philosophical Transactions of the Royal Society B*, **362**, 1601–1613. doi: 10.1098/rstb.2007.2055

Hess, R. D., & Shipman, V. C. (1965). Early experience and the socialization of cognitive modes in children. *Child Development*, **36**(4), 869–886. doi: 10.2307/1126930

Hoff, E. (2003). The specificity of environmental influence: Socioeconomic status affects early vocabulary development via maternal speech. *Child Development*, **74**(5), 1368–1378. doi: 10.1111/1467-8624.00612

Holzinger, K. J., & Swineford, F. (1937). The bi-factor method. *Psychometrika*, **2**, 41–54. doi: 10.1007/BF02287965

Hu, L., & Bentler, P. M. (1999). Cutoff criteria for fit indexes in covariance structure analysis: Conventional criteria versus. *Structural Equation Modeling*, **6**(1), 1–55. doi: 10.1080/10705519909540118

Hubel, D. H., & Wiesel, T. N. (1962). Receptive fields, binocular interaction and functional architecture in the cat's visual cortex. *Journal of Physiology*, **160**(1), 106–154.

Hughes, C., Dunn, J., & White, A. (1998). Trick or treat?: Uneven understanding of mind and emotion and executive dysfunction in "hard-to-manage" preschoolers. *Journal of Child Psychology and Psychiatry*, **39**(7), 981–994. doi: 10.1111/1469-7610.00401

Hughes, C., & Ensor, R. (2005). Executive function and theory of mind in 2 year olds: A family affair? *Developmental Neuropsychology*, **28**(2), 645–668. doi: 10.1207/s15326942dn2802_5

Hughes, C., & Ensor, R. (2007). Executive function and theory of mind: Predictive relations from 2 to 4. *Developmental Psychology*, **43**, 1447–1459. doi: 10.1037/0012-1649.43.6.1447

Hughes, C., & Ensor, R. (2009). How do families help or hinder the emergence of early executive function? *New Directions for Child and Adolescent Development*, **2009**(123), 35–50. doi: 10.1002/cd.234

Hughes, C., Ensor, R., Wilson, A., & Graham, A. (2010). Tracking executive function across the transition to school: A latent variable approach. *Developmental Neuropsychology*, **35**(1), 20–36. doi: 10.1080/87565640903325691

Hughes, C., & Graham, A. (2002). Measuring executive functions in childhood: Problems and solutions? *Child and Adolescent Mental Health*, **7**(3), 131–142. doi: 10.1111/1475-3588.00024

Hughes, C., White, A., Sharpen, J., & Dunn, J. (2000). Antisocial, angry, and unsympathetic: "Hard-to-manage" preschoolers' peer problems and possible cognitive influences. *Journal of Child Psychology and Psychiatry*, **41**(2), 169–179. doi: 10.1017/S0021963099005193

Huizinga, M., Dolan, C. V., & van der Molen, M. W. (2006). Age-related change in executive function: Developmental trends and a latent variable analysis. *Neuropsychologia*, **44**(11), 2017–2036. doi: 10.1016/j.neuropsychologia.2006.01.010

Huttenlocher, P. R. (1990). Morphometric study of human cerebral cortex development. *Neuropsychologia*, **28**(6), 517–527. doi: 10.1016/0028-3932(90)90031-I

Hwang, K., Velanova, K., & Luna, B. (2010). Strengthening of top-down frontal cognitive control networks underlying the development of inhibitory control: A functional magnetic resonance imaging effective connectivity study. *The Journal of Neuroscience*, **30**(46), 15535–15545. doi: 10.1523/JNEUROSCI2825-10.2010

Jaccard, J., & Wan, C. K. (1996). *LISREL approaches to interaction effects in multiple regression* (Vol. 114). Thousand Oaks, CA: SAGE.

Jacobs, R. (2011). Are executive skills primarily mediated by the prefrontal cortex in childhood? Examination of focal brain lesions in childhood. *Cortex*, **47**(7), 808–824.

Jacobsen, C. F. (1935). Functions of frontal association area in primates. *Archives of Neurology and Psychiatry*, **33**(3), 558–569. doi: 10.1001/archneurpsyc.1935.02250150108009

Johnson, M. H. (1995). The inhibition of automatic saccades in early infancy. *Developmental Psychobiology*, **28**(5), 281–291. doi: 10.1002/dev.420280504

Johnson, M. H. (2011). Interactive specialization: A domain-general framework for human functional brain development? *Developmental Cognitive Neuroscience*, **1**(1), 7–21. doi: 10.1016/j.dcn.2010.07.003

Johnson, M. H., Posner, M. I., & Rothbart, M. K. (1991). Components of visual orienting in early infancy: Contingency learning, anticipatory looking, and disengaging. *Journal of Cognitive Neuroscience*, **3**(4), 335–344. doi: 10.1162/jocn.1991.3.4.335

Jones, L. B., Rothbart, M. K., & Posner, M. I. (2003). Development of executive attention in preschool children. *Developmental Science*, **6**(5), 498–504. doi: 10.1111/1467-7687.00307

Kishiyama, M. M., Boyce, W. T., Jimenez, A. M., Perry, L. M., & Knight, R. T. (2009). Socioeconomic disparities affect prefrontal function in children. *Journal of Cognitive Neuroscience*, **21**(6), 1106–1115. doi: 10.1162/jocn.2009.21101

Kline, R. B. (2010). *Principles and practice of structural equation modeling*. New York, NY: Guilford Press.

Klingberg, T., Forssberg, H., & Westerberg, H. (2002). Training of working memory in children with ADHD. *Journal of Clinical and Experimental Neuropsychology*, **24**(6), 781–791. doi: 10.1076/jcen.24.6.781.8395

Kloo, D., Perner, J., Kerschhuber, A., Dabernig, S., & Aichhorn, M. (2008). Sorting between dimensions: Conditions of cognitive flexibility in preschoolers. *Journal of Experimental Child Psychology*, **100**(2), 115–134. doi: 10.1016/j.jecp.2007.12.003

Knudsen, E. I. (2004). Sensitive periods in the development of the brain and behavior. *Journal of Cognitive Neuroscience*, **16**(8), 1412–1425. doi: 10.1162/0898929042304796

Kochanska, G., Murray, K., Jacques, T. Y., & Koenig, A. L. (1996). Inhibitory control in young children and its role in emerging internalization. *Child Development*, **67**(2), 490–507. doi: 10.2307/1131828

Kochanska, G., Murray, K. T., & Harlan, E. T. (2000). Effortful control in early childhood: Continuity and change, antecedents, and implications for social development. *Developmental Psychology*, **36**(2), 220–232. doi: 10.1037/0012-1649.36.2.220

Korkman, M., Kirk, U., & Kemp, S. (1998). *NESPY: A developmental neuropsychological assessment*. San Antonio, TX: The Psychological Corporation.

Kraybill, J. H., & Bell, M. A. (2013). Infancy predictors of preschool and post-kindergarten executive function. *Developmental Psychobiology*, **55**(5), 530–538. doi: 10.1002/dev.21057

Lahey, B., Pelham, W., Loney, J., Kipp, H., Ehrhardt, A., Lee, S., et al. (2004). Three-year predictive validity of DSM-IV attention deficit hyperactivity disorder in children diagnosed at 4–6 years of age. *American Journal of Psychiatry*, **161**(11), 2014–2020. doi: 10.1176/appi.ajp.161.11.2014

Lahey, B. B., Applegate, B., McBurnett, K., Biederman, J., Greenhill, L., Hynd, G. W., et al. (1994). DMS-IV field trials for attention deficit hyperactivity disorder in children and adolescents. *The American Journal of Psychiatry*, **151**(11), 1673–1685.

Lahey, B. B., Pelham, W. E., Stein, M. A., Loney, J. A. N., Trapani, C., Nugent, K., et al. (1998). Validity of DSM-IV attention-deficit/hyperactivity disorder for younger children. *Journal of the American Academy of Child and Adolescent Psychiatry*, **37**(7), 695–702. doi: 10.1097/00004583-199807000-00008

Landry, S. H., Miller-Loncar, C. L., Smith, K. E., & Swank, P. R. (2002). The role of early parenting in children's development of executive processes. *Developmental Neuropsychology*, **21**(1), 15–41. doi: 10.1207/S15326942DN2101_2

Lawson, G. M., Hook, C. J., Hackman, D. A., & Farah, M. J. (2015). Socioeconomic status and neurocognitive development: Executive function. In J. A. Griffin, L. S. Freund, & P. McCardle (Eds.), *Executive function in preschool children: Integrating measurement, neurodevelopment, and translational research*. Washington, DC: American Psychological Association.

Lee, K., Bull, R., & Ho, R. M. H. (2013). Developmental changes in executive functioning. *Child Development*, **84**(6), 1933–1953. doi: 10.1111/cdev.12096

Lee, V. E., & Burkham, D. T. (2002). *Inequality at the starting gate: Social background differences in achievement as children begin school.* Washington, DC: Economic Policy Institute.

Lehto, J. E., Juujärvi, P., Kooistra, L., & Pulkkinen, L. (2003). Dimensions of executive functioning: Evidence from children. *British Journal of Developmental Psychology,* **21**(1), 59–80. doi: 10.1348/026151003321164627

Lerner, M. D., & Lonigan, C. J. (2014). Executive function among preschool children: Unitary versus distinct abilities. *Journal of Psychopathology and Behavioral Assessment,* **36**(4), 626–639. doi: 10.1007/s10862-014-9424-3

Li-Grining, C. P. (2007). Effortful control among low-income preschoolers in three cities: Stability, change, and individual differences. *Developmental Psychology,* **43**(1), 208–221. doi: 10.1037/0012-1649.43.1.208

Linver, M. R., Brooks-Gunn, J., & Kohen, D. E. (2002). Family processes as pathways from income to young children's development. *Developmental Psychology,* **38**(5), 719–734. doi: 10.1037/0012-1649.38.5.719

Lipina, S., Segretin, S., Hermida, J., Prats, L., Fracchia, C., Camelo, J. L., et al. (2013). Linking childhood poverty and cognition: Environmental mediators of non-verbal executive control in an Argentine sample. *Developmental Science,* **16**(5), 697–707. doi: 10.1111/desc.12080

Luria, A. R. (1973). *The working brain: An introduction to neuropsychology.* New York, NY: Basic Books.

Macmillan, N. A., & Creelman, C. D. (2005). *Detection theory: A user's guide* (2nd ed.). Mahwah, NJ: Lawrence Erlbaum.

Margulies, D. S., Kelly, A., Uddin, L. Q., Biswal, B. B., Castellanos, F. X., & Milham, M. P. (2007). Mapping the functional connectivity of anterior cingulate cortex. *NeuroImage,* **37**(2), 579. doi: 10.1016/j.neuroimage.2007.05.019

Mariani, M. A., & Barkley, R. A. (1997). Neuropsychological and academic functioning in preschool boys with attention deficit hyperactivity disorder. *Developmental Neuropsychology,* **13**(1), 111–129. doi: 10.1080/87565649709540671

Marsh, H. W., Wen, Z., & Hau, K.-T. (2004). Structural equation models of latent interactions: Evaluation of alternative estimation strategies and indicator construction. *Psychological Methods,* **9**(3), 275–300. doi: 10.1037/1082-989X.9.3.275; 10.1037/1082-989X.9.3.275. supp (Supplemental).

Martel, M., Roberts, B., Gremillion, M., Eye, A., & Nigg, J. (2011). External validation of bifactor model of ADHD: Explaining heterogeneity in psychiatric comorbidity, cognitive control, and personality trait profiles within DSM-IV ADHD. *Journal of Abnormal Child Psychology,* **39**(8), 1111–1123. doi: 10.1007/s10802-011-9538-y

Martel, M. M., von Eye, A., & Nigg, J. (2012). Developmental differences in structure of attention-deficit/hyperactivity disorder (ADHD) between childhood and adulthood. *International Journal of Behavioral Development,* **36**(4), 279–292. doi: 10.1177/0165025412444077

Martel, M. M., Von Eye, A., & Nigg, J. T. (2010). Revisiting the latent structure of ADHD: Is there a "g" factor? *Journal of Child Psychology and Psychiatry,* **51**(8), 905–914. doi: 10.1111/j.1469-7610.2010.02232.x

McCabe, D. P., Roediger, H. L., III, McDaniel, M. A., Balota, D. A., & Hambrick, D. Z. (2010). The relationship between working memory capacity and executive functioning: Evidence for a common executive attention construct. *Neuropsychology,* **24**(2), 222–243. doi: 10.1037/a0017619

McClelland, M. M., & Cameron, C. E. (2012). Self-regulation in early childhood: Improving conceptual clarity and developing ecologically valid measures. *Child Development Perspectives*, **6**(2), 136–142. doi: 10.1111/j.1750-8606.2011.00191.x

McClelland, M. M., Cameron, C. E., Connor, C. M., Farris, C. L., Jewkes, A. M., & Morrison, F. J. (2007). Links between behavioral regulation and preschoolers' literacy, vocabulary, and math skills. *Developmental Psychology*, **43**(4), 947–959. doi: 10.1037/0012-1649.43.4.947

McLoyd, V. C. (1990). The impact of economic hardship on Black families and children: Psychological distress, parenting, and socioemotional development. *Child Development*, **61**(2), 311–346. doi: 10.2307/1131096

McLoyd, V. C. (1998). Socioeconomic disadvantage and child development. *American Psychologist*, **53**(2), 185–204. doi: 10.1037/0003-066X.53.2.185

Melby-Lervåg, M., & Hulme, C. (2012). Is working memory training effective? A meta-analytic review. *Developmental Psychology*, **49**(2), 270–291. doi: 10.1037/a0028228

Merz, E. C., Landry, S. H., Williams, J. M., Barnes, M. A., Eisenberg, N., Spinrad, T. L., et al. (2014). Associations among parental education, home environment quality, effortful control, and preacademic knowledge. *Journal of Applied Developmental Psychology*, **35**(4), 304–315. doi: 10.1016/j.appdev.2014.04.002

Miller, E. K., & Cohen, J. D. (2001). An integrative theory of prefrontal cortex function. *Annual Review of Neuroscience*, **24**, 167–202. doi: 10.1146/annurev.neuro.24.1.167

Miller, M. R., Giesbrecht, G. F., Müller, U., McInerney, R. J., & Kerns, K. A. (2012). A latent variable approach to determining the structure of executive function in preschool children. *Journal of Cognition and Development*, **13**(3), 395–423. doi: 10.1080/15248372.2011.585478

Milner, B. (1963). Effects of different brain lesions on card sorting: The role of the frontal lobes. *Archives of Neurology*, **9**, 90–100. doi: 10.1001/archneur.1963.00460070100010

Miyake, A., & Friedman, N. P. (2012). The nature and organization of individual differences in executive functions. *Current Directions in Psychological Science*, **21**(1), 8–14. doi: 10.1177/0963721411429458

Miyake, A., Friedman, N. P., Emerson, M. J., Witzki, A. H., & Howerter, A. (2000). The unity and diversity of executive functions and their contributions to complex "frontal lobe" tasks: A latent variable analysis. *Cognitive Psychology*, **41**(1), 49–100. doi: 10.1006/cogp.1999.0734

Moos, R. H. (1995). Development and applications of new measures of life stressors, social resources, and coping responses. *European Journal of Psychological Assessment*, **11**(1), 1–13. doi: 10.1027/1015-5759.11.1.1

Moos, R. H., & Moos, B. S. (1994). *The life stressors and social resources inventory*. Odessa, FL: Psychological Assessment Resources.

Moriguchi, Y., & Hiraki, K. (2009). Neural origin of cognitive shifting in young children. *PNAS Proceedings of the National Academy of Sciences of the United States of America*, **106**(14), 6017–6021. doi: 10.1073/pnas.0809747106

Morton, J. B., & Munakata, Y. (2002). Active versus latent representations: A neural network model of perseveration, dissociation, and decalage. *Developmental Psychobiology*, **40**(3), 255–265. doi: 10.1002/dev.10033

Müller, U., Zelazo, P. D., Hood, S., Leone, T., & Rohrer, L. (2004). Interference control in a new rule use task: Age-related changes, labeling, and attention. *Child Development*, **75**(5), 1594–1609. doi: 10.1111/j.1467-8624.2004.00759.x

Munakata, Y., Herd, S. A., Chatham, C. H., Depue, B. E., Banich, M. T., & O'Reilly, R. C. (2011). A unified framework for inhibitory control. *Trends in Cognitive Sciences*, **15**(10), 453–459. doi: 10.1016/j.tics.2011.07.011

Munakata, Y., Snyder, H. R., & Chatham, C. H. (2012). Developing cognitive control: Three key transitions. *Current Directions in Psychological Science*, **21**(2), 71–77. doi: 10.1177/0963721412436807

Mungas, D., Widaman, K., Zelazo, P. D., Tulsky, D., Heaton, R. K., Slotkin, J., et al. (2013). VII. NIH Toolbox Cognition Battery (CB): Factor structure for 3 to 15 year olds. *Monographs of the Society for Research in Child Development*, **78**(4), 103–118. doi: 10.1111/mono.12037

National Institute of Child Health and Human Development Early Child Care Research Network. (2005). Duration and developmental timing of poverty and children's cognitive and social development from birth through third grade. *Child Development*, **76**(4), 795–810. doi: 10.1111/j.1467-8624.2005.00878.x

National Research Council and Institute of Medicine. (2000). *From neurons to neighborhoods: The science of early childhood development*. Washington, DC: National Academy Press.

Nelson, J. M., James, T. D., Chevalier, N., Clark, C. A. C., & Espy, K. A. (2016). Structure, measurement, and development of preschool executive function. In J. A. Griffin, P. McCardle, & L. S. Freund (Eds.), *Executive function in preschool-age children: Integrating measurement, neurodevelopment, and translational research*. Washington, DC: American Psychological Association.

Nelson, J. M., James, T. D., & Espy, K. A. (2016). The latent structure of Attention-Deficit/Hyperactivity Disorder (ADHD) symptoms in preschool children. Manuscript submitted for publication.

Nigg, J. T. (2006). *What causes ADHD?: Understanding what goes wrong and why*. New York, NY: The Guilford Press.

Nigg, J. T., Willcutt, E. G., Doyle, A. E., & Sonuga-Barke, E. J. S. (2005). Causal heterogeneity in attention-deficit/hyperactivity disorder: Do we need neuropsychologically impaired subtypes? *Biological Psychiatry*, **57**(11), 1224–1230. doi: 10.1016/j.biopsych.2004.08.025

Noble, K. G., McCandliss, B. D., & Farah, M. J. (2007). Socioeconomic gradients predict individual differences in neurocognitive abilities. *Developmental Science*, **10**(4), 464–480. doi: 10.1111/j.1467-7687.2007.00600.x

Noble, K. G., Norman, M. F., & Farah, M. J. (2005). Neurocognitive correlates of socioeconomic status in kindergarten children. *Developmental Science*, **8**(1), 74–87. doi: 10.1111/j.1467-7687.2005.00394.x

Nolan, E. E., Gadow, K. D., & Sprafkin, J. (2001). Teacher reports of DSM-IV ADHD, ODD, and CD symptoms in schoolchildren. *Journal of the American Academy of Child and Adolescent Psychiatry*, **40**(2), 241–249. doi: 10.1097/00004583-200102000-00020

Norman, D., & Shallice, T. (1986). Attention to action: Willed and automatic control of behavior. In R. Davidson, R. G. Schwartz, & D. Shapiro (Eds.), *Consciousness and self-regulation: Advances in research and theory* (pp. 1–18). New York, NY: Plenum Press.

Normand, S., Flora, D. B., Toplak, M. E., & Tannock, R. (2012). Evidence for a general ADHD factor from a longitudinal general school population study. *Journal of Abnormal Child Psychology*, **40**(4), 555–567. doi: 10.1007/s10802-011-9584-5

Ozonoff, S., & Jensen, J. (1999). Brief report: Specific executive function profiles in three neurodevelopmental disorders. *Journal of Autism and Developmental Disorders*, **29**(2), 171–177. doi: 10.1023/A:1023052913110

Patrick, C. J., Hicks, B. M., Nichol, P. E., & Krueger, R. F. (2007). A bifactor approach to modeling the structure of the Psychopathy Checklist-Revised. *Journal of Personality Disorders*, **21**(2), 118–141. doi: 10.1521/pedi.2007.21.2.118

Pauli-Pott, U., & Becker, K. (2011). Neuropsychological basic deficits in preschoolers at risk for ADHD: A meta-analysis. *Clinical Psychology Review*, **31**(4), 626–637. doi: 10.1016/j.cpr.2011.02.005

Pennington, B. F., Bennetto, L., McAleer, O., & Roberts, R. J. (1996). Executive functions and working memory: Theoretical and measurement issues. In G. R. Lyon, & N. A. Krasnegor (Eds.), *Attention, memory and executive function* (pp. 327–348). Baltimore, MD: Brookes Publishing.

Pennington, B. F., & Ozonoff, S. (1996). Executive functions and developmental psychopathology. *Journal of Child Psychology & Psychiatry*, **37**, 51–87.

Petterson, S. M., & Albers, A. B. (2001). Effects of poverty and maternal depression on early child development. *Child Development*, **72**(6), 1794–1813. doi: 10.1111/1467-8624.00379

Polka, L., & Werker, J. F. (1994). Developmental changes in perception of nonnative vowel contrasts. *Journal of Experimental Psychology: Human Perception and Performance*, **20**(2), 421–435. doi: 10.1037/0096-1523.20.2.421

Posner, M. I., Rothbart, M. K., Sheese, B. E., & Voelker, P. (2012). Control networks and neuromodulators of early development. *Developmental Psychology*, **48**(3), 827–835. doi: 10.1037/a0025530

Rabitt, P. (1997). Introduction: Methodologies and models in the study of executive function. In P. Rabbit (Ed.), *Methodologies of frontal and executive function* (pp. 1–34). London: Psychology Press.

Ragozin, A. S., Basham, R. B., Crnic, K. A., Greenberg, M. T., & Robinson, N. M. (1982). Effects of maternal age on parenting role. *Developmental Psychology*, **18**(4), 627–634. doi: 10.1037/0012-1649.18.4.627

Raikes, H. A., & Thompson, R. A. (2005). Efficacy and social support as predictors of parenting stress among families in poverty. *Infant Mental Health Journal*, **26**(3), 177–190. doi: 10.1002/imhj.20044

Rapport, M. D., Scanlan, S. W., & Denney, C. B. (1999). Attention-deficit/hyperactivity disorder and scholastic achievement: A model of dual developmental pathways. *Journal of Child Psychology and Psychiatry*, **40**(8), 1169–1183. doi: 10.1111/1469-7610.00534

Raver, C. C., Blair, C. B., & Willoughby, M. T. (2012). Poverty as a predictor of 4-year-olds' executive function: New perspectives on models of differential susceptibility. *Developmental Psychology*, **49**(2), 292–304. doi: 10.1037/a0028343

Reimers, S., & Maylor, E. A. (2005). Task switching across the life span: Effects of age on general and specific switch costs. *Developmental Psychology*, **41**(4), 661–671. doi: 10.1037/0012-1649.41.4.661

Reise, S. P., Morizot, J., & Hays, R. D. (2007). The role of the bifactor model in resolving dimensionality issues in health outcomes measures. *Quality of Life Research: An International Journal of Quality of Life Aspects of Treatment, Care and Rehabilitation*, **16**(Suppl 1), 19–31. doi: 10.1007/s11136-007-9183-7

Rhoades, B. L., Greenberg, M. T., Lanza, S. T., & Blair, C. (2011). Demographic and familial predictors of early executive function development: Contribution of a person-centered perspective. *Journal of Experimental Child Psychology*, **108**(3), 638–662. doi: 10.1016/j.jecp.2010.08.004

Riggs, K. J., Jolley, R. P., & Simpson, A. (2013). The role of inhibitory control in the development of human figure drawing in young children. *Journal of Experimental Child Psychology*, **114**(4), 537–542. doi: 10.1016/j.jecp.2012.10.003

Riley, C., DuPaul, G. J., Pipan, M., Kern, L., Van Brakle, J., & Blum, N. J. (2008). Combined type versus ADHD predominantly hyperactive-impulsive type: Is there a difference in functional impairment? *Journal of Developmental and Behavioral Pediatrics*, **29**(4), 270–275. doi: 10.1097/DBP.0b13e31816b6afe

Robinson, A. L., Heaton, R. K., Lehman, R. A., & Stilson, D. W. (1980). The utility of the Wisconsin Card Sorting Test in detecting and localizing frontal lobe lesions. *Journal of Consulting and Clinical Psychology*, **48**(5), 605–614. doi: 10.1037/0022-006X.48.5.605

Roth, T. L., & David Sweatt, J. (2011). Annual research review: Epigenetic mechanisms and environmental shaping of the brain during sensitive periods of development. *Journal of Child Psychology and Psychiatry*, **52**(4), 398–408. doi: 10.1111/j.1469-7610.2010.02282.x

Rubia, K., Smith, A. B., Woolley, J., Nosarti, C., Heyman, I., Taylor, E., et al. (2006). Progressive increse of frontostriatal brain activation from childhood to adulthood during event-related tasks of cognitive control. *Human Brain Mapping*, **27**, 973–993. doi: 10.1002/hbm.20237

Sagvolden, T., Johansen, E. B., Aase, H., & Russell, V. A. (2005). A dynamic developmental theory of attention-deficit/hyperactivity disorder (ADHD) predominantly hyperactive/impulsive and combined subtypes. *Behavioral and Brain Sciences*, **28**(3), 397–468. doi: 10.1017/S0140525X05000075

Sameroff, A. J., Seifer, R., Baldwin, A., & Baldwin, C. (1993). Stability of intelligence from preschool to adolescence: The influence of social and family risk factors. *Child Development*, **64**(1), 80–97. doi: 10.1111/1467-8624.ep9309015108

Sarsour, K., Sheridan, M., Jutte, D., Nuru-Jeter, A., Hinshaw, S., & Boyce, W. T. (2011). Family socioeconomic status and child executive functions: The roles of language, home environment, and single parenthood. *Journal of the International Neuropsychological Society*, **17**(1), 120–132. doi: 10.1017/S1355617710001335

Schaie, K. W. (1965). A general model for the study of developmental problems. *Psychological Bulletin*, **64**(2), 92–107. doi: 10.1037/h0022371

Schmitt, S. A., Pratt, M. E., & McClelland, M. M. (2014). Examining the validity of behavioral self-regulation tools in predicting preschoolers' academic achievement. *Early Education and Development*, **25**(5), 641–660. doi: 10.1080/10409289.2014.850397

Schoemaker, K., Bunte, T., Wiebe, S. A., Espy, K. A., Deković, M., & Matthys, W. (2012). Executive function deficits in preschool children with ADHD and DBD. *Journal of Child Psychology and Psychiatry*, **53**(2), 111–119. doi: 10.1111/j.1469-7610.2011.02468.x

Schuck, S. E. B., & Crinella, F. M. (2005). Why children with ADHD do not have low IQs. *Journal of Learning Disabilities*, **38**(3), 262–280. doi: 10.1177/00222194050380030701

Schwarz, G. (1978). Estimating the dimension of a model. *The Annals of Statistics*, **6**(2), 461–464. doi: 10.2307/2958889

Scolari, M., Vogel, E. K., & Awh, E. (2008). Perceptual expertise enhances the resolution but not the number of representations in working memory. *Psychonomic Bulletin and Review*, **15**(1), 215–222. doi: 10.3758/PBR.15.1.215

Shallice, T. (1988). *From neuropsychology to mental structure*. Cambridge, England: Cambridge University Press.

Sheese, B. E., Rothbart, M. K., Posner, M. I., White, L. K., & Fraundorf, S. H. (2008). Executive attention and self-regulation in infancy. *Infant Behavior & Development*, **31**(3), 501–510. doi: 10.1016/j.infbeh.2008.02.001

Sherman, L. E., Rudie, J. D., Pfeifer, J. H., Masten, C. L., McNealy, K., & Dapretto, M. (2014). Development of the default mode and central executive networks across early adolescence: A longitudinal study. *Developmental Cognitive Neuroscience*, **10**, 148–159. doi: 10.1016/j.dcn.2014.08.002

Shing, Y. L., Lindenberger, U., Diamond, A., Li, S.-C., & Davidson, M. C. (2010). Memory maintenance and inhibitory control differentiate from early childhood to adolescence. *Developmental Neuropsychology*, **35**(6), 679–697. doi: 10.1080/87565641.2010.508546

Shipstead, Z., Redick, T. S., & Engle, R. W. (2012). Is working memory training effective? *Psychological Bulletin*, **138**(4), 628–654. doi: 10.1037/a0027473

Siegler, R. S. (1983). Cognitive development: The development of mathematical thinking. *Science*, **221**(4615), 1042–1043. doi: 10.1126/science.221.4615.1042

Simpson, A., & Riggs, K. J. (2006). Conditions under which children experience inhibitory difficulty with a "button-press" go/no-go task. *Journal of Experimental Child Psychology*, **94**(1), 18–26. doi: 10.1016/j.jecp.2005.10.003

Smith, L. B. (2005). Cognition as a dynamic system: Principles from embodiment. *Developmental Review*, **25**, 278–298. doi: 10.1016/j.dr.2005.11.001

Snyder, H. R., & Munakata, Y. (2010). Becoming self-directed: Abstract representations support endogenous flexibility in children. *Cognition*, **116**(2), 155–167. doi: 10.1016/j.cognition.2010.04.007

Sonuga-Barke, E., Sergeant, J., Nigg, J., & Willcutt, E. (2008). Executive dysfunction and delay aversion in attention deficit hyperactivity disorder: Nosologic and diagnostic implications. *Child and Adolescent Psychiatric Clinics of North America*, **17**(2), 367–384. doi: 10.1016/j.chc.2007.11.008

Sonuga-Barke, E. J. S. (2005). Causal models of attention-deficit/hyperactivity disorder: From common simple deficits to multiple developmental pathways. *Biological Psychiatry*, **57**(11), 1231–1238. doi: 10.1016/j.biopsych.2004.09.008

Sonuga-Barke, E. J. S., Dalen, L., Daley, D., & Remington, B. (2002). Are planning, working memory, and inhibition associated with individual differences in preschool ADHD symptoms? *Developmental Neuropsychology*, **21**(3), 255–272. doi: 10.1207/S15326942DN2103_3

Sonuga-Barke, E. J. S., Dalen, L., & Remington, B. (2003). Do executive deficits and delay aversion make independent contributions to preschool attention-deficit/hyperactivity disorder symptoms? *Journal of the American Academy of Child and Adolescent Psychiatry*, **42**(11), 1335–1342. doi: 10.1097/01.chi.0000087564.34977.21

Sonuga-Barke, E. J. S., & Halperin, J. M. (2010). Developmental phenotypes and causal pathways in attention deficit/hyperactivity disorder: Potential targets for early intervention? *Journal of Child Psychology and Psychiatry*, **51**(4), 368–389. doi: 10.1111/j.1469-7610.2009.02195.x

St Clair-Thompson, H. L., & Gathercole, S. E. (2006). Executive functions and achievements in school: Shifting, updating, inhibition, and working memory. *The Quarterly Journal of Experimental Psychology*, **59**(4), 745–759. doi: 10.1080/17470210500162854

Stevens, C., Lauinger, B., & Neville, H. (2009). Differences in the neural mechanisms of selective attention in children from different socioeconomic backgrounds: An event-related brain potential study. *Developmental Science*, **12**(4), 634–646. doi: 10.1111/j.1467-7687.2009.00807.x

Swanson, J. M., Kraemer, H. C., Hinshaw, S. P., Arnold, L. E., Conners, C. K., Abikoff, H. B., et al. (2001). Clinical relevance of the primary findings of the MTA: Success rates based on severity of ADHD and ODD symptoms at the end of treatment. *Journal of the American Academy of Child and Adolescent Psychiatry*, **40**(2), 168–179. doi: 10.1097/00004583-200102000-00011

Swanson, J. M., Sandman, C. A., Deutsch, C., & Baren, M. (1983). Methylphenidate hydrochloride given with or before breakfast: I. Behavioral, cognitive, and electrophysiologic effects. *Pediatrics*, **72**(1), 49–55.

Szyf, M., & Bick, J. (2013). DNA methylation: A mechanism for embedding early life experiences in the genome. *Child Development*, **84**, 49–57. doi: 10.1111/j.1467-8624.2012.01793.x

Tamm, L., Menon, V., & Reiss, A. L. (2002). Maturation of brain function associated with response inhibition. *Journal of the American Academy of Child & Adolescent Psychiatry*, **41**(10), 1231–1238. doi: 10.1097/00004583-200210000-00013

Thatcher, R. W. (1992). Cyclic cortical reorganization during early childhood. *Brain and Cognition*, **20**(1), 24–50. doi: 10.1016/0278-2626(92) 90060-Y

Thatcher, R. W., North, D. M., & Biver, C. J. (2008). Development of cortical connections as measured by EEG coherence and phase delays. *Human Brain Mapping*, **29**(12), 1400–1415. doi: 10.1002/hbm.20474

Thorell, L., Lindqvist, S., Bergman, S., Bohlin, G., & Klingberg, T. (2009). Training and transfer effects of executive functions in preschool children. *Developmental Science*, **12**, 106–113. doi: 10.1111/j.1467-7687.2008.00745.x

Thorell, L. B., & Wåhlstedt, C. (2006). Executive functioning deficits in relation to symptoms of ADHD and/or ODD in preschool children. *Infant and Child Development*, **15**(5), 503–518. doi: 10.1002/icd.475

Toplak, M., Pitch, A., Flora, D., Iwenofu, L., Ghelani, K., Jain, U., et al. (2009). The unity and diversity of inattention and hyperactivity/impulsivity in ADHD: Evidence for a general factor with separable dimensions. *Journal of Abnormal Child Psychology*, **37**(8), 1137–1150. doi: 10.1007/s10802-009-9336-y

Toplak, M. E., Sorge, G. B., Flora, D. B., Chen, W., Banaschewski, T., Buitelaar, J., et al. (2012). The hierarchical factor model of ADHD: Invariant across age and national grouping? *Journal of Child Psychology and Psychiatry*, **53**(3), 292–303. doi: 10.1111/j.1469-7610.2011.02500.x

Tranel, D., Anderson, S. W., & Benton, A. (1994). Development of the concept of "executive function" and its relationship to the frontal lobes. In F. Boller & J. Grafman (Eds.), *Handbook of neuropsychology* (Vol. 9, pp. 125–148). Amsterdam, Netherlands: Elsevier.

van der Sluis, S., de Jong, P. F., & Van der Leij, A. (2007). Executive functioning in children, and its relations with reasoning, reading, and arithmetic. *Intelligence*, **35**(5), 427–449. doi: 10.1016/j.intell.2006.09.001

van der Sluis, S., de Jong, P. F., & Van der Leij, P. (2004). Inhibition and shifting in children with learning deficits in arithmetic and reading. *Journal of Experimental Child Psychology*, **87**, 239–266.

Vygotsky, L. S. (1978). *Mind in society: The development of higher psychological processes* (M. Cole, Ed.). Cambridge: Harvard University Press.

Wang, J., Zuo, X., & He, Y. (2010). Graph-based network analysis of resting-state functional MRI. *Frontiers in Systems Neuroscience*, **4**(16), 16. doi: 10.3389/fnsys.2010.00016

Wapner, S., & Demick, J. (2000). Assumptions, methods and research problems of the holistic, developmental systems-oriented perspective. In S. Wapner, J. Demick, T. Yamamoto, & S. Minami (Eds.), *Theoretical perspectives in environment-behavior research: Underlying assumptions, research problems and methodologies* (Vol. 7–19, pp. 7–19). New York, NY: Kluwer Academic.

Watanabe, H., Forssman, L., Green, D., Bohlin, G., & von Hofsten, C. (2012). Attention demands influence 10- and 12-month-old infants' perseverative behavior. *Developmental Psychology*, **48**(1), 46–55. doi: 10.1037/a0025412

Waxer, M., & Morton, J. B. (2011). The development of future-oriented control: An electrophysiological investigation. *NeuroImage*, **56**(3), 1648–1654. doi: 10.1016/j.neuroimage.2011.02.001

Welsh, J. A., Nix, R. L., Blair, C., Bierman, K. L., & Nelson, K. E. (2010). The development of cognitive skills and gains in academic school readiness for children from low-income families. *Journal of Educational Psychology*, **102**(1), 43–53. doi: 10.1037/a0016738

Welsh, M. C. (1991). Rule-guided behavior and self-monitoring on the Tower of Hanoi disk-transfer task. *Cognitive Development*, **6**(1), 59–76. doi: 10.1016/0885-2014(91)90006-Y

Wender, P. H. (1975). The minimal brain dysfunction syndrome. *Annual Reviews of Medicine*, **26**, 46–62. doi: 10.1146/annurev.me.26.020175.000401

Werner, H. (1957). The concept of development from a comparative and organismic point of view. In D. B. Harris (Ed.), *The concept of development* (pp. 125–148). Minneapolis: University of Minnesota Press.

Wiebe, S. A., Espy, K. A., & Charak, D. (2008). Using confirmatory factor analysis to understand executive control in preschool children: I. Latent structure. *Developmental Psychology*, **44**(2), 575–587. doi: 10.1037/0012-1649.44.2.575

Wiebe, S. A., Sheffield, T., Nelson, J. M., Clark, C. A. C., Chevalier, N., & Espy, K. A. (2011). The structure of executive function in 3-year-olds. *Journal of Experimental Child Psychology*, **108**(3), 436–452. doi: 10.1016/j.jecp.2010.08.008

Wiebe, S. A., Sheffield, T. D., & Espy, K. A. (2012). Separating the fish from the sharks: A longitudinal study of preschool response inhibition. *Child Development*, **83**(4), 1245–1261. doi: 10.1111/j.1467-8624.2012.01765.x

Willcutt, E. G., Doyle, A. E., Nigg, J. T., Faraone, S. V., & Pennington, B. F. (2005). Validity of the executive function theory of attention-deficit/hyperactivity disorder: A meta-analytic review. *Biological Psychiatry*, **57**(11), 1336–1346. doi: 10.1016/j.biopsych.2005.02.006

Willoughby, M. (2002). Developmental course of ADHD symptomatology during the transition from childhood to adolscence: A review with recommendations. *Journal of Child Psychology & Psychiatry*, **44**, 88–160. doi: 10.1111/1469-7610.t01-1-00104

Willoughby, M. T., Blair, C. B., Wirth, R. J., & Greenberg, M. (2010). The measurement of executive function at age 3 years: Psychometric properties and criterion validity of a new battery of tasks. *Psychological Assessment*, **22**(2), 306–317. doi: 10.1037/a0018708

Willoughby, M. T., Blair, C. B., Wirth, R. J., & Greenberg, M. (2012). The measurement of executive function at age 5: Psychometric properties and relationship to academic achievement. *Psychological Assessment*, **24**(1), 226–239. doi: 10.1037/a0025361

Willoughby, M. T., Kupersmidt, J. B., & Voegler-Lee, M. E. (2012). Is preschool executive function causally related to academic achievement? *Child Neuropsychology*, **18**(1), 79–91. doi: 10.1080/09297049.2011.578572

Willoughby, M. T., Pek, J., & Greenberg, M. T. (2012). Parent-reported attention deficit/hyperactivity symptomatology in preschool-aged children: Factor structure, developmental change, and early risk factors. *Journal of Abnormal Child Psychology*, **40**(8), 1301–1312. doi: 10.1007/s10802-012-9641-8

Willoughby, M. T., Wirth, R. J., & Blair, C. B. (2012). Executive function in early childhood: Longitudinal measurement invariance and developmental change. *Psychological Assessment*, **24**(2), 418–431. doi: 10.1037/a0025779

Wolfe, C. D., & Bell, M. A. (2004). Working memory and inhibitory control in early childhood: Contributions from physiology, temperament, and language. *Developmental Psychobiology*, **44**(1), 68–83. doi: 10.1002/dev.10152

Woodcock, R. W., McGrew, K. S., & Mather, N. (2001). *Woodcock-Johnson III tests of cognitive abilities*. Itasca, IL: Riverside Publishing.

Yap, P.-T., Fan, Y., Chen, Y., Gilmore, J. H., Lin, W., & Shen, D. (2011). Development trends of white matter connectivity in the first years of life. *PLoS ONE*, **6**(9), e24678. doi: 10.1371/journal.pone.0024678

Yeung, W. J., Linver, M. R., & Brooks-Gunn, J. (2002). How money matters for young children's development: Parental investment and family processes. *Child Development*, **73**(6), 1861–1879. doi: 10.1111/1467-8624.t01-1-00511

Yuan, K.-H., & Bentler, P. M. (2000). Three likelihood-based methods for mean and covariance structure analysis with nonnormal missing data. *Sociological Methodology*, **30**(1), 165–200. doi: 10.1111/0081-1750.00078

Zanto, T. P., Rubens, M. T., Thangavel, A., & Gazzaley, A. (2011). Causal role of the prefrontal cortex in top-down modulation of visual processing and working memory. *Nature Neuroscience*, **14**(5), 656–661. doi: 10.1038/nn.2773

Zelazo, P. D., Frye, D., & Rapus, T. (1996). An age-related dissociation between knowing rules and using them. *Cognitive Development*, **11**(1), 37–63. doi: 10.1016/S0885-2014(96)90027-1

Zelazo, P. D., Müller, U., Frye, D., & Marcovitch, S. (2003). The development of executive function in early childhood. *Monographs of the Society for Research in Child Development*, **68**(3), 11–27. doi: 10.1111/j.1540-5834.2003.06803001.x

Zelazo, P. D., Reznick, J. S., & Spinazzola, J. (1998). Representational flexibility and response control in a multistep multilocation search task. *Developmental Psychology*, **34**(2), 203–214. doi: 10.1037/0012-1649.34.2.203

ACKNOWLEDGMENTS

This article is part of the issue "The Changing Nature of Executive Control in Preschool" Espy (Issue Editor). For a full listing of articles in this issue, see: http://onlinelibrary.wiley.com/doi/10.1111/mono. v81.4/issuetoc.

This work was supported by a National Institutes of Health Grant MH065668 awarded to Kimberly Andrews Espy. The authors gratefully acknowledge members of the Developmental Cognitive Neuroscience Laboratory at the University of Nebraska-Lincoln for their assistance with data collection, coding, and processing. A special thank you to all the children and families who graciously gave up their time to participate in the study.

DOI: 10.1111/mono.12275

COMMENTARY

COMMENTARY ON THE CHANGING NATURE OF EXECUTIVE CONTROL IN PRESCHOOL

Michael T. Willoughby

This article is part of the issue "The Changing Nature of Executive Control in Preschool" Espy (Issue Editor). For a full listing of articles in this issue, see: http://onlinelibrary.wiley.com/doi/10.1111/mono. v81.4/issuetoc.

In this commentary, I provide a critical evaluation of Espy and colleagues' proposal to use a bifactor modeling approach to characterize children's performance on executive control tasks. I draw attention to an old idea regarding treating items as causal or effect indicators of their latent constructs. I remind readers that factor analytic approaches, including the bifactor model that is proposed here, assume that executive control tasks are effect indicators of the latent construct of executive control. I suggest that executive control tasks may be better conceptualized as causal indicators. I further suggest that these different modeling approaches will result in markedly different conclusions about the nature of executive control—including predictors and outcomes of executive control that were the focus of this monograph.

OVERVIEW

In this well-written and provocative monograph, Espy and colleagues propose a solution to a "measurement impurity" problem as it applies to the

Corresponding author: Michael T. Willoughby, RTI International, Hobbs 349, Research Triangle Park, NC 27709. E-mail: mwilloughby@rti.org
DOI: 10.1111/mono.12276

assessment of executive control among preschool-aged children. The measurement impurity problem refers to a concern that an individual's performance on executive control tasks is the results of a range of cognitive processes. As a result, the observed variation in executive control task scores represents a combination of executive control and nonexecutive control abilities (i.e., the observed tasks are "impure" indicators of true executive control ability). In this monograph, a strong distinction was made between executive control abilities (ECA) and foundational cognitive abilities (FCA). Espy and colleagues emphasize that both ECA and FCA contribute to children's performance on executive control tasks.[1] Espy and colleagues propose that when specific measures of ECA and FCA are available, bifactor structural equation models can be used to partition children's performance on executive control tasks into ECA- and FCA-specific variation. This partitioning of the observed task score variation into ECA and FCA components is purported to solve the measurement impurity problem. As a result of applying this approach to new data, Espy and colleagues arrive at a number of provocative conclusions that contradict previous studies. The implication is that many previous results may have been spurious due to the failure of previous studies to distinguish ECA from FCA. Given the seminal contributions that Espy and her colleagues have made to the measurement of executive control in early childhood, these conclusions are likely to take on greater gravity than would be the case if they were reported by others.

Despite my admiration for the programmatic work of Espy and her colleagues in this area, I have concerns with the approach that they propose here, and with the conclusions that result from it. In this commentary, I propose that neither the application of traditional factor analytic models (exploratory or confirmatory) nor specific elaborations of those models (i.e., bifactor models) are optimal for characterizing children's performance across a battery of executive control tasks. My proposal builds on ideas that I have elaborated in greater detail elsewhere (Willoughby, 2014; Willoughby, Holochwost, Blanton, & Blair, 2014; Willoughby, Blair, & Family Life Project, 2016).

Early Childhood as a Unique Development Period for Measuring Executive Control

Before detailing my points of disagreement with the approach advocated in this monograph, I want to highlight what I consider one of its central contributions. Building on her pioneering contributions to the measurement of ECA in young children (Espy, 1997; Espy & Kaufmann, 2001; Espy, Kaufmann, & Glisky, 1999; Espy, Kaufmann, McDiarmid, & Glisky, 1999; Espy, Kaufmann, Glisky, & McDiarmid, 2001), Espy and colleagues articulate a strong, developmentally informed rationale for why the measurement of ECA should not be conceived as a simple downward extension of its measurement in older children or adults. To set this stage, ECAs are described metaphorically as the "conductor" of an orchestra that consists of "fundamental sensory, perceptual, language, motor, and other subordinate mental processes" (p. 3). In mature adults, these fundamental or foundational aspects of cognition are what ECAs "direct." That is, executive control abilities are conceptualized as a hierarchically situated set of attentional control processes that serve to modify (inhibit, augment, prioritize) sensory, perceptual, language, motivational, and motor processes.

Espy and colleagues remind the reader that both ECAs and the FCAs (upon which ECAs act) are undergoing substantial developmental change and reorganization during early childhood. Hence, early childhood is not only characterized as a period in which ECAs undergo quantitative changes (e.g., in efficiency of inhibitory control or length of working memory span) and qualitative changes (e.g., in the specific strategies that are used to solve executive tasks), it is also a period in which there are marked individual differences in semantic processing of task demands, general processing speed, language production, and motor control processes that are necessary to complete many executive tasks. Although not explicitly discussed in the monograph, a number of other emerging child attributes (e.g., temperamental or motivational factors related to engaging in novel tasks or willingness to respond to adult requests) likely also contribute to individual differences in ECA task performance, although they do not reflect underlying ECAs, per se. The important point is that early childhood may be a period in which it is uniquely challenging to measure ECA abilities due not only to developmental changes in ECAs but also to concomitant changes in FCAs upon which ECAs act. This perspective departs from many research studies in current applied literature in which ECAs are often treated, either implicitly or explicitly, as independent of FCAs. Moreover, this perspective underscores the importance of using tasks that were specifically developed for young children, the value of adopting a longitudinal approach to discern whether and when changes in the underlying construct of ECA occur, and the importance of obtaining direct assessments of both executive control and general cognitive abilities in young children. This monograph was unique in that it attended to all of these issues.

A 30,000-Foot Perspective of Measurement Models

Both classic and modern measurement theories share the assumptions that (1) although latent variables are not directly measurable, specific manifestations of those latent variables are, and (2) the specific manifest indicators of a latent construct are *effect* indicators. Effect indicators are defined as specific instantiations of an underlying latent variable (equivalently, latent variables are said to "give rise" to effect indicators). For example, parent ratings of the frequency with which a child hits, kicks, or bites others can be conceived of as three specific indicators of the latent construct of aggression. Although aggression cannot be directly measured, these specific manifestations of the construct can be. Due to their shared association with the underlying construct of aggression, these indicators will be positively correlated with each other. These positive correlations form the basis for making inferences about the precision of measurement (reliability) of the underlying construct (Bollen, 1984).

Although less commonly considered, the association between manifest indicators and a latent construct can be reversed. That is, some latent constructs may be defined by (rather than giving rise to) their manifest indicators. In these cases, the latent construct is described as having causal indicators. The canonical example is socioeconomic status, which can be conceived of as resulting from one's educational attainment, job prestige, and household income. Importantly, there is no presumption that a set of causal indicators of a latent construct be positively correlated with each other (e.g., there is no requirement that as one's household income increases that his/her educational attainment or job prestige will also necessarily increase). To the extent that this is true, it renders traditional indices of precision of measurement (reliability) irrelevant (Bollen, 1984; Bollen & Lennox, 1991).

The crux of my concern with the measurement approach that is being advocated by Espy and colleagues is that executive control tasks are assumed to be effect indicators of the latent construct of executive control. To be clear, all studies that use factor analytic models to represent individual differences in the latent construct of executive control implicitly treat executive control tasks as effect indicators—this is not unique to the bifactor model that is being proposed here. My contention is that bifactor models exacerbate the problems of treating executive control tasks as effect indicators of the latent construct of executive control abilities.

Bollen and Bauldry (2011) recently drew a distinction between causal indicators, composite indicators, and covariates (what they called the "3 Cs" of measurement). Although a full characterization of these differences is beyond the scope of this commentary, two points are noteworthy. First, causal and effect indicators both assume conceptual unity. That is, they are chosen because they correspond to a shared understanding of the meaning of the underlying latent construct to which they are associated. Moreover, irrespective of whether a construct is defined by effect indicators, causal indicators, or some combination thereof, it is latent because it is not directly observable. Second, although covariates are typically only considered in the context of regression models, they can also play a role in measurement models. Specifically, covariates are variables that are associated with a latent variable and/or its (causal and/or effect) indicators. Covariates do not share conceptual unity with a latent variable; however, their omission has the potential to bias the estimates of the association between indicators and their corresponding latent variables. Conceiving of FCAs as covariates represents an alternative strategy for acknowledging their involvement in ECAs that does not require the adoption of a bifactor model.

A final idea that is necessary to follow my arguments below is an appreciation for different levels of measurement (see Willoughby et al., 2014). Measurement models can be applied to (1) item-level data from individual EC tasks in order to create EC task scores and (2) task-level data across tasks in order to create EC battery-wide scores. The former and latter can be conceived of as lower- and higher-order measurement models, respectively. For example, the individual responses to the Big-Little Stroop task can be conceived of as indicators of the underlying construct of inhibitory control. This lower-order level of measurement is not a focus of this monograph. Instead, this monograph focuses entirely on a higher-order level of measurement in which specific tasks are used as indicators of the construct of executive control. For example, the Big-Little Stroop task is considered along with the Shape School task (Inhibit condition) and the modified Snack Delay tasks as specific indicators of inhibitory control (a higher-order construct). This distinction between lower- and higher-order measurement is important because whereas individual executive control tasks are appropriately characterized by traditional measurement models (i.e., the items on any specific task are reasonably conceived of as effect indicators of the specific cognitive process that the task is attempting to measure), the higher-order construct of executive control may not be (i.e., individual task scores may be better conceived of as causal indicators).

Performance-Based Executive Control Tasks Are Weakly Correlated

Espy and colleagues report bivariate associations between executive control and foundational cognitive tasks separately by each age group (see Table 3). Notably, the correlations between children's performance across these tasks were quite modest. The mean correlations among the executive control tasks were $r=.20$ (3 years, 0 months), $r=.21$ (3 years, 9 months), $r=.20$ (4 years, 6 months), and $r=.17$ (5 years, 3 months) across the four assessments. The magnitude of these inter-task correlations is consistent with many other studies involving direct assessments of executive control in samples of children and adults of varying ages (Willoughby et al., 2014). Modest correlations among EC tasks is the rule, not the exception. Three points are worth emphasizing. First, on average, children's performance on any two EC tasks in this study shared approximately 2% to 9% of their variation, despite the fact that they were purportedly measuring the same underlying construct. In practice, when factor analytic models are applied to executive control tasks that are weakly associated, a majority of the observed variation in any task is relegated to the residual variance term (i.e., most of the variance in any task is conceived of as task-specific and/or measurement error). Second, given the modest associations among EC tasks, it is not surprising that most confirmatory factor analysis and bifactor models will result in excellent fit to the observed data. Excellent fit demonstrates that the models do a good job of reproducing the small amounts of variation shared among the set of tasks—it does not provide any assurance that the construct of executive control has been measured well. Third, all factor analytic (including bifactor) models assume that their (effect) indicators are interchangeable. That is, the addition or removal of individual EC tasks is assumed to have no impact on the meaning of the latent construct. Although this assumption seems plausible when tasks are moderate to strongly correlated, it becomes less so when tasks are only weakly correlated.

A unifying idea of all of the foregoing concerns is that the correlations among executive control tasks may be *too small* to be useful in factor analytic models of any type (e.g., exploratory, confirmatory, bifactor, hierarchical). However, Espy and colleagues suggest that the observed correlations between EC tasks are actually *too big* (see Figure 2). That is, from their perspective, not only do the correlations among EC tasks reflect individual differences in EC abilities, they also reflect individual differences in foundational cognitive abilities. The bifactor model is introduced as a specific strategy for attending to this problem. Specifically, the bifactor model extends traditional confirmatory factor models by introducing additional parameters that partition the (already modest amounts of) shared variation among EC tasks into executive control and foundational cognitive ability components.

Concerns With Applying a Bifactor Model to Executive Control Task Data

I have four concerns with the use of the bifactor modeling approach that was proposed in this monograph. First, bifactor models define the latent construct of executive control exclusively as that variation that is shared across the EC tasks. This does not confirm to modern theoretical definitions, which emphasize that executive control is an umbrella term that refers to a range of cognitive processes that collectively contribute to problem-solving and goal-setting pursuits. The bifactor modeling approach results in the latent construct of executive control that is defined entirely by the limited amount of variation that is shared across the set of cognitive processes that are measured by specific EC tasks. An alternative appropriate approach might characterize the latent construct of executive control as the summation of these cognitive processes, which may better utilize the nonoverlapping variance between tasks.

My second concern with applying the bifactor model to EC task data is that it forces the constructs of executive control and foundational cognitive abilities to be orthogonal. Imposing orthogonality on foundational cognitive and executive control abilities contradicts a large literature that has documented positive correlations between fluid cognition (including executive control abilities) and crystallized (including foundational cognitive abilities) aspects of general intelligence (Ackerman, Beier, & Boyle, 2005; Blair, 2006; Conway, Kane, & Engle, 2003; Kane, Hambrick, & Conway, 2005). Imposing an orthogonal association between ECA and FCA constructs also contradicts Espy and colleagues' earlier characterization of these constructs as hierarchically organized (i.e., ECAs act on FCAs; Chapter I).

My third concern with applying the bifactor model to EC task data is that it implicitly "stacks the deck" toward having better measurement of the FCA construct than the ECA construct. The FCA construct is based on 12 indicators, of which 9 overlap with executive control and 3 are unique. In contrast, the ECA construct is based entirely on the nine indicators that are shared with the FCA construct. The three indicators that are unique to the foundational cognitive abilities construct (i.e., Verbal Comprehension, Concept Formation, and Visual Matching subtests from the WJ-III Brief Intellectual Assessment) are arguably the best measures available because they involve testing children's limits (i.e., item difficulty increases across trials until form termination criteria are met). Given these differences, it is perhaps not surprising that the FCA construct is reported to have three times as much variance as the ECA construct at the age 4 year 6 month assessment (ψs $= .21$ and $.07$) and four times as much variance at the age 5 year 3 month assessment (ψs $= .22$ and $.05$). These differences in measurement and variability in constructs likely contribute to some of the provocative conclusions that result from pitting foundational cognitive and executive control abilities against each other as predictors and outcomes.

My fourth concern with applying the bifactor model to EC task data is that it distorts the across-time stability of the construct. Although consideration of longitudinal associations are unfortunately not a central feature of this monograph, the authors note in passing that the ECA construct was highly stable across time, with stability coefficients of .73–.94 across the four measurement occasions (see Discussion, Chapter III). The across-time stability of the latent construct was likely much larger than the across-time stability of individual tasks. This would be consistent with recent work in which my colleagues and I demonstrated how the across-time stability of the latent construct of executive function (analogous to executive control here) was markedly larger (and perhaps implausibly large) when tasks were treated as effect versus causal indicators (Willoughby et al., 2016b). We attributed these differences in stability to a statistical artifact of factoring tasks that are weakly correlated (i.e., although it is not clear what is being extracted from executive control tasks that are weakly associated, whatever it is, it is highly stable). When the latent construct of executive control exhibits large stability estimates across early childhood, it has the potential to be interpreted as evidence that individual differences in executive control are nearly completely determined early in life. This contradicts evidence that executive control abilities are malleable across the lifespan (Hsu, Novick, & Jaeggi, 2014).

Concerns With Monograph Conclusions

Through their application of the bifactor model to executive control data, Espy and colleagues arrive at three provocative conclusions that demand close attention and follow-up study. First, they conclude that executive control does not exist as a construct separate from foundational cognitive abilities until children are 4 years old or older (see Chapter III). By implication, prior to age 4, children's executive control abilities are apparently so completely enmeshed with general cognitive abilities that they cannot be conceived of as a separate construct—at least not using performance-based measures (the prospect of differentiating it at the level of neurophysiology is briefly noted in Chapter VI). This conclusion appears to call into question the efforts of a number of research groups to develop and evaluate performance-based measures of executive control for use with children between 2 and 4 years old (Carlson, Faja, & Beck, 2015; Garon, Smith, & Bryson, 2014; Mulder, Hoofs, Verhagen, van der Veen, & Leseman, 2014; Willoughby, Blair, Wirth, Greenberg, & the Family Life Project Investigators, 2010). This conclusion also appears to call into question the rationale for and interpretation of studies that have linked individual differences in neural functioning with performance on measures of executive control (working memory) in infancy (Cuevas & Bell, 2011; Cuevas, Raj, & Bell, 2012; Short et al., 2013). These studies are predicated on the idea that executive control is a distinct construct in infancy; however, the results of this monograph suggest otherwise. In my opinion, we should be wary of suggestions that executive control is somehow not amenable to empirical study as an independent construct prior to age 4 solely on the basis of a statistical characterization of data that may be predicated on inappropriate assumptions.

The second provocative conclusion is that measures of socio-familial adversity are predictive of foundational cognitive abilities, but not of executive control (Chapter IV). The authors state

Findings indicate that the mechanism by which socio-familial adversity relates to executive task performance at ages 4;6 and 5;3 is through its relation to foundational

cognitive abilities, the substrates upon which the EC processes act to enable well-regulated, goal-directed thoughts and behaviors. More specifically, distal and proximal aspects of children's socio-familial environments explained variance that was common to both EC and foundational cognitive tasks during the late preschool period but showed little to no independent relation to EC-specific variance in the bifactor models. Thus, children's access to concrete learning supports and stimulation appears to foster the development of foundational cognitive abilities that are drawn upon by EC in the dynamic context of performing executive tasks and yet show no identifiably distinctive relation to the construct engaged specifically in EC tasks. Such findings have important theoretical and applied implications.

Findings were substantively different when EC was modeled using a bifactor approach as opposed to more traditional approach incorporating only the executive tasks. Results from the traditional, unitary models correspond with several studies reporting decrements in EC performance among children exposed to socio-familial adversity, with effect sizes being quite substantial (socio-familial factors explained 15–17% of the variance in latent EC). However, results from the bi-factor models argue against the notion that EC is uniquely or specifically vulnerable, with effect sizes dropping to < 6%. The benefits of the bifactor approach are immediately apparent, as the approach identifies potential mechanisms of socio-familial effects within executive task performance itself. Specifically, it is the general skills that are brought to bear when performing any cognitive task, rather than more discrete control processes per se, that are most related to social risk in this age group.

. . .Essentially, if the foundational cognitive skills are deleteriously affected, then EC cannot properly integrate the weaker representations, which will result in poorer observed performance on executive tasks.

It is important to point out that this interpretation invokes the idea that executive control and foundational cognitive abilities are hierarchically organized constructs. Socio-familial risk factors are characterized as impacting executive control by undermining the development of foundational cognitive skills. However, this interpretation departs from what was actually modeled. The models depicted in Figures 12 and 13 do not permit any inferences about indirect associations between socio-familial adversity and the construct of executive control through intervening effects on foundational cognitive abilities. As noted earlier, the bifactor parameterization treats the executive control and foundational cognitive ability constructs as orthogonal.

This interpretational problem notwithstanding, these conclusions appear to undermine the results of a number of recent studies that have linked socioeconomic status (which is correlated with socio-familial adversity) to individual differences in executive control (Brown, Ackerman, & Moore, 2013; Fernald, Weber, Galasso, & Ratsifandrihamanana, 2011; Hackman, Gallop, Evans, & Farah, 2015; Nesbitt, Baker-Ward, & Willoughby, 2013; Raver, Blair, Willoughby & the Family Life Project Investigators, 2013). From the vantage of Espy and colleagues, these recent studies may have generated spurious results due to their failure to differentiate executive control from foundational cognitive abilities. Espy and colleagues raise an important point. Many recent studies have focused on associations between early measures of socioeconomic adversity and executive control (or equivalently executive function) without consideration of other aspects of children's cognitive function. This approach has the potential to reify ideas that socioeconomic adversity is uniquely (or preferentially) related to executive control. Considering a wide range of cognitive processes that may be negatively impacted through socio-familial adversity makes good conceptual sense. However, these cognitive processes are more appropriately considered as correlated outcomes, which departs from what was done here.

The third provocative conclusion is that foundational cognitive abilities but not executive control are uniquely predictive of children's overall level of attention deficit/hyperactivity disorder (ADHD) behaviors (Chapter V). Although it is well established that general indices of cognitive function are related to ADHD (Frazier, Demaree, & Youngstrom, 2004), the suggestion that executive control is unrelated to ADHD behaviors contradicts the available meta-analytic evidence involving preschool and school-aged samples (Pauli-Pott & Becker, 2011; Willcutt, Doyle, Nigg, Faraone, & Pennington, 2005). Once again, the insinuation is that these previous conclusions were spurious given their failure to attend to the distinction between foundational cognitive and executive control processes that is emphasized here. Although the authors also report that executive control is uniquely predictive of a hyperactive subcomponent of ADHD (which was modeled as orthogonal to general risk for ADHD), this conclusion contradicts other studies that have emphasized that executive control processes are related to inattentive but not hyperactive-impulsive aspects of ADHD (Martel & Nigg, 2006; Martel, Nigg, & Lucas, 2008; Martel, Nigg, & von Eye, 2009). I am suspect of Espy and colleagues' novel conclusions, given my previous concerns that their modeling approach (1) mischaracterizes the construct of EC tasks (as effect indicators); (2) mischaracterizes the association between EC constructs (as orthogonal not correlated); and (3) privileges the measurement of foundational cognitive over executive control abilities (due to the availability of more and better indicators).

An Alternative Approach

It would be presumptuous for me or anyone else to suggest that there was a singular best way for Espy and colleagues to have analyzed their data. Here, I briefly sketch an alternative modeling approach.

1. Fit formal measurement models to executive control task data. It is often the case that executive control tasks are scored using arbitrary or "common sense" approaches. These approaches do not attend to measurement error at the item-level data for individual tasks. Fitting formal measurement models has the benefit of creating indicators for latent constructs of executive control that have been purged of measurement error that occurs at the level of individual tasks (see Willoughby, Wirth, & Blair, 2011). If there are concerns that the item-level data reflect some combination of foundational cognitive and executive control abilities, consider using proxies for foundational cognitive abilities as covariates in task-level measurement models (see Bollen & Bauldry, 2011).

2. Consider using executive control task scores as causal or composite indicators of the latent construct of executive control. The specific approach will depend on the motivating questions being asked and the available data. The important idea is to characterize the latent construct of executive control as the summation of abilities that are assessed by individual tasks. This represents a counterpoint to current characterizations of executive control as exclusively that variation that is common or shared across a set of individual tasks.

3. Contrast the results from models that are built using these two general steps (above) with those obtained from fitting models that use factor analytic approaches for aggregating task-level data (this includes traditional confirmatory factor analytic models, as well as the bifactor models that were the focus of this monograph). In my work, these comparisons have revealed markedly different conclusions about the apparent continuity and change in executive control abilities across intervals ranging from 2 weeks to 2 years (Willoughby, Kuhn, Blair, Samek, & List, 2016). I expect that these comparisons would results in markedly different conclusions about predictors and outcomes of executive control as well.

CONCLUSIONS

Over the last 15 years, I have reviewed hundreds of manuscripts that were submitted to developmental and cognitively oriented journals, and many of these manuscripts have focused on executive control and related topics. Over this time, there have been very few manuscripts that I have enjoyed reading as much as this monograph. Espy and colleagues are to be commended on their efforts to "push the envelope" in terms of the way that the field both conceives of and models executive control task data. I was especially appreciative of the effort that was made to link a developmentally informed conceptualization of the construct of executive control with an explicit modeling approach. The ways in which we conceive of and model constructs are intricately bound, and I would argue are bidirectional in nature (e.g., new modeling approaches challenge us to think more clearly about how we conceive of constructs). The logic and rationale for the approach that Espy and colleagues used was reasoned, and their resulting conclusions were audacious. As I noted at the outset, none of this is surprising, given the pioneering contributions that Espy and her colleagues have made to the measurement of executive control in children.

Despite my enthusiasm for the general objectives of this work, as well as the concerted efforts to apply a developmental perspective to the development and modeling of executive control abilities, I have concerns with the specific approach that has been advocated here. Many of us who were trained in the principles of psychological measurement, myself included, reflexively assume that all constructs conform to conventional measurement wisdom. As a result, we assume that executive control tasks are best conceptualized as effect indicators of the latent construct of executive control. This has given rise to the widespread use of factor analytic (and related) models for modeling executive control task data. The bifactor modeling approach that was endorsed here is entirely consistent with that tradition. However, many researchers are not aware that they are making any assumption about the nature of the latent construct of executive control when they fit factor analytic (including bifactor) models.

My primary objective in this commentary has been to draw attention to the possibility that executive control tasks may be better conceptualized as causal indicators of the latent construct of executive control. I use the word "may" because I am not completely convinced that this is accurate and am unaware of any single approach for definitively testing this possibility. Instead, I expect that a combination of theoretical, empirical, and pragmatic evidence will need to be marshaled to inform the best way to model the latent construct of executive control. All of the provocative conclusions that were put forth in this monograph were predicated on the application of a bifactor model to executive control and foundational cognitive ability data. In this commentary, I have highlighted reasons that we should be skeptical of applying bifactor models to executive control data and have sketched a potential alternative approach. I am hopeful that others will bring their own data to bear on these important questions.

NOTE

1. I adopt the terminology of executive control that is used in the monograph. For purposes of this commentary, I consider executive control to be synonymous with executive functions and to be partially overlapping with some characterizations of effortful control. That is, I assume that these differences in terminology originate from different disciplinary emphases and that they refer to the same (or highly overlapping) cognitive processes.

REFERENCES

Ackerman, P. L., Beier, M. E., & Boyle, M. O. (2005). Working memory and intelligence: The same or different constructs? *Psychological Bulletin*, **131** (1), 30–60. Retrieved from <Go to ISI>://WOS: 000226272000002

Blair, C. (2006). How similar are fluid cognition and general intelligence? A developmental neuroscience perspective on fluid cognition as an aspect of human cognitive ability. *Behavioral and Brain Sciences*, **29**(2), 109–+. Retrieved from <Go to ISI>:// 000237215900001

Bollen, K. A. (1984). Multiple indicators: Internal consistency or no necessary relationship? *Quality and Quantity*, **18**, 377–385.

Bollen, K. A., & Bauldry, S. (2011). Three Cs in measurement models: Causal indicators, composite indicators, and covariates. *Psychological Methods*, **16**(3), 265–284. doi: 10.1037/A0024448

Bollen, K., & Lennox, R. (1991). Conventional wisdom on measurement—A structural equation perspective. *Psychological Bulletin*, **110**(2), 305–314. Retrieved from <Go to ISI>://A1991GE03600009

Brown, E. D., Ackerman, B. P., & Moore, C. A. (2013). Family adversity and inhibitory control for economically disadvantaged children: Preschool relations and associations with school readiness. *Journal of Family Psychology*, **27**(3), 443–452. doi: 10.1037/A0032886

Carlson, S. M., Faja, S., & Beck, D. M. (2015). Incorporating early development into measurement approaches: The need for a continuum of measures across development. In J. A. Griffin, L. S. Freund, & P. McCardle (Eds.), *Executive function in preschool age children: Integrating measurement, neurodevelopment, and translational research*. Washington, DC: American Psychological Association.

Conway, A. R. A., Kane, M. J., & Engle, R. W. (2003). Working memory capacity and its relation to general intelligence. *Trends in Cognitive Sciences*, **7**(12), 547–552. Retrieved from <Go to ISI>://WOS: 000187223400011

Cuevas, K., & Bell, M. A. (2011). EEG and ECG from 5 to 10 months of age: Developmental changes in baseline activation and cognitive processing during a working memory task. *International Journal of Psychophysiology*, **80**(2), 119–128. Retrieved from <Go to ISI>:// WOS: 000290648300005

Cuevas, K., Raj, V., & Bell, M. A. (2012). Functional connectivity and infant spatial working memory: A frequency band analysis. *Psychophysiology*, **49**(2), 271–280. Retrieved from <Go to ISI>://WOS: 000299335600015

Espy, K. A. (1997). The shape school: Assessing executive function in preschool children. *Developmental Neuropsychology*, **13**(4), 495–499.

Espy, K. A., & Kaufmann, P. M. (2001). Individual differences in the development of executive function in children: Lessons from the delayed response and A-not-B tasks. In D. L. Molfese & V. J. Molfese (Eds.), *Developmental variations in learning: applications to social, executive function, language, and reading skills* (pp. 113–137). Mahwah: Lawrence Erlbaum.

Espy, K. A., Kaufmann, P. M., & Glisky, M. L. (1999). Neuropsychologic function in toddlers exposed to cocaine in utero: A preliminary study. *Developmental Neuropsychology*, **15**(3), 447–460. Retrieved from <Go to ISI>://WOS: 000080446100008

Espy, K. A., Kaufmann, P. M., Glisky, M. L., & McDiarmid, M. D. (2001). New procedures to assess executive functions in preschool children. *The Clinical Neuropsychologist*, **15**(1), 46–58.

Espy, K. A., Kaufmann, P. M., McDiarmid, M. D., & Glisky, M. L. (1999). Executive functioning in preschool children: Performance on A-not-B and other delayed response format tasks. *Brain and Cognition*, **41**(2), 178–199.

Fernald, L. C. H., Weber, A., Galasso, E., & Ratsifandrihamanana, L. (2011). Socioeconomic gradients and child development in a very low income population: Evidence from Madagascar. *Developmental Science*, **14**(4), 832–847. doi: 10.1111/j.1467-7687.2010.01032.x

Frazier, T. W., Demaree, H. A., & Youngstrom, E. A. (2004). Meta-analysis of intellectual and neuropsychological test performance in attention-deficit/hyperactivity disorder. *Neuropsychology*, **18**(3), 543–555. doi: 10.1037/0894-4105.18.3.543

Garon, N., Smith, I. M., & Bryson, S. E. (2014). A novel executive function battery for preschoolers: Sensitivity to age differences. *Child Neuropsychology*, **20**(6), 713–736. doi: 10.1080/09297049.2013.857650

Hackman, D. A., Gallop, R., Evans, G. W., & Farah, M. J. (2015). Socioeconomic status and executive function: Developmental trajectories and mediation. *Developmental Science*, **18**(5), 686–702. doi: 10.1111/desc.12246

Hsu, N. S., Novick, J. M., & Jaeggi, S. M. (2014). The development and malleability of executive control abilities. *Frontiers in Behavioral Neuroscience*, **8**, 1–16. doi:10.3389/ fnbeh.2014.00221

Kane, M. J., Hambrick, D. Z., & Conway, A. R. A. (2005). Working memory capacity and fluid intelligence are strongly related constructs: Comment on Ackerman, Beier, and Boyle (2005). *Psychological Bulletin*, **131**(1), 66–71. Retrieved from <Go to ISI>://WOS: 000226272000004

Martel, M. M., & Nigg, J. T. (2006). Child ADHD and personality/temperament traits of reactive and effortful control, resiliency, and emotionality. *Journal of Child Psychology and Psychiatry*, **47**(11), 1175–1183. doi: 10.1111/j.1469-7610.2006.01629.x

Martel, M. M., Nigg, J. T., & Lucas, R. E. (2008). Trait mechanisms in youth with and without attention-deficit/hyperactivity disorder. *Journal of Research in Personality*, **42**(4), 895–913. Retrieved from <Go to ISI>://000257131100008

Martel, M. M., Nigg, J. T., & von Eye, A. (2009). How do trait dimensions map onto ADHD symptom domains? *Journal of Abnormal Child Psychology*, **37**(3), 337–348. Retrieved from<Go to ISI>://000264483400004

Mulder, H., Hoofs, H., Verhagen, J., van der Veen, I., & Leseman, P. P. M. (2014). Psychometric properties and convergent and predictive validity of an executive function test battery for two-year-olds. *Frontiers in Psychology*, **5**, 1–17. doi: 10.3389/Fpsyg.2014.00733

Nesbitt, K. T., Baker-Ward, L., & Willoughby, M. T. (2013). Executive function mediates socio-economic and racial differences in early academic achievement. *Early Childhood Research Quarterly*, **28**(4), 774–783. doi: 10.1016/j.ecresq.2013.07.005

Pauli-Pott, U., & Becker, K. (2011). Neuropsychological basic deficits in preschoolers at risk for ADHD: A meta-analysis. *Clinical Psychology Review*, **31**(4), 626–637. doi: 10.1016/j.cpr.2011.02.005

Raver, C. C., Blair, C., Willoughby, M., & the Family Life Project Investigators. (2013). Poverty as a predictor of 4-year-olds' executive function: New perspectives on models of differential susceptibility. *Developmental Psychology*, **49**(2), 292–304. doi: 10.1037/A0028343

Short, S. J., Elison, J. T., Goldman, B. D., Styner, M., Gu, H. B., Connelly, M., et al. (2013). Associations between white matter microstructure and infants' working memory. *Neuroimage*, **64**, 156–166. Retrieved from <Go to ISI>://WOS: 000312504200015

Willcutt, E. G., Doyle, A. E., Nigg, J. T., Faraone, S. V., & Pennington, B. F. (2005). Validity of the executive function theory of attention-deficit/hyperactivity disorder: A meta-analytic review. *Biological Psychiatry*, **57**(11), 1336–1346. Retrieved from <Go to ISI>://000229570500017

Willoughby, M. T. (2014). Formative versus reflective measurement of executive function tasks: Response to commentaries and another perspective. *Measurement: Interdisciplinary Research and Perspectives*, **12**(4), 173–178. doi: 10.1080/15366367.2014.981074

Willoughby, M. T., Blair, C. B., & the Family Life Project Investigators. (2016). Measuring executive function in early childhood: A case for formative measurement. *Psychological Assessment*, **28**(3), 319–30. doi: 10.1037/pas0000152

Willoughby, M. T., Blair, C. B., Wirth, R. J., Greenberg, M., & the Family Life Project Investigators. (2010). The measurement of executive function at age 3 years: Psychometric properties and criterion validity of a new battery of tasks. *Psychological Assessment*, **22**(2), 306–317. Retrieved from<Go to ISI>://000278665600011

Willoughby, M. T., Holochwost, S. J., Blanton, Z. E., & Blair, C. B. (2014). Executive functions: Formative versus reflective measurement. *Measurement: Interdisciplinary Research and Perspectives*, **12**(3), 69–95. doi: 10.1080/15366367.2014.929453

Willoughby, M.T., Kuhn, L. J., Blair, C. B., Samek, A., & List, J. A. (2016). The test-retest reliability of the latent construct of executive functions depends on whether task are used as causal or effect indicators. *Child Neuropsychology*, 1–16.

Willoughby, M. T., Wirth, R. J., & Blair, C. B. (2011). Contributions of modern measurement theory to measuring executive function in early childhood: An empirical demonstration. *Journal of Experimental Child Psychology*, **108**(3), 414–435.

CONTRIBUTORS

This article is part of the issue "The Changing Nature of Executive Control in Preschool" Espy (Issue Editor). For a full listing of articles in this issue, see: http://onlinelibrary.wiley.com/doi/10.1111/mono. v81.4/issuetoc.

Kimberly Andrews Espy, Ph.D., is the Senior Vice President for Research at the University of Arizona and Director of the Developmental Cognitive Neuroscience Laboratory at the University of Nebraska–Lincoln. Her research focuses on identifying the antecedents of learning, attention, and behavioral disorders in medically at-risk populations, including those born prematurely, those exposed to substances of abuse during pregnancy, and those exposed to neurotoxins in the environment. For the past two decades, she has studied the normative development of emergent executive control skills in young children and infants.

Nicolas Chevalier, Ph.D., is a Chancellor's Fellow in the Department of Psychology at the University of Edinburgh (Edinburgh, UK). His work addresses cognitive development, especially executive function, during childhood. He is particularly interested in how children determine what they need to do and how to best engage control based on environmental information, available cognitive means, and previous experiences.

Hye-Jeong Choi, Ph.D., is an Assistant Research Scientist and an Adjunct Assistant Professor in Quantitative Methodology in the Department of Educational Psychology at the University of Georgia. Her expertise is in applied statistics with a focus on psychometric and latent variable models. Her research focuses on item response theory and diagnostic measurement.

DOI: 10.1111/mono.12277

Caron A. C. Clark, Ph.D., is an Assistant Professor in the Department of Educational Psychology at the University of Nebraska-Lincoln. Her research focuses on the development of self-regulation, with specific interests in the relation of perinatal experiences and early adversity to executive control development and in the influence of executive control on mathematics learning.

John P. Garza, Ph.D., is a Senior Research Associate in the Developmental Cognitive Neuroscience Laboratory at the University of Nebraska–Lincoln. His broad research interest is in the development of selective attention and executive control across the lifespan. He uses behavioral and electrophysiological measures to examine contextual sources of attentional bias.

Tiffany D. James, M.A., is the statistical analyst in the Developmental Cognitive Neuroscience Laboratory at the University of Nebraska–Lincoln. Her research interests lie in quantitative methodology, with a focus on advanced uses of structural equation modeling.

Jennifer Mize Nelson, Ph.D., is a Research Assistant Professor, Director of Administration in the Center for Brain, Biology and Behavior, and Program Site Director of the Developmental Cognitive Neuroscience Laboratory at the University of Nebraska–Lincoln. Her research interests are at the intersection of clinical, developmental, and cognitive neuroscience approaches. Specifically, her research focuses on the development of executive control in childhood, with an eye toward how this development relates to mental health and social adjustment.

Sandra A. Wiebe, Ph.D., is an Associate Professor in the Department of Psychology and a member of the Neuroscience and Mental Health Institute at the University of Alberta. Her research uses behavioral and electrophysiological methods to examine the development of children's ability to regulate their thoughts, actions, and emotions in the early years, and the impact of environmental and genetic factors on these developing skills.

Michael T. Willoughby, Ph.D., is a Fellow and Senior Public Health Analyst at RTI International. His program of research is focused on the developmental causes, course, and consequences of self-regulatory abilities with a specific interest in their relevance to disruptive behavior disorders and academic readiness.

STATEMENT OF EDITORIAL POLICY

The SRCD *Monographs* series aims to publish major reports of developmental research that generates authoritative new findings and that foster a fresh perspective and/or integration of data/research on conceptually significant issues. Submissions may consist of individually or group-authored reports of findings from some single large-scale investigation or from a series of experiments centering on a particular question. Multiauthored sets of independent studies concerning the same underlying question also may be appropriate. A critical requirement in such instances is that the individual authors address common issues and that the contribution arising from the set as a whole be unique, substantial, and well integrated. Manuscripts reporting interdisciplinary or multidisciplinary research on significant developmental questions and those including evidence from diverse cultural, racial, and ethnic groups are of particular interest. Also of special interest are manuscripts that bridge basic and applied developmental science, and that reflect the international perspective of the Society. Because the aim of the *Monographs* series is to enhance cross-fertilization among disciplines or subfields as well as advance knowledge on specialized topics, the links between the specific issues under study and larger questions relating to developmental processes should emerge clearly and be apparent for both general readers and specialists on the topic. In short, irrespective of how it may be framed, work that contributes significant data and/or extends a developmental perspective will be considered.

Potential authors who may be unsure whether the manuscript they are planning would make an appropriate submission to the SRCD *Monographs* are invited to draft an outline or prospectus of what they propose and send it to the incoming editor for review and comment.

Potential authors are not required to be members of the Society for Research in Child Development nor affiliated with the academic discipline of psychology to submit a manuscript for consideration by the *Monographs*. The significance of the work in extending developmental theory and in contributing new empirical information is the crucial consideration.

Submissions should contain a minimum of 80 manuscript pages (including tables and references). The upper boundary of 150–175 pages is more flexible, but authors should try to keep within this limit. Manuscripts must be double-spaced, 12pt Times New Roman font, with 1-inch margins. If color artwork is submitted, and the authors believe color art is necessary to the presentation of their work, the submissions letter should indicate that one or more authors or their institutions are prepared to pay the substantial costs associated with color art reproduction. Please submit manuscripts electronically to the SRCD *Monographs* Online Submissions and Review Site (Scholar One) at http://mc.manuscriptcentral.com/mono. Please contact the *Monographs* office with any questions at monographs@srcd.org.

The corresponding author for any manuscript must, in the submission letter, warrant that all coauthors are in agreement with the content of the manuscript. The corresponding author also is responsible for informing all coauthors, in a timely manner, of manuscript submission, editorial decisions, reviews received, and any revisions recommended. Before publication, the corresponding author must warrant in the submissions letter that the study has been conducted according to the ethical guidelines of the Society for Research in Child Development.

A more detailed description of all editorial policies, evaluation processes, and format requirements can be found under the "Submission Guidelines" link at http://srcd.org/publications/monographs.

Monographs Editorial Office
e-mail: monographs@srcd.org

Editor, Patricia J. Bauer
Department of Psychology, Emory University
36 Eagle Row
Atlanta, GA 30322
e-mail: pjbauer@emory.edu

Note to NIH Grantees

Pursuant to NIH mandate, Society through Wiley-Blackwell will post the accepted version of Contributions authored by NIH grantholders to PubMed Central upon acceptance. This accepted version will be made publicly available 12 months after publication. For further information, see http://www.wiley.com/go/nihmandate.

SUBJECT INDEX

Page numbers in *italics* represent figures and tables.

CURRENT